The Evolution of Banking Regulation in the European Union

The Evolution of Banking Regulation in the European Union

An Economic Approach

Nikolay Gertchev

LEXINGTON BOOKS
Lanham • Boulder • New York • London

Published by Lexington Books
An imprint of The Rowman & Littlefield Publishing Group, Inc.
4501 Forbes Boulevard, Suite 200, Lanham, Maryland 20706
www.rowman.com

86-90 Paul Street, London EC2A 4NE

British Library Cataloguing in Publication Information Available

Library of Congress Cataloging-in-Publication Data

Names: Gertchev, Nikolay, 1979- author.
Title: The evolution of banking regulation in the European Union : an economic
    approach / Nikolay Gertchev.
Description: Lanham, Maryland : Lexington Books, 2023. | Includes bibliographical
    references and index.
Identifiers: LCCN 2023024619 (print) | LCCN 2023024620 (ebook) |
    ISBN 9781666937190 (cloth) | ISBN 9781666937206 (epub)
Subjects: LCSH: Banking law--European Union countries. | Financial institutions--Law
    and legislation--European Union countries. | Banks and banking--Economic aspects--
    European Union countries.
Classification: LCC KJE2188 .G47 2023 (print) | LCC KJE2188 (ebook) |
    DDC 346.24/082--dc23/eng/20230613
LC record available at https://lccn.loc.gov/2023024619
LC ebook record available at https://lccn.loc.gov/2023024620

To Marie-Madeleine and Théodore

Contents

List of Figures and Tables

FIGURES

TABLES

Acknowledgments

This book project would not have come to fruition without the enthusiastic support of Guido Hülsmann, professor at the University of Angers, France, to whom I also owe much of my development as an economist. I am also forever grateful to the late Professor Bertrand Lemennicier who vividly encouraged my penchant for controversial discussions and ignited my love for economics at the University of Paris II Panthéon–Assas some twenty years ago. I am also thankful to the Mises Institute in Auburn, Alabama, which has played an important role in my discovery of the intellectual universe of economic science in the Austrian tradition. An anonymous referee should be thanked for their careful reading of the original draft and the thoughtful observations that contributed to its improvement.

The views expressed in this book are my own and do not represent my employer in any way. All errors or inconsistencies are of my own responsibility.

Nikolay Gertchev
Brussels, Belgium
March 2023

Introduction

This book is an introduction to the economics of banking regulation, with a special focus on the European Union. To start, operate, or even terminate their activity, banks are subject to specific business requirements that aim at ensuring their safety and soundness at any moment. For instance, mandatory capital ratios and additional capital buffers request banks to build up and keep a minimum level of own funds. The intention is to guarantee their solvency even under circumstances of acute stress in the economy. Similarly, liquidity requirements aim to ensure that banks have enough available assets at the time when their liabilities fall due. The intention here is to guarantee they do not miss a single payment. In no other industry are the actors subject to operational rules of this type. In practice, all such requirements are applied through a myriad of often complex numerical indicators that allow for an on-going monitoring of compliance. The specialized authorities in charge of the surveillance, that is, the banking sector supervisors, are vested with intrusive powers that allow them to examine banks' books at any time and to impose changes to their business operations and strategies. In a word, banking is the most heavily regulated commercial activity worldwide.

Yet concerns about banks' safety and soundness have not become a thing of the past. The history of banking is essentially the history of crises, and the history of banking regulation is the history of continuously expanding requirements, both in scope and in content. Even before newly introduced rules have been fully implemented, authorities discuss already the next expansion of the regulatory toolkit. From the outset, these incessant dynamics invite various plausible interpretations. The evolving regulation might be a response, as adequate as possible, to the evolving risks of banking itself. Regulators might be closing previously undiscovered loopholes. They might be pursuing other political or personal objectives. Or maybe the regulatory requirements bring about adverse effects and unintended consequences of their own that a further regulatory expansion attempts to correct. Understanding the dynamics of banking regulation is a difficult issue of paramount importance for grasping its efficiency. It is of interest not only for the regulation-makers, but also for the intended ultimate beneficiaries, that is, all of us who hold bank accounts.

1

This book refers to the essential teachings of economics, and especially that part of the economic science that deals with the study of money, to shed new light on the logic, content, and consequences of banking regulation.

The topic of banking regulation has received much public attention in the aftermath of the global financial crisis (GFC) of 2007–2008. The policy response to this twin banking and sovereign debt crisis included an ambitious overhaul of the regulatory and supervisory framework worldwide, known as the new Basel Standards, or Basel III. The implementation of these new norms in the EU effectively transformed the European Monetary Union (EMU), commonly referred to as the Euro Area (EA), into a fully fledged Banking Union (BU), where since 2014 the European Central Bank (ECB) has assumed the additional role of chief banking sector supervisor. To operationalize the BU, the EU and the national authorities set up many new institutions which they endowed with powerful and broad mandates to fix micro- and macro-prudential policy and standards, to restructure banks, and to provide new supra-national guarantees and safeguards.

These major changes in the regulatory and supervisory framework over the last decade did not come out of nowhere. Basel III evolved out of Basel II, which was the successor to Basel I. This simple observation, namely that the bank regulatory architecture has been subject to continuous change and reform, naturally raises some commonsense questions. What brought these successive reforms? Were they timely responses to new challenges arising from changes in the practice of banking, that is, financial innovation? Or, alternatively, did any new round of Basel Standards address some unforeseen shortcoming or adverse effect caused by the latest regulation itself? How successful were these reforms, notably to reduce banks' vulnerabilities and to improve their resilience to shocks? Can we consider them as progressive steps in the direction of strengthening financial stability? Or, to the contrary, is one reform correcting some failure of a previous reform? So far, these and similar questions about the recent development and achievements of banking regulation have attracted the attention mostly of lawyers, decision-makers, and practitioners.[1] Economists, on the other hand, have shown a less-than-enthusiastic interest for the content and consequences of banking regulation.[2] Banking regulation lacks even a framework for passing the test of the now popular cost-benefit analysis, which has become a standard prerequisite for justifying new norms in any business area.[3] This lack of a systematic analysis of banking sector requirements from a broader economic point of view is both problematic and surprising.

The problem is not tiny—the study of banking regulation is too important a subject to be left to lawyers only. Law students and practitioners, biased by modern positivism, are imbued with a legalistic instinct, that is, the belief that legislation can solve any social problem. In line with this view, policymakers are under the impression that government regulations provide a quick and efficient fix to any issue, including the stability of the banking system. The major achievement of economic science, however, is to demonstrate that specific market forces, directed by the purposeful choices of individuals, drive social outcomes. If government decrees alone could determine prices, production, and industrial organization according to a stable socially desired pattern, it would be pointless to search for economic laws and cause-to-effect regularities in society. That would mean the end of economic science altogether.[4] By implication, to the extent that economic theory exists, it necessarily must find and point at some undesired or adverse effects of government interventions. Hence, economists have an important role to play in checking the too rosy "solve-it-by-regulation" legalistic attitude. Insofar as economists can prove indeed that banking regulation brings about some undesired or adverse effects, they even have the moral duty to develop their argument and to present their alternative—economic—point of view.

Economists' lukewarm interest for a more comprehensive analysis of the present-day banking regulation also comes as a surprise because of a great original contribution. In his 1873 description of the financial sector in England (the money market), Walter Bagehot laid down what would be considered nowadays a full-fledged blueprint of a reform program for financial stability. The economic profession has retained two major lessons from this seminal study. First, the existence of a central bank that centralizes commercial banks' reserves and can act as a lender of last resort—that is, as an ultimate provider of cash—creates moral hazard. As a result of their reliance on the expected liquidity support from the central bank, banks lower their individual cash reserves, to which they substitute interest-bearing loans that increase their profits. This moral hazard renders banks' balance sheets more fragile and objectively prone to illiquidity. Second, during the frequent crises that this inherent fragility is bound to bring about, to avoid a total panic the central bank must act resolutely through quick and massive liquidity loans to the requesting banks. The central bank should provide its emergency refinancing at a penalty rate and against collateral of good quality only. Yet the story told in Lombard Street goes much deeper.

Bagehot focuses on what he considers the most salient feature of the banking sector—the fact that all domestic banks, and even some foreign institutions, keep their gold reserves at the Bank of England. He sees this "one reserve system" as a serious anomaly that is contrary to nature: "I have tediously insisted that the natural system of banking is that of many banks keeping their own cash reserve, with the penalty of failure before them if they neglect it" (Bagehot 1979, 160). He links this anomalous concentration of the entire country's gold reserve to several government privileges bestowed upon the Bank of England—the exclusive possession of the government's deposit, the monopoly on issuing banknotes in England and their legal tender privilege, and the monopoly of limited liability. Moreover, he proves that this unnatural system has negative and unforeseen consequences in terms of higher indebtedness, amplified business cycles, risk of sudden stop of funding, and risk of contagion through debt that could escalate an individual crisis into a generalized panic. Beyond the richness and modernity of these and many other findings,[5] the truly remarkable element in Lombard Street is Bagehot's analytical approach. First, he examines the outstanding fundamental features of the banking system as such. Among them, he distinguishes between natural aspects related to the free practice of the banking business and anomalous aspects caused by the government's involvement. Second, in the anomalous aspects of banking he finds an inherent cause for the instability of banks. Third, considering that it is too late to correct these anomalies at the root, he outlines a remedial plan that takes the system, however anomalous, for granted. The plan itself focuses on stronger *judgmental prudence* with respect to both the size and the use of the single reserve and the general management of all banks.[6] In a sense, this was a plan for regulating the banking activity within the one reserve system.

Bagehot's analysis remained the standard approach to banking regulation for as long as the one reserve system was in place. With many modifications, among which the migration of the world's single reserve from the Bank of England to Fort Knox, this system lasted until 1971, when the US government definitively suspended the convertibility of the dollar into gold. The ultimate demonetization of gold totally transformed the international monetary system. Gold was no longer the single anchor of the national currencies. The latter remained convertible into each other, but only at a flexible exchange rate. The national central banks became truly independent, as they were no longer constrained by the obligation to convert their paper monies into gold. From the bankers' banks, the central banks became independent fiat money producers. Naturally, this new context, which introduced the foreign exchange and the international settlement risks, provided the institutional ground for a change in the economists' approach to banking regulation.

The burgeoning field of information economics[7] added a new analytical angle to this new reality. The so-called Diamond–Dybvig framework redefines the banking activity as liquidity and maturity transformation. This framework, like the one of Bagehot, also sees an inherent instability in banks. However, unlike in Lombard Street, the cause of this instability would not be due to the way the banking system is organized. Rather, it would originate in banks' transformation activity, which consists in the investment of short-term liquid liabilities into long-term illiquid assets. The government's involvement, notably through a mandatory deposit insurance, would be a solution to this problem of instability, rather than a contributing factor (Diamond and

Dybvig 1983). More generally, followers of this new approach study a broad category of regulatory instruments—the lender of last resort, deposit interest rate ceilings, reserve requirements, capital requirements, deposit guarantees, and so on—as targeted solutions to specific market failures (Freixas and Rochet 2008, 305–48). In turn, the market failures would originate in widespread information asymmetries between principals and agents, lenders and borrowers, owners and managers. From that perspective, banking regulation would be justified by its positive contribution to the safety and soundness of the industry, notably by protecting deposits and hence preventing bank runs.

Overall, deposit protection has become the single most fundamental rationale for banking regulation. Even though analysts have used different arguments, they all agree on the need to guarantee bank deposits. The provision of risk-free "transactions account balances" has sometimes been presented as a social justice requirement ensuring that even the financially unsophisticated and relatively poor individuals get access to demand deposits (Kareken 1986).[8] A very similar reason, rooted in depositors' insufficient knowledge of banking risks and their incapacity to ensure that bankers manage these risks properly, is the so-called representation hypothesis "that the prudential regulation of banks is primarily motivated by the need to represent small depositors and to bring about an appropriate corporate governance for banks" (Dewatripont and Tirole 1994, 35). Macroeconomic arguments have also been brought forward to support an institutional protection of deposits. One of the implications of a deposit guarantee is to keep the stock of deposits, and hence the aggregate money supply in the broad sense, unchanged in the event of bank failures. In other words, it removes a significant cause of possible deflation. Thus, mainstream macroeconomic theory sees deposit insurance as a necessary and effective tool to bring about the full employment of resources (Meltzer 1967, 496).[9]

Irrespective of the concrete reason that justifies government deposit protection, the standard modern case for banking regulation rests on *utilitarian* grounds. Some expected benefits from the authorities' involvement in the banking sector would speak in favor of the regulation. Ultimately, this favorable view about banking regulation stems from its expected contribution, in one way or another, to social utility. In other words, the government would be bringing about an improvement in welfare by better aligning the conflicting private interests with the properly understood social interest. Regulation would compensate for market failures, protect the consumers (depositors), and set up a level playing field for the producers (banks). In this intellectual universe, the textbook economic discussion of banking regulation boils down to a relative comparison of the efficiency of the different regulatory instruments in offsetting various aspects of the alleged instances of market failure. From that point of view, the specific case for regulating banks does not appear different from the general case for regulating any other industry. Banking regulation is specific only insofar as it prescribes treatment of instances of market failure that are exclusive to the functioning of the banking sector.

This utilitarian case for banking regulation suffers from an obvious limitation, beyond the innate pitfalls of utilitarianism[10]—it does not provide an answer to the basic question why banks are the most intrusively regulated commercial activity. At their start of business, banks are subject to prior approval by the public authorities. The cessation of their activities also cannot happen without an official sanction. Throughout their existence, banks must comply with a myriad of strictly enforced rules. Specialized financial analysts, employed by public agencies, scrutinize their balance sheets practically on a daily basis. Any deviation from some externally imposed ratios and targets gives rise to a request for a corrective action, including changes to the business model itself. Why do banks bear such a regulatory and supervisory burden, unmatched by any other sector in the economy? An answer to that simple and primary question requires an investigation into what is specific and unique in the *very nature* of banking itself. What is so special with the product of the banking industry and with the organization of its production? Is there a definite reason, rooted in the very essence of modern banks, which would incentivize governments to control them so closely? We contend that the defining feature of modern banks is their contribution to the production of money, and that therefore these questions cannot be answered properly without a focus on that specific point. Hence, this book[11] espouses an approach to the study of banking regulation that is based on an informed understanding of banks' specific *monetary role* in the economy.[12]

This economic approach to banking regulation could be seen as a proposed return to the foundational analysis that Bagehot laid down in his *Lombard Street*. Additionally, an investigation that is primarily concerned by the nature and role of banks provides an objective framework for an impartial assessment of both the consequences and limitations of banking regulation. As it goes beyond a one-sided enumeration of the expected benefits of banking regulation, the economic approach of this book is more balanced and conducive to purely descriptive cause-to-effect relationships. That way, it also contributes to dissipate irreconcilable disagreements stemming from divergent moral or political judgments.

The first chapter sets the scene. It describes the main function of modern banks and highlights the important, and yet fragile, place they hold in the economy. In particular, the chapter highlights banks' contribution to the production of a specific category of goods that are the cornerstone of human societies—media of exchange. The presentation focuses on two different monetary regimes, depending on whether banks can or cannot add to the stock of media of exchange. This distinction turns out very useful for grasping the difference between what banking regulation would have been on the free market and what it is nowadays. The ability of banks to add to the stock of media of exchange appears as the most instrumental reason for a first type of regulation, directly by the central bank, with a view to exercising control over the supply of money in the broad sense. The analytical integration of this liquidity-based regulation of banks into the study of banking regulation is one of the contributions of this book. Furthermore, the chapter argues that the other, industrial, types of banking regulation, in the form of prudential requirements, owe their raison d'être to the fact that the liquidity-based regulation of banks is either insufficient—that is modern banks have found ways to circumvent it—or deficient—that is, it brings about adverse effects of its own or even has become inoperative. The description of how liquidity is created in the Eurosystem, of its absorption by the commercial banks and of the workings of the euro-area interbank market and of loans securitization illustrates the theoretical conclusions.

The remaining three chapters present the prudential regulatory environment of banks and discuss its implications for the banking sector itself and for the economy as a whole. They develop a progressive presentation of the various forms of prudential regulatory requirements, grouped in three broad categories—micro-prudential regulation, macro-prudential regulation, and safety nets and backstops. The presentation is progressive insofar as it attempts to establish a connection between and within these categories, whereby every next requirement is shown as an attempt to solve a problem that a previous intervention has either left unaddressed or has contributed to create. This suggests that there is an underlying relation between the different forms of banking regulation, based on their relative efficiency. This relation introduces a common thread between regulatory forms and helps connect the analytical presentation of the different categories of banking regulation along the remaining three chapters of the book. This is one of the advantages of our economic approach in comparison to other approaches, which often present the various pillars of banking regulation as separate stand-alone blocks.

The second chapter focuses on micro-prudential regulation and supervision, that is, the set of institution-specific rules that aim at ensuring the individual safety and soundness of banks considered in isolation from each other. In essence, the chapter details the Basel Committee capital and liquidity requirements, as implemented in the EU. Faithful to the economic approach of this book, it also examines broader macro-economic questions, such as the effect of these requirements on the type of bank credit and of investments, their implications for the monetary transmission mechanism and the business cycle, their capacity to account for credit risk properly, or their own optimality. The chapter also describes the main building blocks of the contemporary post-GFC banking supervision, that is, asset quality reviews and stress tests, and concludes with an economic reflection about its broader implications for the banking sector.

The third chapter goes beyond the individual bank requirements and critically examines the main tenets of the broader macro-prudential regulation, which aims at ensuring the stability of the system as a whole. This novel "macro-pru" approach, as opposed to the traditional "micro-pru" view of banking regulation, is also a by-product of the GFC, and, in particular, of the realization that individual institutional requirements do not suffice to bring about financial stability. Macro-prudential regulation pays special attention to the interconnectedness between banks, including across countries. The concept of systemic risk captures the relevance of macro-prudential requirements for financial stability. The chapter critically examines this concept through a discussion of the market externalities that are meant to drive systemic risk, namely credit deleveraging and fire sales of assets. In particular, the chapter raises the question whether the true cause of systemic risk does not lie in the very organization of the present-day monetary system rather than only in banks' contingent behavior during the downturn of the economic cycle. This broader view sheds new light on the increasing importance of macro-prudential policy, notably in relation to monetary policy.

The last and fourth chapter delves into the regulatory response to a problem that seems to have remained unresolved despite the multifarious evolution of banking regulation lately. This problem is the too-big-to-fail issue and, more generally, the question of moral hazard in banking. Banks that credibly expect that governments will bail them out and central banks will refinance them in times of crisis become less careful in their assessment of risks and tend to grow their balance sheets excessively. This reckless attitude, which arguably becomes even more complacent in case of compliance with the existing regulations, becomes a factor that brings about the feared crisis. To address this pressing issue of moral hazard, and in light of the lessons from the GFC, the EU authorities reformed the existing and introduced new safety nets, backstops, and guarantees of public rescue. The last chapter offers a succinct presentation of these reforms, as they are part of the overall regulatory framework, and critically examines their contribution to solving the moral hazard issue. It pays special attention to the building blocks of the post-GFC regime for the restructuring of failed or failing banks, known as bank resolution. More specifically, it examines to what extent the newly established resolution regime promotes market-consistent solutions to bank failures or, to the contrary, is still a case of government interventionism not without adverse effects of its own. Indeed, without a clear answer to that question it is impossible to gauge the extent to which the reform of bank resolution has addressed the underlying moral hazard problem.

To some extent, this book might appear incomplete. Indeed, it has a narrow focus on banks only and considers neither the other financial institutions, instruments, or infrastructures nor their regulatory environment. It is definitely far from being exhaustive and, in some cases, it might not be up-to-date with respect to the latest amendment. To the author's comfort, the myriad of implementation details evolves at such a speed that any presentation would need regular updating.[13] More importantly, however, the book offers a consistent economic framework that goes beyond the simply formalistic and descriptive content that is so common for discussions of banking regulation. This emphasis on the economic point of view offers a new opportunity for a broader understanding of banking regulation. For that same reason, technicalities are detailed only insofar as they relate to a relevant economic argument that needs to be highlighted.[14] In order not to lose its analytical unity, the text deals with the many involved public agencies only in connection with the underlying issues that determine their policy or implementation mandate.

Despite these limitations and shortcomings, there is a sense in which the analysis of banking regulation presented in this book could be considered complete. Indeed, the adopted economic approach is consistently applied throughout banks' entire lifecycle—from their inception as stand-alone business units (micro-pru), through their integration into the financial system (macro-pru), until their dissolution (rescue and restructuring). That way, the book relates, within a single framework, regulatory aspects that hitherto have been considered in isolation from each other. Thus, this book offers a novel framework, from the economic standpoint, for a holistic understanding and critical assessment of the many different forms of banking regulation, with a special focus on their main foundations and broader consequences. The author hopes that this approach would be of interest to scholars and students alike, in the fields of economics, finance, and banking, irrespective of whether they are looking to grasp the overarching principles of banking regulation or some nitty-gritty details.

NOTES

1. The latest state-of-the art handbook introduction to the legal principles and content of banking regulation can be found in Chiti and Santoro (2019). Busch and Ferrarini (2020) and Howarth and Schild (2020) contain contributions by legislators and practitioners that focus on the historical, institutional and administrative aspects of the various building blocks of the Banking Union. Teixeira (2020) develops an excellent systematic legal history of banking regulation in the EU and identifies five periods of regulatory consolidation within the broader context of the ongoing European integration: harmonization or rules (1973–1984), competition between intermediaries

(1985–1997), governance improvements (1998–2007), crisis response (2008–2012), and centralization (2013–).

2. Two notable exceptions are worth mentioning. Sironi (2018) offers a very comprehensive assessment of the post-GFC regulatory reform, including many critical elements, in particular, linked to the redundancy of the leverage ratio, the difficulties with properly calibrating the countercyclical capital buffer, the arbitrariness of internal risk models or banks' issues with profitability. Arnaboldi (2020) offers an empirically well-documented account of the challenges for EA banks stemming from some unfinished areas of the Basel III reform, namely the problem with non-performing loans, the difficult-to-value (Level 3) assets, and the risks related to large non-provisioned sovereign exposures. The author proposes a stronger role for market discipline and more risk-sharing as two useful complements to the formalistic regulatory approach. Despite their undeniable value, both contributions follow an ad hoc approach outside of a broader analytical economic framework.

3. Only recently have authors proposed "[. . .] a modest start toward filling this gap" (Posner and Weyl 2013, 393).

4. Ludwig von Mises concludes his discussion of statutory law versus economic law with the following words: "If prices can be fixed by the authority without producing a reaction in the market which is contrary to the intentions of the authority, then it is futile to attempt an explanation of prices on the basis of market forces. The very essence of such an explanation of market forces lies in the assumption that each constellation of the market has a corresponding price structure and that forces operate in the market which tend to restore this—'natural'—structure of prices if it is disturbed" (Mises 1998a, 25).

5. Among his many contributions, Bagehot provides a strikingly clear description of the leverage effect in finance. This effect shows how a higher share of debt finance boosts profits on the invested equity, as long as the cost of debt remains below the return on investment. Bagehot immediately draws the important social implication that new debt can easily destroy old fortunes, because the higher debt-leveraged profits give an advantage to indebted new entrants. Thus, to stay in business and remain competitive under these circumstances, entrepreneurs have to get indebted. Gradually, debt crowds out equity.

6. With respect to the reserve, Bagehot advises to increase it above one-third of liabilities. However, he rejects the American example of a strict minimum ratio, as even a decreasing value without breaching the minimum could trigger loss of confidence and a crisis. Rather, he advises on an "apprehension minimum," that he prefers to increase by successive layers of further conservatism (Bagehot 1979, 159). When it comes to bank management, he insists upon professional governance structures that would check the risk appetite of the daily manager (ibid., 126–28) and on maximum disclosure of information to stop contagion (ibid., 129). His entire plan is based on instilling a prudent behaviour, because "There is a cardinal difference between banking and other kinds of commerce; you can afford to run much less risk in banking than in commerce, and you must take much greater precautions" (ibid., 113).

7. Bhattacharya and Thakor (1993) provide a very comprehensive presentation of the information-based literature on financial intermediation and banking. More

specifically, the authors show how this information-based understanding of banking contributes to solving some theoretical puzzles, that is, the very existence of financial intermediation, banks' denial of credit to potential borrowers instead of charging them higher interest, banks' funding of illiquid assets by liquid liabilities or their role in maturity transformation. Bhattacharya et al. (1998) further focus on the implication of this literature for banking regulation. Their starting point is the finding that government deposit insurance leads to moral hazard that implies excessive risk-taking by banks. The authors then examine possible remedial regulatory measures, such as cash-asset reserve requirements, risk-sensitive capital requirements, stronger market discipline and stricter bank closure policy. In light of the numerous deadweight costs and distortions associated with government-sponsored safety nets, and given the explosive growth of off-balance-sheet (shadow) banking, the authors finally call for a "serious look at the desirability of government deposit insurance" (ibid., 766).

8. Based on his detailed review of the history of federal banking regulation in the US from 1863 to 1986, Kareken is very critical of its efficiency. He argues that 100 percent reserve banking based on Treasury bills as the reserve asset might be a more efficacious means to achieve the proclaimed goals of keeping the banking industry safe and sound. Within the very different theoretical framework of general stochastic equilibrium models, with an explicit favour for the state origin theory of money, Benes and Kumhof (2012) also find support for the superiority of 100 percent reserve banking as advocated by Irving Fisher in his famous 1936 Chicago Plan, including an output gain of around 10 percent.

9. Meltzer reviews, very meticulously, five arguments in favour of government controls in the banking industry. The macro case is built upon i) the monopolistic behaviour of the industry, which restricts output and increases prices and ii) the independent expansion of the banking system on its own volition. The micro case for government controls rests on i) the effects of economies of scale and concentration and ii) the possibility for local monopolies in banking. The fifth argument is the market failure argument based on the cost of bank failures. Meltzer finds no justification in any of the arguments and refers to evidence that "present controls on entry, branching, and merger have costs that exceed their benefits" (Meltzer 1967, 500). Yet he emphasizes the need to preserve the stability of the money supply, that is, to avoid deflation, in order to ensure the full employment of resources. However, even here he makes a proposal for a competitive, market-based system of deposit insurance, in line with his finding that "Government insurance provides a partial safeguard against a precipitous decline in the money supply" (ibid., 500). Meltzer does not elaborate on the link between monetary deflation and unemployment of resources, which he takes for granted. Thornton (2003), Bagus (2003; 2015), and Hülsmann (2008a) disentangle this mainstream view and build up a positive case for deflation.

10. On the grounds of revealed preference, Rothbard (1956) provides a thoughtful criticism of standard social utility-based welfare economic analysis. Rothbard (2000) offers a broader discussion of the limitations of utilitarianism with respect to property rights and justice.

11. The immediate trigger for this book is a course that the author has had the pleasure to teach as part of the Master Program, Law and Finance at the Université d'Angers (France) since 2020.

12. The economic approach adopted here is *essentialist* because of its focus on the most essential features—that is, the very nature—of modern banks. By opposition, the standard utilitarian approach can be considered *nominalist*. I am indebted to Professor Guido Hülsmann for drawing my attention to the subtle observation that utilitarianism is a form of nominalism.

13. Many financial companies publish regulatory radars with the latest updates. The European Central Bank monthly supervisory newsletter and the European Banking Federation daily newsletter are also worth highlighting.

14. The technical glossary of BU-related concepts developed by Heimbüchel et al. (2018) can serve therefore as a useful complement.

Chapter 1

Monetary Regimes and the Liquidity-Based Regulation of Banks

Prima facie, for the modern specialist in economics or finance, a chapter on money and its production under different regimes might surprise, particularly in a book with a primary focus on the analysis of banking regulation. Yet, as argued later, economic analysis cannot ignore the necessarily monetary nature of any economy. Thus, the study of money appears as a prerequisite for the analysis of any economic problem. This is even truer when it comes to modern banks, which actively take part in the production of money in the broader sense. Hence, a chapter on money at the beginning of a book on banking regulation has more than one advantages. First, it reveals the economic nature, that is, the essence and hence the vulnerabilities, of modern banks, which are the very same entities that are the object of the regulation under study. This is indeed an unavoidable step for the critical assessment of the regulatory measures that purport to alleviate these vulnerabilities. Second, such a broader general framework offers original insights into the reasons for the very detailed regulation and very intrusive supervision to which the banking industry is subject presently. Moreover, this broader framework brings back the economic analysis of banking regulation where it started in Bagehot's *Lombard Street* and where it truly belongs—the comparative analysis of monetary regimes.

The first section reminds the reader of the crucial role of money for a market economy, draws an important implication for economic analysis and highlights two monetary laws of particular importance. The second section brings banks and their specific monetary contribution into the discussion and suggests how their activity would be regulated on the free market. This sets the scene for presenting, in the third section, the modern fractional-reserve banking system, especially as regards its role in the production of money in the broader sense. It is precisely banks' credit expansion and its impact on the overall stock of media of exchange in the economy that motivates a liquidity-based regulation of their activity by the central bank. The case of the euro area (EA) provides a real-world illustration of this hierarchical relation between modern central banks and the commercial banks under their jurisdiction. The last section shows the limits of that liquidity-based regulation, as banks successfully avoid it through the interbank market or thanks to loans securitization, or due to its own destabilizing effects.

1.1 THE NECESSITY OF THE MONETARY ECONOMY

Media of exchange are a special category of goods that individuals hold neither for consumption nor for production purposes. Their raison d'être stems from the solution they provide to the intricate difficulties associated with the direct exchange of goods and services. The improbable double coincidence of wants, whereby A and B would mutually offer each other exactly what the other party expects in type, quantity and quality, and the unequal divisibility and storability of the various objects of exchange imply that, if ever possible, direct transactions would be very limited in scope and extent. A human society that had not discovered a more evolved technology of exchange, that is, one that bypasses the tremendous difficulties of direct exchange, would have remained at a very primitive stage of development. Indeed, the simple prospect of only very limited successful exchanges would have discouraged specialized production for the market. As a result, autarky would have remained predominant and the productivity gains from individuals' comparative advantages could not have materialized. The major driver of civilization—interpersonal association based on, and promoting, individual talents—would have remained inoperative. The human person known to us as a social being with spiritual aspirations, intellectual inclinations, and cultural achievements would have not developed.[1]

The more evolved technology for carrying out transactions is therefore necessarily roundabout. In the indirect exchange, a third good, that is neither demanded nor supplied for its services in consumption or in production, mediates the transactions.[2] Individuals accept to hold it, in exchange for their market supplies, only because they realize that others accept it too with the same intentions. Because of this enhanced acceptability, the originally third good becomes the fittest means to acquire the object of one's market demands, that is, it becomes a medium of exchange demanded specifically for its capacity to mediate exchanges. Although adding an intermediary step in the chain of transactions, the technology of the indirect exchange makes feasible trades that otherwise could not have been effected at all. Media of exchange naturally[3] evolve out of the most marketable goods, the liquidity of which increases further as more and more individuals use them as such.[4] A medium of exchange that is commonly used as such is referred to as money (Mises 1998b, 398). The nexus of all monetary exchanges, that is, of all transactions of goods and services against money, transforms society into a monetary economy.

The most salient feature of the monetary economy is that it makes possible the division of labor, specialized production, and capital accumulation. As units of money are exchanged against units of any other goods and services,[5] all exchange ratios have the same denominator, that is, all prices are monetary. Thanks to these monetary prices, economic calculation becomes possible (Mises 1990). To the extent that prices are ratios relative to units of the same medium of exchange, market participants know, or at least can conceptualize, how many units of money they should provide or could receive in a market transaction. This precisely makes incurred costs comparable to expected returns, which in turn sets up the framework without which entrepreneurs could not possibly come into being. It is only in a monetary economy that the acting investors could compare purchases of factors of production to the sales of products according to the same stick. Thus, media of exchange provide the most essential institutional framework without which acting individuals could not possibly know whether their investment decisions could lead to profit or to loss, to capital accumulation or to capital consumption. In a sense, any economy must be monetary for rational future-oriented action to take place.

A corollary of this conclusion is that a realistic science of economics cannot avoid focusing primarily on the study of the monetary economy. Although useful for grasping some aspects of human action, the imaginary constructions of the Robinson Crusoe world (autistic exchange) and of the barter fiction (direct exchange) do not describe a segment of our reality in any meaningful way. Rather, they help us understand our world only to the extent that they provide us with a description of what is essentially unrealizable and impossible. From that perspective, economic theory is monetary *par excellence*. In particular, as money is foundational to the economy and to the actual market process, it is no longer permissible to discuss price formation and all related processes in the economy in isolation, without an explicit reference to the monetary aspect that all transactions have. The strived-after realism and concreteness of the analysis command the economist to keep in mind that any supply of good A or B is, at the same time, a demand for units of the medium of exchange M, and vice versa. The recognition that money is an integral and constitutive element of the market process implies that, analytically, monetary considerations should permeate the theory of market exchanges. This implies that it is no longer permissible to separate economics into the study

of the "real economy" and the "real determinants" of consumption and investment on the one hand, and of monetary phenomena on the other hand.[6] Yet,
due to knowledge specialization, monetary theory in the strict sense refers
exclusively to the study of media of exchange themselves and of their relation to other goods and services, present and future. Two major conclusions of
monetary theory—two monetary laws—need to be stressed because of their
relevance for the study of banking regulation.

The first law states that any aggregate supply of media of exchange is
optimal as changes in that quantity bring about no social benefit.[7] There are
different ways to demonstrate the validity of this first monetary law. The
very nature of media of exchange is such that they are neither consumption
nor production goods. Hence, a higher quantity of media of exchange does
not satisfy additional needs, be it directly and immediately through increased
consumption or indirectly and in the future through enlarged production.

Another way to derive this first law is based on the key insight that media
of exchange do not embed physically or technologically their specific monetary services in the way in which for instance glasses, pens or radios embed
their own specific services of, respectively, improved vision, writing capacity, or sound transmission. This is the case because the capacity of media of
exchange to intermediate transactions, that is, to acquire units of other goods
and services, ultimately depends on the other market participants' willingness
to accept to hold the monetary units in their cash balances.[8] The more willingness there is in the market to hold units of media of exchange, the higher their
monetary services, that is, their purchasing power. Indeed, a stronger willingness to hold media of exchange means that more individuals require a higher
compensation in terms of other goods and services to part with one unit of
the media of exchange. This higher demand for monetary services triggers
actual exchanges at higher prices for money in terms of the other goods and
services or alternatively at lower monetary prices. One unit of the media of
exchange can buy more of the other goods. The crucial point to emphasize is
that changes in the demand for monetary services are addressed by changes
in the purchasing power of the media of exchange. This direct[9] and automatic
process occurs in the market, through the monetary transactions themselves,
and does not require any change in the supply of media of exchange.

Moreover, an increase in the aggregate supply of media of exchange could
not possibly satisfy a stronger demand for monetary services. A larger supply
of media of exchange contributes to inflate monetary prices, as at least some
of the beneficiaries of the new money would exchange it for other goods and
services, thereby bidding up their prices. This process engenders a tendency
toward a decline in the purchasing power of money. Thus, in fine any single
unit of the media of exchange would be providing fewer, not more, monetary
services. The final outcome of less monetary services per unit of money

goes in the exactly opposite direction of what would be needed to satisfy individuals' higher demand for monetary services. This is due to the fact that an increase in the supply of money contributes to a deterioration, rather than an improvement, of the monetary services rendered by any single unit of the media of exchange.[10]

This brings us to the second monetary law of particular relevance for understanding banking regulation. This law states that increases in the supply of media of exchange trigger wealth redistribution effects, according to which the first users of the newly created media of exchange benefit at the expense of any later money-holders. These so-called Cantillon effects stem from the fact that any additional units of the media of exchange enter the economy at a specific point and then spread among money-users through sequential spending transactions.[11] This sequential spending raises monetary prices, one after the other as actual transactions take place, above what they would have been otherwise. This process continues until, at the lowered purchasing power of money, all units held of the media of exchange provide the monetary services demanded by the money-users. Until that new monetary equilibrium is reached, those who were first to spend the new media of exchange are relatively better off, because they could acquire extra goods and services before the price increases had materialized fully. Inversely, those who were last to spend the new media of exchange are relatively worse off, as they had to face a generally higher price structure.

The Cantillon effects confirm the first monetary law according to which an increase in the supply of media of exchange brings no aggregate benefit to society. They point out that such an increase unavoidably divides society into winners and losers. This second law of monetary theory implies that money can never be neutral and that any alleged distinction between the short-term and longer-term effects of an increase in the stock of media of exchange is irrelevant in that regard. Moreover, the resulting conflictual frictions and the associated individual attempts to join the winners' club and stay away from the losers' group explain why regulating the production of media of exchange is of such a special interest, including politically.

1.2 THE COMPETITIVE REGULATION OF FREE-MARKET MEDIA OF EXCHANGE

The spontaneous process of the most marketable commodities becoming progressively media of exchange results in the appearance of commodity monies. Free-market competition regulates their production in two distinct ways. First, several commodities might compete simultaneously as parallel media of exchange, especially as they likely present specific advantages for different types of transactions. One commodity might be preferred for intermediating higher-value transactions, while others might be better fit for smaller-value exchanges. The natural emergence of media of exchange needs not result in the selection of a single money. The parallel use of gold and silver offers a historical illustration of that possible outcome. Second, the production and supply of commodity monies fall under the same commercial principles that apply to the competitive production and distribution of any other good in the economy.

The economically most relevant feature of this competitive production process is that the law of scarcity and the general price mechanism naturally guide and limit the supply of money in the economy. To expand the production of money, entrepreneurs must bid up labor and capital out of the other sectors in the economy. At the resulting higher costs, the rate of return in money production remains competitive, or at par with other productive ventures, only if money holders are ready to pay higher prices for money in terms of other goods, in other words if money's purchasing power increases under the effect of a stronger demand for monetary services. Thus, thanks to the market process, where all entrepreneurs, irrespective of their specific sector, compete on equal footing for labor services and capital goods, the supply of additional media of exchange naturally responds to changes in the demand for monetary services. This means that consumers' preferences to hold money, relative to other goods, successfully regulate and direct money production as well as the production of any other good or service.[12] No third-party involvement is required to ensure that society is supplied with enough media of exchange, exactly as no third-party involvement is necessary to ensure that consumers get enough cars or books.

In addition, this competitive market process leads to a specific case of monetary stability. A higher demand for monetary services increases money's purchasing power, which renders an expansion of the production of money, vis-à-vis the other goods and services, competitive enough. In turn, the higher supply of money brings about a counterbalancing tendency in money's purchasing power and therefore moderates its final increase. Conversely, a lower demand for monetary services lowers money's purchasing power, thereby diverting labor and capital from the production of money toward other sectors that can employ them at relatively higher returns. The resulting lower supply of money brings an offsetting tendency in the original change of money's purchasing power, which again moderates its final decline. One way or another, the competitive production of commodity monies dampens preferences-driven changes in their purchasing power. In that sense, the free market brings about purchasing power stability. This natural monetary stability is propitious for long-term planning and investment and makes economic calculation as stable as possible.

Second, and furthermore, the market-driven entrepreneurial competition spurs continuous innovation in the production of media of exchange. These competitive pressures incentivize producers to supply and transform the monetary units in the size and form that best fit consumers' preferences. In addition to constantly improving the shape of coins, this innovative process has brought about an invention of tremendous economic relevance, namely the money warehousing.[13] The possibility of money warehousing arises from the very specificity of the monetary services. Namely, money provides its services by means of being held in cash balances, for exchange against any other good at any future moment. When that future exchange occurs, money is held again, though in the cash balances of the counterparty to the transaction. Thus, money is being held in someone's cash balances at any single moment.[14] Precisely because money provides its services while and through being held, it needs not be transferred physically between buyers and sellers during exchanges. The transfer of a title of ownership over the agreed quantity of money (the transaction price) is perfectly sufficient.

Monetary theory refers to such representative titles of ownership that take the place of money in actual exchanges as money substitutes (Mises 1980, 64). There are two reasons why market participants would accept money substitutes. First, transacting with the substitutes might offer distinctive advantages to transacting with the money they represent, for example, avoiding wear and tear, reducing the risk of accidental loss, or even easing the very process of exchange thanks to broadening the opportunities for divisibility of the monetary unit. Depending on how strongly individuals value the services of these substitutes, they would be ready to pay a price for them. To the extent that this price is sufficiently high to compensate alert entrepreneurs for the storage, safeguarding, issuance, and other costs related to money warehousing, the money substitutes will come into existence. Second, transaction counterparties would accept to hold the substitutes instead of money itself only if they are certain, beyond any doubt, that the substitutes can be redeemed upon demand at any moment, that is, they are fully convertible.

Such money substitutes that are fully convertible in money are also known as monetary certificates, irrespective of the form they might take (a token, a banknote, or a deposit certificate, whether in metal, paper, or electronic form). The money warehouses that first started issuing monetary certificates are the predecessors of our modern banks. To effectively ensure their instant convertibility in money, banks must keep in reserve and available at any given moment all monetary units that have been entrusted, that is, deposited, with them. In other words, the banks must hold a one-to-one reserve of money for any monetary certificate that they issue. Such hundred percent reserve banks issue monetary certificates only against the transfer of the corresponding amount of money, which is thereby deposited with them. Any type of record, whether material or digital, to the extent that it is an easy-to-recognize and commonly accepted proof of that deposit, fulfils the functions of a monetary certificate.

By its very nature, hundred percent reserve banking promotes systemic financial stability in two different ways. First, the full reserve implies that every bank is, indeed, able to redeem the monetary certificates it has issued, should their holders require to get back the deposited units of money. In that sense, a hundred percent reserve bank is immune to a liquidity crisis. Some warehousing entrepreneurs might underestimate the storage- and issuance-related costs of banking. However, although such entrepreneurial errors could lead to the insolvency of the bank, the latter would still be able to redeem upon request all the monetary certificates it has issued. It would then simply close business, without any impact on the solvency or liquidity of any of its clients or of any other bank. From that perspective, a full-reserve banking system is also immune to contagion.

Second, full-reserve banks exert no influence of their own on the supply of or demand for money. Rather than consisting of money proper only, cash holdings consist now of money held in cash balances and monetary certificates that represent money withheld from cash balances and deposited with banks. Although the relative composition of media of exchange between these two types of monetary objects might evolve due to changes in preferences, the aggregate stock of media of exchange remains unaffected. Moreover, the requirement to keep a full reserve, and hence the impossibility to add to the stock of media of exchange, prevents full-reserve banks from financing additional credit transactions, that is, exchanges that would involve future goods. Consequently, full-reserve banking affects neither money's purchasing power nor interest rates.

More specifically, all credit transactions in the economy, whether for investment or consumption, must be funded exclusively out of prior savings, that is, with effectively available resources. An increase (decrease) in the availability of savings, implied by a lower time preference, results in a lower (higher) interest rate, at which more (less) investments become competitive than at the previously higher interest rate. Thanks to this intertemporal resource-allocation process, saving and investment decisions are coordinated in such a way that the sufficient availability of resources is guaranteed throughout the investment period until its completion. Although accidental entrepreneurial errors of overestimating the availability of resources or of underestimating the investment costs are of course possible, such errors cannot be attributed to the intertemporal resource-allocation process itself, an integral part of which is the very operation of credit markets. In this sense, full-reserve banking—because it has no influence of its own on credit markets and on investment and saving decisions—is also conducive to financial stability.

1.3 THE CASE FOR SELF-REGULATION IN BANKING

It appears, therefore, that from the aggregate point of view of the economy, full-reserve banks need no special regulation. No particular risk, stemming from their operation, could justify public authorities' interventions aiming to prevent or mitigate an alleged socially damaging vulnerability. Moreover, as their activity has no bearing on the total supply of media of exchange, on the operation of credit markets, or on investment and production decisions, there would be no political motivation to regulate full-reserve banks. However, this insulation from inherent risks and political interests does not imply yet that full-reserve banks would not abide by specific industry standards.

The issuance of monetary certificates relies on bank customers' confidence in their instant money convertibility upon demand. Hence, the establishment and continuous operation of any bank relies on a crucial condition—the impeccable reputation of being able to ensure the constant convertibility of the money substitutes. The particularity of this special type of banking reputation is that it should be created and constantly kept among all market participants, not only among the current bank clients. Save for that universality, the monetary certificates would lack the necessary certainty about their universal and unconditional acceptability in any transactions, which would compromise their essential function of money substitutes. From a simple condition for establishment at individual level, this fundamental problem of gaining and keeping the universal reputation of all market participants becomes a common business concern for the entire banking industry as a whole. Thus, all banks share a joint and solidary interest in gaining the confidence of all holders of money substitutes, including those issued by competitors.[15]

This shared solidarity leads banks to adopt and consistently follow widespread good practices or industry standards. The ultimate goal of these standards is to facilitate the use of monetary certificates and to ensure full confidence in their convertibility in money. As the standards' efficiency depends greatly on the customers' trust and knowledge of them, banks have all the incentives to make these standards easy to understand by all market participants, and to publicize their own adherence to them. One paramount means to enforce such industry standards, while guaranteeing their maximum disclosure and transparency, is the membership into a professional association or business federation. In this sense, the banking sector is naturally self-regulated, notably through the professional association of peers who

condition membership to their self-established business club on the continuous respect of some commonly designed industry standards.

The exact design and content of these industry standards are a specific
business decision that cannot be known or described with absolute certainty,
outside of a specific historical context. They are subject to entrepreneurial
discovery and to banks' specific understanding, at a given historical moment,
of how their customers perceive their reputation. The essential aspect of these
standards, which are also de facto conditions for admission in the banking
business, is that they purport to build and keep the confidence in the money
convertibility of all monetary certificates. Such industry standards would
include, for instance, i) a minimum wealth requirement for any new prospective banker, ii) a commitment to redeem monetary certificates issued by
other members, iii) contributions to an insurance fund for accidental losses
of money and to a receivership fund for unclaimed certificates in the event
of cessation of business, iv) regular inspections and audits of the money
warehouses by a certified company, or v) minimum disclosure requirements.
These norms would also evolve, as deemed necessary, to respond to changes
in customers' perception of what a reputable bank is. Irrespective of their
specific design, three broad considerations deserve special mention because
of their economic relevance.

First, these self-adopted and self-imposed industry standards contribute to
strengthen the application of the full-reserve principle. The standards result
in a de facto increase in the cost of entry in the banking business, which
remains nevertheless free and unrestricted by privileges. This translates, one
way or another, into a minimum wealth requirement that is tantamount to a
contingent guarantee, provided by the banks themselves, for the availability
of an even larger than the full reserve. Consequently, by reinforcing the full
reserve, the market-based self-regulation of the full-reserve banking sector
reaffirms its lack of influence on the money supply and on credit markets.

Second, none of the norms involves any complex requirements, in particular, based on relations between balance sheet items. As only a simple and
single rule binds all banks' balance sheets, namely the hundred percent correspondence between money warehoused and monetary certificates issued,
there is no need for any further requirement. Naturally, the industry standards
have implications for the banks, in terms of own funds necessary to start
operations, incurred liabilities and corresponding assets. The structure of their
balance sheets reflects these implications. However, the norms themselves do
not consist in minimum numerical ratios between balance sheet items and the
monitoring of their observance is not limited to the verification of mechanical compliance with such ratios. As a matter of fact, such ratios would not be
necessary because the single and simple rule of the full reserve is sufficient.

Third, neither the discovery nor the enforcement of any of the standards needs government involvement.[16] Given that reputation is a shared interest for banks, no collective action problem would justify a centralized and externally imposed regulation. Banks are first and directly concerned by the fundamental problem of banking, and therefore they are best placed to identify efficacious solutions. Public authorities have no competitive advantage in finding out how to build and keep confidence in banks. Moreover, the involvement of the government in banking would meet strong skepticism, if not outright resistance. To fund their activities, governments rely exclusively on taxation of private property and on borrowing from private owners. This means that money owners and their trustees have a strong incentive to keep governments away from where the money is, that is, away from the banks.

To sum up, under competitive market conditions where property rights are respected, banks operate as warehouses for commodity money and issue fully covered monetary certificates that are all instantaneously redeemable upon demand. Banks' activity is regulated by the continuous adherence to the principle of the full reserve and there is a strong case for the self-regulation of the banking industry through the voluntary adoption of industry standards that reinforce the full-reserve principle.

The case of modern fractional-reserve banking is fundamentally different.

1.4 THE MONOPOLISTIC REGULATION OF FIAT MONEY AND OF FIDUCIARY MEDIA OF EXCHANGE

As the use of monetary certificates spreads through the economy and more individuals hold them as part of their cash holdings, the requests for their actual redemption become less frequent. The banks realize that in such a context of already established reputation, and therefore of significantly lower risk of seeing the money substitutes returned to them for actual redemption in money, they need to keep available in reserves only a fraction of the deposited money. From the limited perspective of ensuring the convertibility of those certificates that return to the banks' cashiers for redemption on a regular basis, the full reserve appears as an excessive requirement. Moreover, the banks can lend out that part of their accumulated money reserves that exceeds the strict minimum that would be necessary to ensure the redemption of the money substitutes under regular business circumstances. In this way they could benefit from an additional income stream stemming from the interest attached to that portion of the money reserve that has been lent out.

When banks start lending part of the money that has been deposited with them, they stop being exclusively warehouses for money and become fractional-reserve banks that are also involved in lending. From that moment, money kept in reserves covers only partially the total amount of issued money substitutes. From monetary certificates, the convertibility of which raises no doubt, the money substitutes become fiduciary media of exchange that rely on the users' confidence in the issuing bank's ability to, somehow, meet all redemption requests, even if they go beyond what typically occurs in the regular course of business. It is important to emphasize that the monetary objects themselves do not undergo a physical transformation. The tokens, banknotes or deposit certificates, whether in metal, paper, or digital, look and appear still the same. However, by depleting part of their money reserve to finance credit transactions, the now fractional-reserve banks alter the economic nature of the money substitutes. This transubstantiation of the money substitutes from monetary certificates into fiduciary media of exchange brings about dire consequences on the banking system, and on the economy as a whole.

1.4.1 The Inherent Instability of Fractional-Reserve Banking

A simple numerical example will be helpful in grasping better these implications. Let us assume that the single banknote-issuing bank in a closed economy becomes aware that, by the end of every week, the clients who accept its banknotes present less than 20 percent of these substitutes for redemption before that money gets redeposited with the bank again. Accordingly, the bank decides to keep a reserve ratio of slightly above 20 percent only, as it estimates that this fractional-reserve ratio allows it to keep its good reputation, to maintain clients' confidence high enough and to respond to an unusual contingency beyond the regular redemption pattern. Let us further assume that, so far, the bank has issued a thousand units of monetary certificates, which represent therefore a thousand units of deposited money. The easiest way for the bank to reduce its effective reserve ratio is to increase its issuance of money substitutes, namely by lending out additional money substitutes, until the available money kept in reserves represents the desired reserve ratio. In this case of a target reserve ratio of slightly above 20 percent, a thousand units of money in reserve could support slightly below five thousand units of money substitutes. The bank could add up to four thousand units of money substitutes to the original monetary certificates. It creates these additional media of exchange out of thin air, by means of financing new loans to the economy. The borrowers are the first recipients of these new media of exchange, which they spend according to their own preferences on other goods and services, thereby triggering the Cantillon effects. This simple example shows the extraordinary power of a fractional-reserve banking system to increase the supply of media of exchange by expanding bank credit,[17] a process commonly referred to as money multiplication.[18]

However, this power comes at the expense of a very significant inherent fragility. First, fractional-reserve banks are exposed, naturally, to liquidity crises. Whenever redemption requests exceed the available reserve, convertibility of the fiduciary media of exchange into money must be suspended, due to lack of money in the banks' vaults, in a situation known as *cours forcé*. The fiduciary media of exchange might continue to circulate as credit money as long as their users keep confidence that the banks will be able to resume redemption in the foreseeable future. The more frequent these suspension events are and the longer they last, the more banks' clients lose confidence. In turn, this leads to higher redemption requests addressed to other banks, thereby propagating an individual liquidity crisis throughout the banking system.

The long historical process of repeated attempts to find a permanent solution to this systemically recurrent problem of fractional-reserve banks' illiquidity has led to the present-day dematerialization of money.[19] Eventually, banknotes were declared inconvertible in the commodity (gold) that they had been representing originally. The ultimate and definitive suspension of redemption transformed banknotes from simple fiduciary media of exchange into fiat paper money. The former bankers' bank in charge of issuing money substitutes in the form of banknotes became a central bank with a national or regional monopoly over the production of money itself. This transubstantiation of banknotes, which boils down to a large-scale expropriation, did not happen without forceful measures by the government. In that regard the state-sponsored privilege of legal tender,[20] which rules out that fiat money could be refused as a medium of exchange, even in private transactions, played a crucial role.

The most outstanding economic aspect of fiat money is that its production, unlike the production of commodity monies, escapes the general law of scarcity and the limitations imposed by the competitive price mechanism. To increase the stock of money, the producer of fiat money does not need to attract factors of production from other alternative business venues. Instead, the central bank creates the additional monetary units practically at a zero marginal cost, that is, out of thin air, and allocates them to banks through collateralized loans or direct purchases of existing assets in the economy. In no way is the central bank economically restrained, either by its own resources or by the prevailing prices for capital and labor, in the maximum amount of money it could produce. Rather, the production of fiat money follows some self-imposed administrative rules that central banks can change unilaterally.[21] This extraordinary feature of fiat monies, which makes them absolutely unique among all goods, also accounts for the central banks having become ultimate lenders of last resort[22] capable of providing never-ending liquidity to the commercial banks established in their respective jurisdictions.[23]

It should be highlighted that the extraordinary nature of fiat paper money necessarily implies the question of how its production should be governed or limited. This is the fundamental question of monetary policy. Indeed, given its zero marginal cost, whoever controls the production of fiat paper money has the exceptional privilege of being able to attract otherwise scarce economic resources, and therefore to change the overall distribution of goods and services in the economy, without having to engage in prior production for exchange. As aptly put, he who prints his own dollars "could consume without producing, and thus seize the output of the economy from the genuine producers" (Rothbard 1991, 23–24). This extraordinary nature of fiat money explains why governments have monopolized their production and have used it, together with taxation and regulation, as a potent tool for income redistribution and general policy financing. Fractional-reserve banks share in this exorbitant privilege, thanks to their capacity to add to the money supply in the broader sense. Thus, the question of their regulation, or of the control over their participation in the overall money production, becomes of paramount importance for any government that has monopolized money production, as is the case with the current fiat money regime.

The emergence of fiat money represents a permanent solution, still in place today, to the systemic problem of fractional-reserve banks' recurrent liquidity crises. Yet individual events of illiquidity have not disappeared, and irrespective of the availability of this permanent solution the history of banking remains a history of illiquidity crises, though admittedly less frequent than in the past. This is the case because fractional-reserve banks issue fiduciary media of exchange in the form of deposits that are only partially covered by fiat money reserves kept in their own vaults and on their accounts with the central bank. At times, this partial coverage turns out insufficient for some banks to meet all their liquidity needs. This requires the intervention of the lender of last resort, which steps in to supply the missing money. Ultimately, such temporary illiquidity events are due to the fact that fractional-reserve banks participate actively in the production of money in the broad sense.[24] They influence the overall supply of broad money by making available additional fiduciary media of exchange (deposits) through an expansion of their bank credits (loans). In a nutshell, fractional-reserve banks share in the central bank's privilege to add to the stock of money. This is the most fundamental structural reason for a hierarchical, liquidity-based regulation of commercial banks' credit expansion by the central bank, lest money production gets out of control.

Before explaining how the liquidity-based regulation of banks operates—in particular, in the euro area—it must be emphasized at this stage that fractional-reserve banks remain fragile because of a second structural source of vulnerability. When expanding bank credit by adding to the stock of fiduciary media of exchange, banks provide monetary financing to fund extra consumption and/or investment, while savings have remained unchanged in society. By its very nature, this bank credit expansion introduces a structural and unavoidable distortion between the objectively available resources in space and time and the monetary reflection of this availability in terms of prices and interest rates in entrepreneurs' calculations.

A bank credit expansion entails a lowering of the market interest rates below the level at which the sole availability of savings and the intertemporal consumption/investment decisions would have fixed them. Indeed, if the interest rates do not decrease, the additional supply of bank loans on the credit markets would meet no demand and hence could not possibly take place. These lower interest rates make entrepreneurs believe that previously sub-marginal investments have become profitable now. However, as time preference itself has not changed, the amount of savings has not expanded. From the aggregate point of view, this means that bank credit expansion necessarily leads to a widespread entrepreneurial overestimation of the resources available in the economy. Investments financed by bank credit expansion are therefore unsustainable, because of a lack of sufficient resources. Hence, an increase in the production of fiduciary media of exchange by the fractional-reserve banks causes the appearance of clusters of investment errors that unfold in two stages. An optimistic boom, that is, the conviction that business is buoyant and that all new investments are profitable, describes the first stage. More characteristically, the boom takes place because credit expansion happens, that is, the banks provide actual financing that allows borrowers to bid up and attract factors of production. This is an implication of banks' great privilege to participate in the production of money in the broad sense. In the second stage, known as the bust, the many projects that cannot be finalized as intended, because of the objective lack of resources, are restructured in an attempt to minimize losses.[25]

Without entering into a detailed theoretical account of the business cycle and how it affects the price and capital structures of the economy,[26] the crucial point here is that the bank credit expansion engineered by fractional-reserve banks structurally and necessarily implies unsustainable booms that result into busts due to malinvestments that squander scarce economic resources. Thus, bank credit expansion is a systemic cause of recurring economic losses that are revealed through regular swings in the aggregate economic activity. These recurring economic losses directly affect banks' balance sheets and produce systemic financial instability. Indeed, the economic losses implied by the malinvestments prevent borrowers from repaying the bank loans which made the malinvestments possible in the first place. Thus, the problem of nonperforming loans (NPLs) becomes endemic to the fractional-reserve banks. These NPLs lead to losses that erode banks' capital, potentially destabilizing the confidence of depositors and of banks' creditors, and hence capable of triggering a liquidity crisis. The crucial point that could not be emphasized enough is that systemic financial instability and recurrent losses due to delinquent loans are not an incidental issue, but a salient feature that is built into contemporary fractional-reserve banking.

In short, the very nature of the two-tier modern banking system offers two distinct and basic rationales for banking regulation by the central bank. First, the production of fiat money at zero marginal cost, which allows monopolistic central banks to provide monetary refinancing to any economic activity without the prior need to attract real resources through the price mechanism, implies the question of how that money production should be circumscribed and directed. To the extent that commercial banks also participate in the production of money in the broader sense, this further raises the question of their regulation by the same public authorities that are in charge of money production. In addition, as the production of media of exchange implies unavoidable Cantillon effects, the question of who the first and early receivers of any new units of money will be becomes of paramount importance, both in general and to support specific government policy initiatives. Hence, the ambition to regulate bank credit expansion is directly linked to the discretionary power of fractional-reserve banks to finance specific economic projects and to the ensuing income redistribution.

Second, when banks exert their privilege to add to the money supply in the broader sense by expanding bank credit, they destabilize the socially coordinated process of intertemporal allocation and economizing of the resources available in the economy. The ultimate losses that result from the malinvestments weaken banks' own balance sheets, which negatively impacts their future capacity to expand credit and to provide financing. This adverse outcome provides another raison d'être for the regulation of banks' credit expansion by the central bank, both to minimize the risk of a crisis that could erode confidence in the monetary system as a whole and to ensure that future credit expansions are not compromised and stay aligned with the broader political objectives.

Thus, the most basic regulation of banking occurs, first and foremost, with respect to the very conditions of the present-day production of money in the broader sense. The next section illustrates how this liquidity-based regulation of banks operates, namely through the so-called open market, in the specific case of the euro area.

1.4.2 The Liquidity-Based Regulation of Banks in the Euro Area

In the course of their daily business, banks must address their own customers' demand for money, in the form of currency in circulation, as well as settle payments toward their own or other customers' accounts at other banks, including at the central bank. Commercial banks need central bank money to finance these daily liquidity outflows. To the extent that such liquidity outflows are outside the central bank's own control, they are considered to be autonomous liquidity-absorbing factors. In addition to these autonomous factors, banks must also keep a minimum amount of required reserves on their own current accounts at the central bank.[27] This minimum reserve requirement, together with all other liquidity-absorbing factors, creates a "captive" demand for liquidity, that is, for central bank money. This structural liquidity deficit, driven by the reserve requirement and the expected aggregate liquidity outflow from the banking system as a whole, forces the commercial banks to express a demand for holding central bank money. In turn, the central bank supplies this liquidity, that is, it credits banks' current accounts with central bank money of its own creation, by lending it out against the pledge of some assets (eligible collateral), or through the outright acquisition of these same assets. The central bank supply of liquidity meets commercial bank's demand for liquidity in the so-called open market.

In essence, the open market is the nexus of liquidity transactions, by means of which the central bank remains in control of the monetary policy interest rate. As long as the banking system faces a structural liquidity deficit, it has to borrow the needed liquidity through the open-market operations that the central bank makes available. Because the central bank has the discretion to decide on the amount, the duration, and the interest rate at which it supplies the needed liquidity, it has the capacity to exert a tight control on banks' liquidity condition. When the central bank lends more liquidity at a lower policy interest rate, banks receive excess liquidity[28] beyond what is needed to cover the reserve requirement and the autonomous liquidity-absorbing factors.[29]

The crucial point that needs to be emphasized is that the banks that receive that excess liquidity can use it to finance new loans to the economy up to the point where the liquidity outflows generated by the newly created media of exchange (in terms of additional required reserves, a higher demand for banknotes and liquidity outflows toward other banks) fully absorb that surplus liquidity. As the newly created media of exchange are spent, the banks that benefit from the related liquidity inflows can, in turn, use this excess liquidity to finance liquidity outflows linked to a second round of additional loans to the economy. Each successive round of new loans and additional fiduciary media of exchange is smaller than the previous one, due to the net liquidity flowing outside the banking system. Thus, this process of increasing the stock of money in the broader sense stops when all the liquidity outflows triggered by the aggregate and sequential bank credit expansion fully absorb the original excess liquidity.[30]

While the provision of individual bank loans is subject to many specific determinants on a case-by-case basis, extra excess liquidity in the banking system is the single limiting factor for an aggregate bank credit expansion. When the central bank loosens banks' liquidity condition through additional liquidity-providing operations at a lower interest rate, it stimulates a bank credit expansion that could not occur otherwise. Conversely, when the central bank tightens banks' liquidity condition, by lifting the reserve ratio or by reducing its liquidity-providing operations notably at a higher policy interest rate, it restrains banks' capacity to finance a credit expansion and might even trigger a credit contraction. The central bank is in the position to exert this liquidity-based regulation of banks' credit expansion and of their production of fiduciary media of exchange thanks to banks' structural liquidity deficit, which leads them to continuously demand central bank money in the open market.

This view of the "mechanics of money," which puts the central bank and its open-market operations in the driving seat of money creation, gained prominence in standard economic theory thanks to the monetary writings of Milton Friedman. Following the rational expectations revolution in economics, it came under criticism, in particular, by the proponents of the post-Keynesian school. Post-Keynesians admit the existence of the so-called money multiplier. However, they consider it as "a purely descriptive tautology" (Moore 1988, 384) and give it an inverted causal interpretation in the sense of a credit divisor, instead of a deposit multiplier, based on the observation, advanced by French bankers in the 1970s, that a bank first provides loans and then seeks refinancing at the central bank. In that view, banks take the initiative to supply the productive part of the economy with that amount of money that corresponds to the borrowers' needs for credit, itself determined by their expected production plans. Money would then be *endogenous*, because produced by the economic system itself, credit-based and demand-determined (Lavoie 1984; Fontana 2002). Banks' reserves at the central bank would not be relevant for the money creation process, as the central bank is deemed bound to accommodate commercial banks' liquidity needs, by virtue of its function as lender of last resort.[31]

This alternative view, which puts the commercial banks in the driving seat of money creation, has gained prominence recently, especially following a 2014 Bank of England report on money creation in the modern economy (McLeay et al. 2014). The report clarified that "whenever a bank makes a loan, it simultaneously creates a matching deposit in the borrower's bank account, thereby creating new money" and that "monetary policy acts as the ultimate limit on money creation" (ibid., 14). In that sense, the Bank of England report has clarified that credit expansion does happen through the additional creation of fiduciary media of exchange. However, this well-deserved emphasis on the active role of commercial banks in the production of money in the broader sense went beyond and has stimulated a burgeoning revisionist literature in defense of the credit theory of money (Hook 2022), often stressing the need for a reform that would allow the public authorities to regain sovereign control over money production (Huber 2017).

This alternative post-Keynesian and modern banking view has the undeniable advantage of focusing on the crucial role played by fractional-reserve banks. Yet this emphasis seems to lead to an over-statement of the exclusive and allegedly independent relevance of bank credit for money creation.[32] First, bank credit does not consist in lending money, but in lending fiduciary media of exchange that are redeemable in money. These are two distinct monetary objects, even though in normal times they intermediate exchanges equally well. As shown earlier, fiduciary media of exchange are valued, and hence demanded, only because of their holders' confidence in their redeemability into money upon demand. Moreover, had they been money, fractional reserve banks would not be subject to any liquidity risk and would not experience any runs. Second, by virtue of being the monopolist money producer, the central bank is effectively in charge of the stock of money, including that part of it which banks hold as their reserves. Ex post, in a historical interpretation, the supply of bank reserves can always be understood as accommodative to some specific circumstances or to economic and political considerations. The crucial point, however, is that the central bank alone decides on the quantity of money produced, as recognized by post-Keynesians themselves: "[. . .]: central banks can and do refuse to fully accommodate increases in the demand for reserves" (Palley 1991, 400). Therefore, the reality of the liquidity-based regulation of banks could hardly be denied, irrespective of the specific technical tools employed by the central bank.[33]

In the EU, the twenty-seven national central banks (NCBs) in each of the Union's member states (MS) and the European Central Bank (ECB) together comprise the European System of Central Banks (ESCB). The Eurosystem refers exclusively to the ECB and the NCBs of those MS (currently twenty) that have adopted the euro as their legal tender national currency. While the governing council of the ECB formulates monetary policy in the euro area and the executive board of the ECB assumes implementation responsibility, the NCBs remain highly relevant. Indeed, the NCBs implement monetary policy in a decentralized way, through the liquidity-providing and liquidity-absorbing operations, with a direct impact on their own balance sheets. The consolidated financial statements of the Eurosystem merely compile the ECB's and the NCBs' individual balance sheets.[34]

The consolidated balance sheet of the Eurosystem conveniently illustrates how the liquidity-based regulation of banks operates and has evolved in the euro area. The weekly main refinancing operations (MROs) and the originally monthly longer-term refinancing operations (LTROs) have been the main lending tools of the Eurosystem through which euro area banks were supplied with liquidity, prior to the GFC of 2007–2008.[35] The MROs used to be larger in volume, thereby reflecting the continuous steering of the policy interest rate. Figure 1.1 shows a dramatic change in the way the Eurosystem has been supplying banks with liquidity over the last decade. In response to the GFC, the ECB introduced various major changes to its framework for providing liquidity to commercial banks, of which two in particular are worth mentioning.[36] First, to provide more certainty and forward guidance, both the duration and the volume of the LTROs were increased.[37] Starting from June 2014, the Eurosystem introduced also the so-called targeted LTROs, which are linked to banks' lending patterns. The more a bank is lending to the real economy, excluding residential loans to households, the more it can access the TLTRO, and at a lower interest rate. The third TLTRO, started in 2019, consists of ten quarterly lending operations, each with a maturity of three years, at an interest rate that could be as low as fifty basis points below the marginal lending facility. As a result of this stronger focus on the LTROs, the MROs have lost

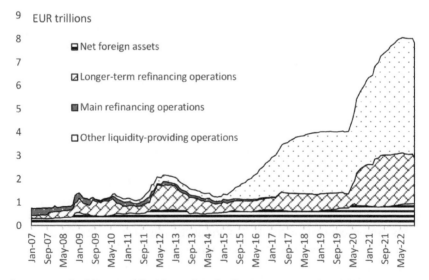

Figure 1.1   Liquidity-Providing Operations by the Eurosystem, 2007–2022.
Source: ECB Statistical Data Warehouse, https://sdw.ecb.europa.eu/browse.do?node=bbn27.

their role, which is also consistent with a policy interest rate that has been fixed at around zero between June 2014 and July 2022.

Second, in addition to its collateralized-lending operations, typical of the euro area open-market, the Eurosystem started having recourse to outright purchases of assets. This policy of quantitative easing, or asset purchase programs (APP), started with initially modest amounts of targeted specific asset classes, such as covered bonds (CB) as from October 2014, asset-backed securities (ABS) as from November 2014, sovereign bonds as from March 2015 and corporate bonds as from June 2016. By the end of 2022, it has expanded into a total volume of assets acquired under the different components of the APP of about EUR 3.3 trillion, out of which public sector debt represented 80 percent. Furthermore, the ECB introduced a Pandemic Emergency Purchase Programme (PEPP) in March 2020, under which it has acquired almost exclusively euro area sovereign debt for around EUR 1.7 trillion by the end of 2022.[38] Although the initial purpose of the quantitative easing was to prevent the price deflation of some specific asset classes, it has de facto expanded into a massive support to public spending that had the effect to supply the banking system with unprecedented volumes of excess liquidity.

The other liquidity-providing operations (OLPOs), which have become the most prominent liquidity-supplying factor since 2015, capture the combined effect of these programs of quantitative easing (see figure 1.1). The prevalence of the OLPOs is unlikely to change in the medium term, as any deliberate exit from these asset purchase programs would deflate the respective assets' prices. This would run against their intended original purpose, notably by increasing the borrowing cost of euro area governments, which does not appear politically feasible.[39] The sixteen years between January 2007 and the end of 2022 can be divided in two equal periods, whereby the total supply of liquidity doubled by October 2014, before more than sextupling in the last eight years.

Figure 1.2 shows the factors that have absorbed this overwhelming liquidity supplied by the Eurosystem. Both the demand for banknotes (currency in circulation) and the national treasuries' deposits with the NCBs have been increasing at a regular rate, which appears to have accelerated in the aftermath of the COVID-19–related lockdowns. However, the most relevant change, and one that is of the highest economic interest, lies in the tremendous ballooning of banks' aggregate liquidity, whether kept on their current accounts, on the deposit facility or as fixed-term deposits with the Eurosystem.[40] The policy of quantitative easing has transformed the structural aggregate liquidity deficit of euro area banks into a structural liquidity surplus. This has removed banks' systemic need to regularly borrow liquidity from the Eurosystem, as evidenced by the fact that the MROs have become, as a matter of fact, irrelevant.

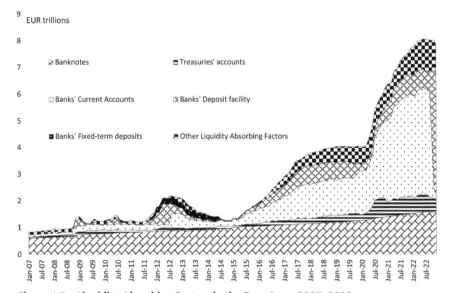

Figure 1.2   Liquidity-Absorbing Factors in the Euro Area, 2007–2022.
Source: ECB Statistical Data Warehouse, https://sdw.ecb.europa.eu/browse.do?node=bbn27.

Banks' excess liquidity, as shown in figure 1.3, became a systemic phenomenon in the aftermath of the monetary response to the GFC in late 2008.
After some volatility and relative stabilization, the volumes of excess liquidity started increasing again in 2015 when the policy of quantitative easing
began and became very significant in early 2018, due to the ECB sovereign
debt purchases program. Against the backdrop of a negative remuneration
rate on the deposit facility (negative since June 2014, fixed at –0.5 percent/
year between September 2019 and July 2022), the ECB undertook a minor
reform of the remuneration of these impressive volumes of excess reserves,
in order to dampen their negative impact on banks' profitability.

From the perspective of the liquidity-based regulation of banks, the crucial
point to emphasize is that in this environment of ample excess liquidity, the
Eurosystem has lost its tight grip on banks' liquidity condition, and hence no
longer controls their credit expansion and their contribution to changes in the
broader money supply. That loss of control is the natural consequence of the
Eurosystem having moved its focus of attention away from purely monetary
developments and toward asset prices stabilization. This is the major lesson
from the evolution of its consolidated balance sheet over the last decade
(figures 1.1 and 1.2). This potentially explosive context, in which banks
have received enough excess liquidity to finance a massive credit expansion,
provides an extremely relevant, though historically contingent, rationale for
imposing other rules and requirements on banks to limit and restrain their

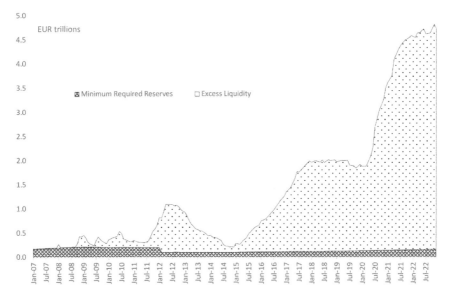

Figure 1.3   Euro Area Banks' Excess Liquidity, 2007–2022.

Source: ECB Statistical Data Warehouse, https://sdw.ecb.europa.eu/browse.do?node=bbn27. Excess liquidity
    is defined as the sum of banks' balances on their current accounts, the deposit facility and the fixed-term
    deposits minus the minimum reserve requirement.

role in the further production of money in the broader sense. In other words,
banking sector requirements beyond the liquidity-based regulation of banks
become even more topical in the present-day context of systemic excess
liquidity.

1.5 FIRST INSTANCES OF REGULATORY
AVOIDANCE AND OF ADVERSE EFFECTS

Even in the absence of systemic excess liquidity, which is a contingent,
though durable, contemporary phenomenon implied by the Eurosystem policy of quantitative easing, banking requirements beyond the liquidity-based
regulation would still be highly relevant. As in the case of any regulated
entity, banks seek and find ways to reduce the central bank's liquidity-based
control of their credit-granting activity, while still complying with the basic
minimum reserve requirement. Attempts of regulatory avoidance offer an
excellent perspective for grasping the essence and economic role of the interbank market and of loans securitization—two crucially important institutions
for banks. Moreover, central banks and their expansionary monetary policies
bring about adverse effects of their own on banks' balance sheets, which reinforce the insufficiency of the liquidity-based regulation of banks.

1.5.1 The Interbank Market

From the outset, lending between banks would appear counterintuitive. Are not banks supposed to lend to households, corporations and governments, that is, to the nonfinancial economy? Would not one more euro lent to a bank mean a euro less lent to the genuinely productive sectors? To understand why the interbank market is actually foundational for the fractional-reserve banking system and for fiduciary media of exchange themselves, we must look into the economic incentives for banks to lend to each other.

Let us assume two banks A and B that are fully loaned up, which means that all of their money reserves are kept as required reserves. In other words, neither A nor B has any excess liquidity. Payments among customers of the same bank do not impact that bank's liquidity condition. The situation, however, is fundamentally different when a customer a of bank A makes a payment to a customer b of bank B. By the very fact of being a customer of the bank B, and not of A, b does not accept to hold the fiduciary media issued by A. Customer b insists upon receiving fiduciary media issued by B. Let us further assume that, at the end of the business day, and after netting all transactions between customers of A and B, it appears that bank A has a net negative liquidity balance x toward B. This creates a dreadful problem for A, which must find a solution how to finance this negative balance x.

The most obvious answer would be to settle this interbank payment in money, by a transfer of liquidity from bank A's account at the central bank to bank B's account. However, this solution would have worked out only in the specific case of bank A having sufficiently large excess reserves, which is excluded by assumption. The fully loaned-up bank A could finance with money only a fraction r of its net negative balance x to B. This fraction $r.x$ corresponds to the reserve that it is no longer required to keep, given that its issued stock of media of exchange has declined by x. The remainder, $(1-r).x$, must be borrowed, either from the central bank, through a liquidity-providing operation, or from another bank, that is, at the interbank loan market. The periodic net negative liquidity balances between banks are the fundamental rationale for the interbank market. Banks' regular needs to borrow in order to finance their interbank liquidity outflows necessarily imply that they must accept to become lenders to each other.

Moreover, there are several compelling reasons why bank B itself, rather than a third party, would accept to lend to A by agreeing on a delayed payment for the remainder $(1-r).x$. First, bank B is in the position of conceding the delayed payment because it needs no more actual liquidity than the portion r to cover, by corresponding central bank money reserves, the increase in the amount of its fiduciary media of exchange. Second, by accepting to lend to A, B can reasonably expect to itself receive a loan from A when the net liquidity impact of customers' transactions will be to A's favor in a future period. Third, the loan to A will yield an interest that will improve B's current income.[41]

At this stage, we should ask the even more fundamental question whether bank B could refuse a loan to bank A. In practice, such a refusal would imply that bank B does not accept to hold the fiduciary media of exchange issued by A. This case of mutual nonrecognition by the banks themselves of their respective fiduciary media of exchange would, however, question mutual trust. If banks do not accept to hold the media of exchange issued by their peers, it is inconceivable that fractional-reserve banks could ever acquire and maintain the confidence of their customers. This crucial finding implies that the interbank market is foundational for fiduciary media of exchange, and hence for fractional-reserve banking itself.

Furthermore, by engaging in mutual refinancing, the apparently decentralized banks can engineer a swiftly coordinated aggregate credit expansion. If a bank notices a permanent increase in its reserves, it can itself lend out a multiple of that excess liquidity up to the point when that excess liquidity is fully absorbed in required reserves covering the newly issued, and retained, fiduciary media of exchange. All other liquidity outflows triggered by the credit expansion, and especially those toward other banks, could be financed on the interbank market. This implies that, thanks to the interbank market, a systemic credit expansion needs no successive rounds of loans by the decentralized banks, whereby in fine each of them would receive a portion of the original excess liquidity in correspondence with its own deposit market share. The multiplication of any new excess liquidity into additional fiduciary media of exchange can occur in one go, through the balance sheet of the single original bank, as long as the other banks accept to refinance it.[42]

The interbank market does not free banks fully from the central bank's control. However, it allows banks to self-finance each other as far as intrabank liquidity outflows are concerned. Thus, banks need central bank money only to finance their aggregate liquidity outflows outside the banking system. Thanks to the interbank market, and as long as mutual recognition of the fiduciary media of exchange goes on, banks can emancipate themselves from the central bank to a significant extent. However, this relative emancipation comes at the expense of increased mutual interdependence. The resulting cross-balance sheet exposures make each bank vulnerable to a sudden denial of rollover of its outstanding refinancing (or redemption of the current loans), which the lending banks could decide, for instance due to a revised appraisal of the borrowing bank's financial health. To minimize this systemic risk of contagion and to protect customers' general confidence in the sector, banks have a strong incentive to adopt similar lending policies, to follow similar risk-management practices and to come to each other's rescue, should an adverse event occur. Hence, even though decentralized, a fractional-reserve banking system has a natural tendency toward uniformity, cartelization, and consolidation.

Different factors determine the extent of the interbank market. The lower the reserve ratio is, the higher the scope for interbank lending. The higher the degree of concentration, the higher the scope for balance netting and hence the lower the remaining need for interbank refinancing. Based on reputation and historical practices, unsecured lending, as opposed to collateralized lending against the pledge of a security, would be more or less spread. Finally, the very presence of a central bank-producer of fiat money that can act as an unconstrained lender of last resort affects banks' incentives. The technical possibility and expectations of unlimited liquidity support is a major cause of moral hazard that tends to lower the risk-assessment standards applied to interbank lending. Thus, banks' stronger willingness to lend to each other translates into an increased size of the interbank market, which makes the whole banking system more exposed to regular banking crises due to a sudden degradation of the trustworthiness among banks. A reassessment of a bank's risk profile by its peer creditors would imply requests for repaying the loans at maturity. This would mean that the borrowing bank has been excluded from the interbank market and must then seek the assistance of the central bank. In short, while the presence of an unconstrained lender of last resort leads to an expansion of the interbank market beyond what its size would have been otherwise, it also contains the seeds for regular swings in interbank loan transactions.

The latest developments in the euro area interbank market provide an empirical illustration of these theoretical points (see figure 1.4). Bank loans to other banks[43] have been growing steadily until the outburst of the GFC. Since then, the massive liquidity injections by the ECB have contributed to crowd out interbank loans. Indeed, banks need refinance each other less in a context where they get ample excess liquidity and direct refinancing from the central bank. Up until mid-2009, interbank lending has evolved in parallel with lending to the economy, of which it used to represent an astounding 50 percent. The crisis-linked loss of confidence and the subsequent liquidity injections by the Eurosystem have kept the interbank lending volumes subdued below their nominal peak of EUR 6.3 trillion from October 2008. Lately, the relative size of the interbank market has declined to around 40 percent of bank loans to the economy, which themselves had stagnated until 2015, before starting to expand again at an average annual rate of around 3 percent since then.

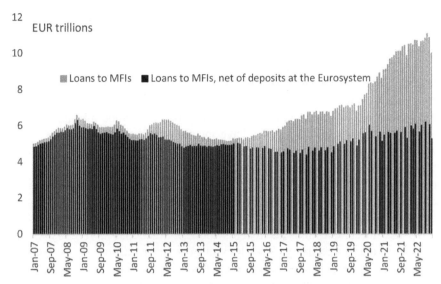

Figure 1.4　Euro Area Bank Loans by Monetary Financial Institutions, 2007–2022.
Source: ECB Statistical Data Warehouse, https://sdw.ecb.europa.eu/browse.do?node=bbn28.

1.5.2 Loans Securitization

Securitization is a technique of structured finance that pools and repackages nonmarketable loans into marketable securities. Such repackaged securities bear the generic name of asset-backed securities (ABS). Specific ABSs might be backed by mortgages (MBS), whether residential (RMBS) or commercial (CMBS). Any type of loans, including corporate loans, student loans, or even leases and credit card balances, can serve as collateral for ABSs. The income stream attached to an ABS derives from the repayments of the underlying loans. To improve their marketability, special purpose vehicles (SPVs) issue the ABSs into tranches that differ by actual risk and expected return.[44] Typically, the issuers retain the riskier tranches (equity and mezzanine) and thus provide a last-resort loss-absorbing guarantee to the investors.[45] The remaining tranches, which may pay their coupons sequentially (pay-through bonds) or pro-rata (pass-through bonds), are sold to institutional or private investors that differ by their risk appetite.[46]

Any company that has receivables on its balance sheet, that is, which has become a lender to the economy, and seeks to liquefy them—to finance a new investment, to repay a maturing debt, or simply to increase its cash reserve—can have recourse to this financial technique that dates back at least to the eighteenth-century "plantation loans." Securitization allows the company to exit financial intermediation, which is not its specialty, and to focus on its principal economic activity. Irrespective of how the securitization proceeds are used, neither the total balance sheet nor the liabilities of the company are affected. Longer-term assets, which are claims on future goods, are exchanged for money, which is the present-day good par excellence. By connecting future claims-holders that look for liquidity to liquidity-holders that look for future claims, securitization expands the intertemporal market for goods. In a sense, securitization epitomizes financial intermediation itself. This leads to a very intriguing question. Why is it that modern banks, rather than the nonfinancial companies, have institutionalized the use of securitization? Are not modern banks already involved in financial intermediation through their loan-granting activity? As lending has become a core part of their business model, would not their intention to liquefy some of their loans appear as the exact opposite of their core business? Finally, what else could banks do with the proceeds from the securitization, but to grant new loans?

To ask these questions as regards modern fractional-reserve banks is already to answer them. A closer look at how securitization affects banks' balance sheets reveals that the investors into ABSs, unless they change their preferences to hold other assets, have to acquire the newly issued ABSs with fiduciary media of exchange. These fiduciary media of exchange are part of banks' liabilities. In consideration for the acquisition of the ABSs, the investors transfer an equivalent amount of bank deposits initially to the SPV, which ultimately transfers these deposits to the same, or another, bank. One way or another, after netting all transactions between banks, the stock of fiduciary media of exchange decreases by the amount of bank loans that have been securitized. Here lies the essence of securitization when applied by banks and its essential difference from the same financial technique when applied by nonbank companies. When banks have recourse to the "originate and distribute" model, as opposed to the "originate and hold" approach, the consolidated balance sheet of the banking system shrinks by the amount of "distributed," that is, securitized, loans. The securitized loans go off-balance sheet and move to the balance sheet of the SPVs. Similarly, the fiduciary media of exchange that the banks created by originating in the first place the now securitized loans are no longer part of their redeemable-on-demand liabilities. Economically, the banks have transformed them into longer-term redeemable-at-maturity securities and managed to move them outside their own balance sheet.

Banks adopt the "originate and distribute" model because it allows them to sterilize the monetary impact of their bank credit expansion. The standard reference to securitization as shadow banking is a rather happily chosen term. Obviously, the SPVs themselves do no banking at all. Yet, they help banks to transfer part of their business off balance sheet, and in that way to avoid the economic and regulatory consequences from credit expansion. In particular, securitization holds back the monetary impact of bank credit expansion. This opens the space for a larger overall credit expansion, as part of it moves into the shadows. The malinvestments of real resources that are so characteristic of the bank credit–fueled boom become deeper and last longer. At the same time, as banks have found in securitization a means to separate credit expansion from balance sheet expansion, the central bank de facto loses its full control of both bank credit expansion and monetary policy.[47] Similar to the interbank market, securitization has become an institutionalized tool that helps banks avoid the liquidity-based regulation by the central bank.[48] Consequently, the central bank has lost part of its strict control over the production of media of exchange.

Securitization volumes in Europe, where the interbank market is so much developed, are much lower than in the United States (US). Moreover, due to regulatory changes introduced in 2014 that make it more difficult for banks to derecognize securitized loans from their balance sheets, outstanding volumes in Europe have been declining since then (see figure 1.5). Thus, if securitized loans represented 11.3 percent of banks' on-balance sheet loans to the non-financial private economy in 2014, that ratio declined to 8 percent in 2021. The stagnation of securitization in Europe contrasts sharply with its expansion in the United States (see figure 1.6), where total outstanding volumes have been growing and even surpassed the on-balance sheet net loans and leases by commercial banks and savings institutions affiliated to the Federal Deposit Insurance Corporation (FDIC).[49] However, the trend of securitization

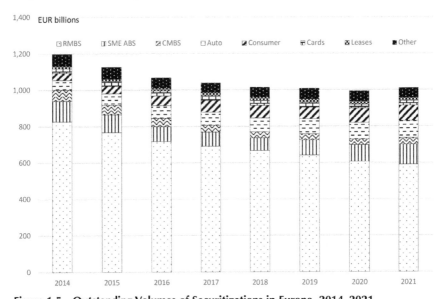

Figure 1.5   Outstanding Volumes of Securitizations in Europe, 2014–2021.
Source: The Association for Financial Markets in Europe (AFME), https://www.afme.eu/Publications/Data-Research/?PageNo=1#category=2188&IncludeFeaturedArticles=False.

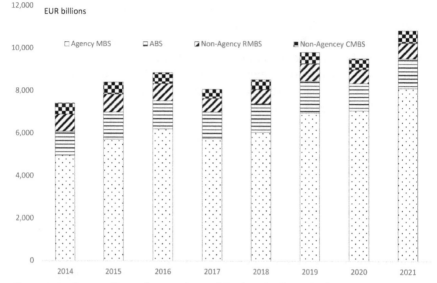

Figure 1.6   Outstanding Volumes of Securitizations in the United States, 2014–2021.
Source: The Association for Financial Markets in Europe (AFME).

in the United States remains dominated by the agency MBSs issued by Fannie Mae, Freddie Mac, and Ginnie Mae.[50] Hence, government policies that aim at promoting home ownership continue to be a major driver of securitization in the United States, as at its origins in the 1970s.

1.5.3 The Adverse Effects of Monetary Policy on Banks' Balance Sheets

The insufficiency of the liquidity-based regulation of banks is not due only to their capacity to avoid it through the interbank market or by loans securitization. This liquidity-based regulation also brings about adverse effects on banks' balance sheets that are undesirable from the point of view of banks' own soundness and stability, that is, from the regulator's own objectives. To begin with, the very existence of a central bank that can act as an unlimited lender of last resort creates wrong incentives for banks' risk appraisal and management. The prospect of being saved out of illiquidity does not promote prudent assessment of credit, counterparty, operational, and other risks. To the very contrary, the unlimited lender of last resort renders a prudent investment attitude excessively costly under these circumstances. The result is a generalized risk mispricing that makes banks structurally weaker than in the absence of a lender of last resort.

In addition, the nowadays standard expansionary monetary policy itself further contributes to a deterioration of the quality of banks' balance sheets, in particular, as reflected in their accumulated equity. The ultimate cause of these additional adverse effects is rooted in the boom-bust cycle engineered by an expansionary monetary policy and a bank credit expansion that lowers the interest rate below its market level. During the boom, when additional credits stimulate economic activity, the higher bank profits reflect the burgeoning economic activity and upbeat profit expectations. In the unavoidable bust, the revealed clusters of entrepreneurial errors and actual bankruptcies translate into NPLs on banks' balance sheets that erode their capital and might even wipe it out completely in cases of very high financial leverage. As many malinvestments cannot be remedied and restructured due to the inconvertibility of some of the capital, the actual losses in the bust are bound to exceed the illusionary profits in the boom. This implies that expansionary monetary policy, on aggregate over the lifetime of the full economic cycle, necessarily weakens banks by causing an erosion of their capital through the postcrisis future correction of the artificially inflated value of their assets.

In the present context of persistently low and even negative interest rates, economists started to acknowledge this adverse impact of monetary policy, though from a different perspective. In particular, they note that banks' own profitability is a key factor for generating capital internally and, if profits are retained instead of distributed, for building a cushion against future losses, thereby contributing to banks' health and stability. The question then is how monetary policy, and especially low interest rate monetary policy, affects banks' profitability. Three channels are typically considered before the empirical examination of their combined effect—net interest margins, revaluation gains, and provisions for NPLs.

First, a low interest rate monetary policy impacts negatively banks' net interest margins, as the return from newly originated loans contracts by more than the interest at which banks remunerate their liabilities. The necessity for banks to retain funding explains why the pass-through of the lower interest rate on their cost of funding is weaker than on their revenue base, thereby resulting in squeezed margins. A very broad empirical study on a sample of 3,385 banks between 2005 and 2013 finds out that a one percentage point interest rate drop implies a decline between eight and twenty basis points in the net interest margin, with the strongest impact at lower interest rates (Claessens et al. 2018, 1).

Second, an off-setting effect comes from the inverse link between interest rates and the value of fixed income assets. A lower interest rate increases the capitalized present-day value of any stream of fixed future incomes due to competition with new assets that pay less now. This fundamental link in finance theory is known to be more sensitive for longer-term assets and at lower rates. To what extent this counter-balancing effect compensates the net interest margin effect on total profitability depends on the share of fixed income assets in banks' balance sheets. The aggregate result is more advantageous for banks with larger holdings of bonds.

Third, because of its initially stimulating effect on economic activity, a lower interest rate reduces the probability of credit default in the short term. The lower share of impaired assets implies a de facto reduction in needed provisions for NPLs, which contributes positively to profits. Demirgüç-Kunt and Huizinga (1999) suggest that thanks to this initially stimulating influence of bank credit expansion on the macroeconomic environment, the combined impact of a lower interest rate of all three effects on profitability is positive.

Later empirical studies qualify this conclusion. Altavilla et al. (2018) find out a neutral combined impact, which might become even negative in prolonged periods of low interest rates. Moreover, the authors also emphasize the existence of additional distortionary effects due to excessive bank risk-taking during the boom and zombie lending/loan ever-greening practices (ibid., 568). Bikker and Vervliet (2017) focus in particular on this latter repercussion of low interest rates on worsening lending standards. They highlight that the reduction in needed provisions for NPLs comes at the expense of a smaller cushion against future credit losses, thereby overstating banks' actual profitability. Ulate (2021) notes, on the basis of an empirically calibrated model, that at the zero rate bound, or below a properly defined low threshold, monetary policy is between 60 and 90 percent as efficient as in positive territory, due to a negative bank equity channel that impedes the transmission of monetary policy. Therefore, the author confirms that, below a point, low interest rates squeeze banks' profits, even though the impact on policy efficiency is found to be rather immaterial.

These most representative empirical studies are not based on a firm theory-based argument that expansionary monetary policy necessarily worsens banks' balance sheets when both stages of the business cycle are considered. Yet they do come to grasps, by means of relentless data gathering and testing, with the finding that monetary policy itself might be deteriorating banks' financial health. To some extent the prominence that macro-prudential regulation has gained in the aftermath of the GFC, which is the subject of the third chapter, is driven precisely by this insight, though from the analytical angle of the specific notion of systemic risk. One way or another, the essential point here is that the liquidity-based regulation of banks, in addition to being insufficient to ensure full control of banks' credit expansion, might also be disrupting for banks' safety and soundness due to its own adverse effects.

1.6 CONCLUSION

This chapter approached the issue of banking regulation from the perspective of commercial banks' participation in the production of fiduciary media of exchange. Three crucial insights offer essentialist, as opposed to utilitarian, reasons why modern fractional-reserve banks have become the most regulated and supervised industry.

First, the privilege of modern banks to operate with fractional reserves and hence to produce fiduciary media of exchange, themselves redeemable in fiat paper money, is immense. Whoever controls bank credit decides which business projects get a nonmarket advantage and how the real resources in the economy are distributed, invested and consumed. Moreover, as media of exchange intermediate all transactions in a market economy, any change in their supply brings about further wealth redistribution effects that divide society into winners and losers. It is thus understandable that governments could not possibly let this immense privilege uncircumscribed. The very monopoly on fiat money production implies already a regulation of the banking sector for the purposes of successfully attaining the publicized goals and the intermediate targets of monetary policy itself, which, for all its functional independence, remains part and parcel of public policy broadly understood. As banks and their bank credit expansion are the most basic vehicle through which monetary policy affects the real economy, the authorities in charge of the present-day fiat money systems could not possibly leave fractional-reserve banks unattended. In a nutshell, this is the very essence of the liquidity-based regulation of banks, which this chapter identified as the most basic and fundamental form of banking regulation.

Second, banks' attempts to avoid the constraints of this liquidity-based regulation of their credit activities, together with the most recent evolution of monetary policy itself, have contributed to a significant loosening of this liquidity-based control that central banks have been exerting historically upon commercial banks. Banks have been successful in circumventing the direct liquidity-based regulation by the central bank thanks to the interbank market and to loans securitization. These two financial institutions have been supporting a tendency toward the uniformity of risk management policies and practices across banks, thereby leading to a de facto cartelization of the industry. At the same time, the central banks' response to the GFC of 2007–2008 has reoriented monetary policy toward stabilizing the prices of financial assets. The resulting structural change, namely permanent excess liquidity for banks, has further eroded the central bank's grip on the commercial banks, which need not go to the open market to finance a structural liquidity deficit that no longer exists. The current historically contingent, yet real, situation of ample excess liquidity in the banking system has rendered the liquidity-based regulation of banks dysfunctional. This naturally calls for the implementation of other regulatory tools and measures that would strengthen the authorities' control over banks' activities.

Third, as privileges, especially when exorbitant, do not come at no expense, fractional-reserve banks are subject to manifold structural vulnerabilities, often described as risks—deposit withdrawal risk, interbank market redemption risk, funding illiquidity risk, contagion risk, reputational risk, capital erosion risk, credit risk, market risk, operational risk, and so on. All these risks can be ascribed to one or another aspect of their activities. The inherent and systemic instability of such a system is a direct consequence of the contradiction between the fractional-reserve principle and the instantaneous redemption promise as regards the fiduciary media of exchange. Furthermore, this inherent instability is exacerbated by the real malinvestments that bank credit expansion necessarily brings about. Hence, nonperforming loans, bank loan losses, erosion of bank capital, and ultimately bank failures can be traced back to the fundamental principle that governs modern banking. This characteristic financial instability, which also has a disturbing influence of its own on the very goals of monetary policy, is the third fundamental rationale for remedial action by the public authorities, that is, for further industry-specific regulation and supervision of the banking sector.

NOTES

1. For that same reason, economists do not consider direct exchange as a viable historical reality. Rather, they see it as an "imaginary construction," a product of our intellect, the sole purpose of which is to serve as a methodological device for grasping the limitations of a nonmonetary economy. On the role of imaginary constructions as the specific method of economic analysis, see Mises (1998b, 236–37).

2. For a detailed presentation of the place of money among all goods, see Mises (1990, 55–68).

3. This natural process of the emergence of money has been noticed already by Turgot (1997, 181–83), Condillac (1966, 283–401), Smith (1994), and Say (1841, 240–44). Menger contributed a seminal and very coherent explanation of the origin of monies in the framework of his general theory of commodities (Menger 1994, 236–86 and Menger, 1892), while Mises has further clarified the conditions under which individuals discover the media of exchange (Mises 1980, 41–49).

4. Moreover, this is the only way in which society could discover and progressively adopt media of exchange. As media of exchange evolve out of commodities and rely on their own marketability and liquidity, it is inconceivable that a ruler, however enlightened and well intentioned, could ever impose goods that are not yet marketable and liquid, that is, already media of exchange or susceptible of becoming media

of exchange on their own, on the ruled. The very use of media of exchange implies adoption and prior, mutually spread, understanding of their benefits.

5. This is sometimes summarised by the saying that "money permeates all markets." Although emphasizing the central role of money, this formulation also implies that each good has a self-contained market of its own. Coming from a businessman specialized in the trade of a few goods, this segmented view would be permissible. However, for the economist, all transactions are interrelated, irrespective of the physical characteristics of the goods and services that exchange for money. Thus, the totality of all monetary transactions comprises the market, in which all prices are interconnected, either horizontally (along the same stage of production) or vertically (across the stages of production). An in-depth presentation of the vertical and horizontal connectivity of prices can be found in Strigl (2000, 37–90).

6. This is the outstanding contribution of the so-called Austrian school of economics, namely to definitively accomplish the integration of money into the modern economic analysis. This achievement was possible thanks to the application of subjective valuation at the margin directly to individuals' holdings of monetary units, relative to units of other goods and services. This allows for a coherent explanation of monetary prices, as they really occur in the market process, based on the modern subjectivist value theory. This definitive monetary integration finally removed the veil of money that plagued classical economics for so long and raised such a mathematical challenge to neoclassical economics. For the same reason, economic analysis in the Austrian tradition does not face the standard mainstream problem of lacking microeconomic foundations for its macroeconomic findings.

7. As aptly put by Rothbard: "One of the most important economic laws, therefore, is: *Every supply of money is always utilized to its maximum extent, and hence no social utility can be conferred by increasing the supply of money*" (Rothbard 2009, 766; original emphasis).

8. This is a crucial specificity of money as a good: "What therefore constitutes the peculiarity of a commodity which has become money is, that *the possession of it* procures for us at any time, that is, at any moment we think fit, assured control over every commodity to be had on the market, and this usually at prices adjusted to the economic situation of the moment: the control, on the other hand, conferred by other kinds of commodities over market goods is, in respect of time, and in part of price as well, uncertain, relatively if not absolutely" (Menger 1892, 251–52; our emphasis).

9. The process is direct in the sense that individuals address their higher demand for media of exchange by their own actions of withholding more monetary units in their cash balances, that is, accepting to sell other goods and services, including labour and assets, at lower monetary prices. No third party intervention is required. This monetary equilibration mechanism is best described in Mises (1998b, 413–21), Rothbard (2009, 756–67) and Salerno (2010, 181–97).

10. For an important development of this argument on how changes in the money supply and the monetary regime itself affect the quality of money and its purchasing power, see Bagus (2009).

11. The important time- and place-specific aspects of any real-world increase in the supply of money and their implications in terms of wealth and income redistribution

have been discovered by Hume (1987, 286–87) and Cantillon (2001, 67 and f.), to whom they owe their name, and further developed by Mises (1980, 237–43) and Rothbard (2009, 811–15). For a modern revival of the relevance of the Cantillon effects, see Thornton (2012) and Dorobat (2015).

12. On this overarching principle of the consumers' ultimate sovereignty through the market process, see Mises (1998b, 270–73).

13. The economic analysis of banking as originating in money warehousing has been very much developed by Rothbard (2008, 85–110; 1991, 42–51; 1994, 37; 2009, 700), Huerta de Soto (1995) and Hülsmann (2000). Huerta de Soto (2005, chapter II) provides important evidence that roman and canonical laws both denied any property right to the bank on the money deposited with it and imposed an obligation on the bank to maintain a hundred percent reserve at any single moment.

14. From that perspective, any reference to the circulation of money in the economy, as epitomized in the notion of velocity of money, raises more questions than it provides answers.

15. On good will and reputation as a very special asset for banks, see Mises's discussion of free banking (1998b, 441–45). Mises espouses the view that reputation is an individual phenomenon, thereby concluding that each bank would be protective of its own exclusive good will, notably by avoiding any association with less reputable institutions.

16. Murray Rothbard also sees no reason for a specific detailed government regulation of banking: "There is one and only one government 'regulation': that they [banks], like any other business, must pay their debts promptly or else be declared insolvent and be put out of business" (Rothbard 2008, 111). However, in this very restrictive view of legitimate regulation by governments, Rothbard refers to banks that do not observe the full-reserve principle. As shown in the next section, the operation of such fractional-reserve banks is subject to specific vulnerabilities and risks. To some extent, these structural weaknesses legitimize governments' attempts to alleviate them, notably through regulating the banking business. How successful that regulation could be is another question, one that this book attempts to answer.

17. On the crucial distinction between circulation (bank) credit, which is financed through additional media of exchange, and commodity (real) credit, which is financed through prior savings, cf. Mises (2008, 296–300) and Huerta de Soto (2005).

18. Strictly speaking, there is no multiplication of money. Rather, there is creation of money substitutes up to a point where they become a well-defined multiple of the money kept in reserves. For the simplest case where the required reserve is the only source of liquidity drain on the banking system, that multiple is equal to the inverse of the targeted reserve ratio.

19. The explanation of monetary and banking history on the basis of this essentialist process of transubstantiation of the monetary objects has been described as a "progression theorem" (Salerno 1991, 371). Hoppe (1994), Huerta de Soto (1995), and Hülsmann (1997) espouse the same approach to monetary history. The centralization of banks' own money reserves into a single institution (the one-reserve system described by Bagehot) and various government privileges (territorial monopoly of issue, government funding, limited liability, *cours forcé*, legal tender, etc.) all played a

role in this very long and progressive process, which was completed with the ultimate demonetization of gold in 1971.

20. Hülsmann (2004) develops the importance of legal tender laws in the process of transforming dematerialized fiduciary media of exchange into fiat paper money.

21. Kuznetsov (2005) aptly describes fiat money as an administrative good. Practically all contemporary developments in monetary theory can be viewed as attempts to rationalize the specific rules for fiat money production, commonly referred to as the objectives and targets of monetary policy.

22. The consecrated term of "unlimited lender of last resort" assumes the lack of any limit to central banks' money production and liquidity support. This view is not entirely correct, as money-holders might lose their confidence in the fiat money to the point of reducing their demand for money down to zero. Such hyperinflationary episodes, which are not that infrequent, imply the economic death of money, which becomes valueless, and reflect the ultimate limit that constrains somewhat the central banks as lenders of last resort.

23. In what follows, the notion of commercial banks, or simply banks, will always refer to fractional-reserve banks. In practice, commercial banks might combine their fractional-reserve banking activity with the business of investment banking, that is, borrowing of funds with the purpose of on-lending them as part of plain-vanilla financial intermediation.

24. Money in the narrow sense refers to money proper only, whether it is fiat paper money or commodity money. It is measured by the monetary aggregate M0 (currency and banks' reserves at the central bank). Money in the broader sense includes, next to money proper outside banks' vaults, all money substitutes. Different broader aggregates, from M1 to M3 depending on the type of money substitutes taken into account, measure money in the broader sense. The very existence of fiduciary media of exchange implies that money in the broader sense (from M1 to M3) is a multiple of money proper (M0). For an enlightening discussion of a proper measure of the "true" money supply, see Salerno (2010, 119–34).

25. The crisis, which is the moment of understanding that resources have been misdirected into malinvestments, ends the boom and starts the bust. While the boom might last quite some time, the crisis itself needs not take long. However, a longer boom means deeper malinvestments, and consequently the need for more intense restructuring during the bust.

26. The bank credit, or monetary, theory of the business cycle, which together with capital theory is a central building block of the Austrian macro-economic theory, is expounded, among others, in Mises (1980; 1998b) and Hayek (1967). Notable modern developments include Hülsmann (1998), on the role of expectations and government interventionism, and Huerta de Soto (2005), on price developments and the Ricardo effect. Bagus (2012) offers a comprehensive and enlightening discussion of the advantages of the Austrian business cycle theory in comparison to alternative modern theories. Macovei (2016) defends the general validity of the monetary theory of the cycle against the assumption that entrepreneurs could arbitrage away inflation-induced clusters of errors.

27. The rules on the minimum reserve requirements in the euro area have been loosened over time, in terms of i) the eligibility of liabilities that determine the reserve base, ii) the minimum reserve ratio or coefficient applied to that base and iii) the allowance to maintain the resulting reserve requirement as an average only over a certain period. Initially set up at 2 percent, the minimum reserve ratio in the euro area was brought down to 1 percent as of February 2012 as part of the policy response to the Greek sovereign debt crisis. Deposits with agreed maturity over two years do not enter in the composition of the reserve base and are exempt from any reserve requirement. Euro area banks' average reserve requirements, for the period from November 2, 2022 to December 20, 2022, amounted to almost EUR 167 billion. At that time, reserves were remunerated at 2 percent, while a penalty rate of 4.75 percent applied to deficiencies.

28. Euro area banks' latest excess reserves have exceeded EUR 4 trillion. In fact, since the various accommodations to monetary policy and in particular the repetitive rounds of quantitative easing, banks in the euro area have been operating with structural excess liquidity since 2009. This excess liquidity, which reached astronomical levels only lately in the context of the COVID-19 policy measures, explains the historically low interest rates on bank loans, especially in real terms when price inflation is considered.

29. The central bank can alter banks' liquidity condition also by changing the minimum reserve requirement ratio. A lower ratio automatically frees part of the available reserves, which become excessive relative to the new (lower) requirement, and thus can serve to finance any liquidity outflows, including those that could be linked to a credit expansion.

30. In the aggregate, the banks' originally excess reserves either change their status by becoming additional required reserves $(r.\Delta D)$ or serve to acquire additional banknotes $(b.\Delta D)$ from the central bank, where r is the reserve ratio and b is the ratio of banknotes to deposits, assumed stable. Then, if EL is the originally excess liquidity created by the central bank, its absorption through credit expansion implies that $EL = r.\Delta D + b.\Delta D$, or $\Delta D = EL.1/(r+b)$. This is precisely the end-result of the "money multiplier."

31. In their empirical review of business cycles, Kydland and Prescott find out that the monetary base is procyclical, or even slightly lagging the cycle. On that basis, they conclude at the "monetary myth" of the monetary base playing an important causal role (Kydland and Prescott 1990, 14).

32. The analytical focus on credit leads to a general overstatement of its role in the broader economy, as evidenced by the claim that "*All* production must be financed by credit" (Lavoie 1984, 792; original emphasis). This is another aspect of the post-Keynesian theory of endogenous money, which reinforces the original Keynesian bias against the critical function of savings for funding investment and sustaining the capital structure of the economy.

33. Post-Keynesians emphasize that central banks control the policy interest rate instead of base money. However, policy rate changes are only one technical instrument, among others (e.g., collateral eligibility, haircuts on collateral, duration and type of the open-market operations, direct asset purchases), for altering the

availability of reserves to banks and the quantity of money produced. Irrespective of the implementing instruments, the quantity of money produced by the central bank remains the single most important real-world factor of relevance: "Hence, in practice, monetary actions are almost always described in terms of their impact on a short-term nominal interest rate—such as the federal funds rate in the United States—*even though, strictly speaking, those actions still begin with open market operations that change the monetary base*" (Ireland 2005, 3; our emphasis).

34. It is worthwhile noting that while profits are collectivized and distributed among the NCBs according to a specific distribution key, potential losses—in particular, those related to the emergency liquidity assistance (ELA)—are not. There are other elements on the individual NCBs' balance sheets, such as the reported volumes of currency in circulation, which are not a truthful reflection of reality, but are based on that same distribution key. The need to correct these rather fictitious numbers is one of the factors that explain the build-up of the so-called intra-Eurosystem claims and liabilities (depending on the direction of the correction). Lately, these intrasystem claims have become particularly important in the context of the so-called Target-2 (im)balances. The build-up of these balances reflects the fact that liquidity provided by one NCB (to banks under its local jurisdiction) has ended up on another NCB's settlement Target-2 account with the ECB (due to that same liquidity having ended up in banks under that other local jurisdiction). Sinn and Wollmershäuser (2012) and Sinn (2020) provide an in-depth theoretical analysis of the nature of the Target-2 balances and show the intra-euro area fiscal redistribution effects implied by the build-up of these balances in the context of the Eurosystem's response to the GFC.

35. In addition, a marginal lending standing facility allows the Eurosystem to provide liquidity, at the margin, to a bank that faces a temporary liquidity need. Conversely, a marginal deposit facility is a tool for absorbing temporary excess liquidity. The fixed-term deposit, which is the third type of banks' deposit account with the Eurosystem, is a tool for attracting, or sterilizing, structural excess liquidity. As a rule, euro area banks hold their available liquidity, whether required or excess, on their current accounts with the Eurosystem.

36. For grasping the full extent of all amendments to the implementation of monetary policy in the euro area, compare the version of the general documentation on the Eurosystem policy instruments and procedures from June 2021 with its pre-GFC version from 2004 (ECB 2004; ECB 2021).

37. Moreover, the ECB has moved to "unlimited allotment" of the tender procedures, which means that it is providing as much liquidity as requested by the banks, without any interest rate-driven rationing.

38. The dedicated webpages https://www.ecb.europa.eu/mopo/implement/app/html/index.en.html and https://www.ecb.europa.eu/mopo/implement/pepp/html/index.en.html contain detailed information on the APP and the PEPP, the two broad programmes of quantitative easing in the EA.

39. In the long term, the liquidity impact of these operations will fade away as the assets mature and if the Eurosystem does not reinvest the proceeds in new assets.

40. The difference between these accounts is essentially institutional. Current accounts serve to settle transactions and their balances enter in the calculation of

Chapter 1

banks' compliance with the period-averaged minimum reserve requirement. The marginal deposit facility absorbs excess liquidity that is considered to be occasional and temporary. The fixed-term deposit sterilizes a longer-term or structural excess liquidity. Thus, base money is defined as the sum between banknotes and banks' reserves, excluding the balances on the fixed-term deposits. The underlying logic is that fixed-term deposits represent inaccessible liquidity, at least for the duration of the fixed term. The concept of central bank money is broader and includes, in addition to base money, the governments' deposits. By extension, all liabilities of a central bank should be considered as part of the so-called central bank money.

41. As refinancing at the central bank is a permanently outstanding option, the rates at which banks can borrow needed liquidity from the central bank, or alternatively deposit their excess liquidity, closely determine the interest rate on interbank loans.

42. For a broader and more detailed presentation of the interbank market, especially in the framework of the debate about the inflationary nature of a free, that is, unprotected by an unlimited lender of last resort, fractional-reserve banking system, see Gertchev (2012).

43. The ECB Statistical Data Warehouse includes both commercial banks and the Eurosystem in the single standalone category of Monetary Financial Institutions (MFIs). The nonmonetary financial institutions include pension funds, insurance corporations and other financial intermediaries. The aggregate balance sheet of the MFIs, excluding the Eurosystem—that is, of commercial banks—reports loans to all MFIs, that is, including banks' deposits at the Eurosystem. To capture the interbank market between commercial banks only, figure 1.4 subtracts banks' deposits at the Eurosystem, as reported in the consolidated balance sheet of the Eurosystem, from the post "loans to MFIs," as reported in the consolidated balance sheet of the MFIs, excluding the Eurosystem.

44. The SPV, whether fully independent from the company or set up by the company itself, is a mere screen between the investors, to whom it sells the ABSs, and the company, from which it acquires the loans.

45. Credit enhancements, additional guarantees and credit ratings by third parties contribute further to the marketability of the ABSs.

46. For a more detailed analysis of the rationale, scope and techniques of securitization, cf. Gertchev (2009).

47. Central bank economists have recognized that securitization decreases the power of monetary policy: "The analysis suggests that securitization has likely weakened the impact of any policy move" (Estrella 2002, 1).

48. More broadly, to the extent that securitization prevents balance sheet expansion, it helps banks to avoid all regulatory requirements that a standard on-balance sheet credit expansion would have triggered. In particular, securitization helps banks economize also on their own funds (capital), as further detailed in the next chapter.

49. For data on US banks' consolidated balance sheet, cf. https://www7.fdic.gov/sdi/main.asp?formname=standard.

50. While the Federal National Mortgage Association (Fannie Mae) and the Federal Home Loan Mortgage Corporation (Freddie Mac) are government-sponsored enterprises, the Government National Mortgage Association (Ginnie Mae) is owned in full by the government.

Chapter 2

Micro-Prudential Regulation and Supervision

The previous chapter established an economic framework for analyzing the regulation of banks based on their specific monetary role. It highlighted several reasons why public authorities have a strong interest in regulating banks—their shared privilege to participate in the production of money in the broader sense, their capacity to influence the distribution of resources in the economy, as well as their structural instability. Furthermore, the chapter stressed that, in the present-day monetary regimes, the control of banks' liquidity condition by the central bank is how banking regulation starts. However, despite all its theoretical potency, this primary regulation of banks can be proven to be either inoperative (as in the current situation of structural excess liquidity), insufficient (due to its avoidance by banks through the interbank loan market or by securitizing loans), or even deficient (due to the adverse effects of expansionary monetary policy on banks' profitability and stability). Against this backdrop, it is only natural that public authorities seek other means to control banks' activities and to limit the related risks. This is the ultimate raison d'être of prudential banking regulation, which aims at reducing and containing banks' default risk.

The economic literature attributes banks' default risk to three fundamental causes: the inherent risk of loans (a specific feature of their assets), the leveraging of that risk through debt (a specific feature of their liabilities), and the funding illiquidity risk (a specific relation between long-term assets and short-term liabilities) (Calomiris 2012). In that conceptual framework, the three sources of risk command a wisely designed combination of three policy tools, namely, a lender of last resort,[1] minimum capital requirements, and minimum liquidity requirements. In the strict sense of the word, prudential regulation, understood either as a policy or as an established set of operational rules, refers to the capital and liquidity requirements that banks should conform to. In that context, the role of supervision is to ensure, through a

55

sufficiently invasive monitoring of banks' actual practices, the effective compliance with the established rules.

This chapter deals with the principal requirements of micro-prudential regulation, the focus of which is to ensure that each bank's individual balance sheet is robust enough against the default risk. In practice, this implies setting up a level playing field of common rules for all banking institutions.[2] The first section offers a succinct history of the coming into place of the so-called Basel Framework. The next section presents the Single Banking Rulebook in the EU legislative context. The third and fourth sections detail, respectively, the capital and the liquidity requirements in that Rulebook and examine their economic impact. The fifth section describes the essentials and implications of banking supervision, with an emphasis on the annual supervisory cycle and the comprehensive reviews of banks in the Banking Union.

2.1 THE THREE PILLARS OF THE BASEL FRAMEWORK

The core principles of regulating and supervising international bank groups, known as the Basel Framework, have come into being only progressively and over the course of several decades. Continuously evolving, they are the result of regular and ongoing international cooperation, coordinated by the Basel Committee on Banking Supervision (BCBS) hosted by the Bank for International Settlements (BIS). At its creation in 1974, the BCBS comprised the central bank governors of the G10 countries, joined by Switzerland and Luxembourg. Today, the Basel Committee has expanded to twenty-eight jurisdictions and includes even international agencies, such as the International Monetary Fund (IMF) and the European Commission (EC).[3] Although the Committee has no formal authority, its members recognize it as an international standards-setter. It belongs to national authorities to make these standards legally binding.[4]

The immediate trigger for setting up the BCBS came from the notorious failure of a rather small German bank that has become a textbook example of settlement and contagion risks. After finding out that the Herstatt Bank had suffered forex-related losses that exceeded ten times its own capital, the German banking regulator decided to liquidate the bank in the afternoon of June 26, 1974.[5] All of a sudden, counterparties in the United States, where markets were still open, realized that Herstatt would never settle its dollar-denominated liabilities. Because of the ensuing uncertainty about how losses coming from now unrecoverable claims on Herstatt would affect other banks' exposures and their own capital, the international interbank market is said to have frozen for several days. Although the magnitude of this accident might be exaggerated to some extent, it seriously disturbed the international financial community and alerted central banks about the risky implications of uncoordinated supervisory actions. It should also be recognized that, even though not new, settlement and contagion risks have acquired new relevance since the 1971 suspension of the dollar convertibility into gold and the establishment of an international system of floating exchange rates since 1973. In this new reality of multiple paper monies, regulatory and supervisory cooperation has been developing as only one aspect of the broader international cooperation between independent central banks. Though the Herstatt incident might have been instrumental indeed in accelerating these coordination efforts, it is not accidental that the Basel Committee started gaining prominence only after the Bretton Woods agreements collapsed.[6]

The first steps toward international cooperation were rather slow and hesitant. It took eight years before the very first report on the supervision of banks' foreign establishments (BCBS 1975) resulted in the adoption of two quite broad, though clear, principles, in a succinct seven-page document known as the Concordat (BCBS 1983). No foreign banking establishment should be able to escape supervision, and that supervision should be adequate. The Concordat laid down the implications of these two simple principles in terms of responsibility sharing and information exchange between home and host supervisors, depending on the type of the foreign banking establishment (branch, subsidiary, or joint venture) and the object of supervision (liquidity, solvency, or foreign exchange positions). The distribution of responsibilities between the home supervisor, in charge of the parent institution at consolidated level, and the host supervisor, in charge of the standalone subsidiaries,[7] dates back to that same document. In 1990, the Committee supplemented these broad principles with rules on the cross-border exchange of information between bank supervisors and oversight bodies in securities transactions. This work prepared the adoption, two years later, of four minimum standards for the supervision of international banking groups in another rather humble six-page document (BCBS 1992).[8]

These 1992 minimum standards explicitly aimed at ensuring that the Concordat principles were effectively applied. Enforceability was achieved through the mutual agreement that host supervisors could prohibit the local establishment of a foreign bank, whose home supervisor would not abide, or would be considered as not abiding, by the Concordat principles (fourth standard). This enforcement mechanism turned out very successful, including in securing commercial banks' own endorsement of the principles, as they were the ultimate target of the threat. From that point onward, the Concordat principles grew quickly into the more detailed twenty-five core principles for effective banking supervision that the Committee adopted in 1997. By making these principles the backbone of their Financial Sector Assessment Programs (FSAPs), the IMF and the World Bank were instrumental in promoting their quick endorsement throughout the world. Since then, the Committee has expanded and revised these core principles into twenty-nine norms, covering the two broad areas of supervisory powers, responsibilities and functions, and of prudential regulation and requirements (BCBS 2012).

Beyond the harmonization and dissemination of supervisory best practices and guidelines, the Committee has been playing a crucial role in shaping banks' regulatory environment. The evolving set of rules—known as Basel I, II, and III—aimed at addressing the evolving risks to banks' soundness and safety.[9] The original Basel Accord (Basel I), approved in 1988 and implemented by international banks in 1992, focused on banks' capacity to absorb losses and set up the minimum capital requirement as the backbone of micro-prudential regulation. Basel I introduced the concept of risk-weighted capital adequacy, meaning that banks need to build up and keep at least as much capital as required by a ratio (8 percent) of their risk-weighted assets (RWAs). Basel I had two primary goals. First, it aimed at ensuring sufficient capitalization of large banks, in particular, in the aftermath of the Latin American debt crisis from the early 1980s. Second, it strived at setting a "level playing field" for banks by removing nonmarket advantages due to the leniency of some supervisory jurisdictions (regulatory forbearance).[10] In that way, it attempted to remove incentives for regulatory arbitrage. Yet, the single most essential element and achievement of the Basel Accord was the adoption of the concept of risk-weighted capital adequacy.

Indeed, all subsequent revisions and expansions of the original Basel Accord can be seen as refinements of that concept. How should RWAs account for noncredit, that is, market, counterparty or operational, risks? How should off-balance sheet elements, such as guarantees or contingent exposures, be included in the RWAs? Which is the proper asset portfolio segmentation and the most accurate means to estimate the associated risks and to determine the risk weights? Which liabilities would be eligible as capital instruments? Should there be deductions? How should loan loss provisions be treated? What is the appropriate level of the capital adequacy ratio? Should banks be required to keep one or more buffers above that minimum ratio? Should there be a differentiation between banks, based on their systemic relevance? Many questions of this nature have inspired lengthy and ongoing debates. This chapter will address some of them from the economic point of view. For the sake of completing this introductory historical overview, this section needs only to mention the two major upgrades of Basel I.[11]

In response to the financial innovation in the early 1990s, a new capital framework, known as Basel II, was proposed in 1999 and released to banks in 2004. It went beyond Basel I in three specific areas. First, it crystallized the three pillars of modern banking regulation: i) minimum regulatory requirements, focused primarily on banks' capital needs, ii) supervisory review by competent authorities of the implementation of these requirements, and iii) transparency/disclosure requirements to boost market discipline. Second, it expanded the concept of RWAs beyond credit exposures, with the view of incorporating market and operational risks. Third, and most crucially, to improve banks' understanding of their own risks, it promoted the use of internal methods of risk assessment through probabilistic models based on historical data. In that respect, Basel II endorsed a major complexification of regulatory compliance that has become the primary cause of the new phenomenon of regulatory capture. Regulatory capture refers to the growing difficulties of the regulator/supervisor to understand, and hence circumscribe, the risks related to the activities of the regulated entities.[12]

The ex post analysis of the financial sector weaknesses exposed by the GFC of 2007–2008 and the related European sovereign debt crisis led to the subsequent revision of the framework into Basel III. Too much leverage, arbitrary external ratings, inadequate liquidity buffers, insufficient stable funding, poor governance, and insufficient risk management practices were perceived as the main factors of the crisis, and hence necessitating adequate solutions.[13] The updated Basel III Capital and Liquidity Standards (2010) aimed at addressing these deficiencies by strengthening the first, regulatory pillar of the Basel framework. First, to improve banks' capacity to absorb losses, the quality of required capital was reinforced through a stronger emphasis on equity, as opposed to hybrid and debt instruments that do not absorb losses on an ongoing basis. Second, to alleviate the possible adverse effects of risk-weighting, in particular, as applied by the internal methods of risk assessment, a standard nonweighted leverage ratio was introduced. Third, additional capital requirements were adopted in the form of capital buffers, either general for all banks or only specific to the systemically important institutions. Fourth, to mitigate the negative spill-overs of fire sales, whereby untimely sales of assets reduce their marketability and bring about effective insolvency through sale-induced losses, Basel III also explicitly addressed the issue of banks' funding structure through the introduction of liquidity requirement ratios.[14] Fifth, to minimize both regulatory arbitrage and capture, the enforcement of rules received a renewed emphasis, notably through the regularized use of asset quality reviews and stress tests.

Thus, Basel III went much beyond the original intention of the first Basel Accord, notably by expanding the regulatory framework to include rules that are meant to address issues of liquidity, of pro-cyclicality, and of systemic risk. The specific problem of systemic risk, and more broadly of the system's overall stability, is of concern for macro-prudential regulation, which is the subject of the next chapter. This chapter remains focused on the Basel III-related micro-prudential regulation and its implementation in the EU through the Single Banking Rulebook. This naturally calls for a short detour through the essential architecture of the legal foundations of the European Union.

2.2 THE SINGLE RULEBOOK IN THE EU LEGISLATIVE CONTEXT

The constitutional setup of the EU is fixed by two pieces of primary legislation, namely the Treaty on the Functioning of the European Union (TFEU), which sets up the founding principles and the role of the EU across various policy areas, and the Treaty on European Union (TEU), which defines the prerogatives of the different European Institutions (EIs).[15] The policies, which over the years have gradually expanded to encompass practically every aspect of human activity in the EU, are grounded—originally and still nowadays—in the four foundational freedoms of movement of the people, of capital transfers, of trade in goods, and of establishment for providing services. In other words, the EU is designed as a unified economic space (the single market) where investment and production of goods and services are free in principle and governed by the same rules in all member states (MS) of the Union. This is what the primary law of the EU upholds.

The concrete rules for carrying out economic activity in specific areas, for instance banking and financial services, as well as the respective roles of MS and the EU in limiting and controlling that specific activity, are set up in secondary legislation by policy area. Regulations and directives are the two main secondary legal instruments in the EU. Regulations are directly applicable and enforceable in all MS. To enter into force, directives need to be transposed in national laws within a given time frame. Decisions, implementing acts and delegated acts are other secondary legislative tools that do not carry a new political meaning but rather clarify or apply various aspects of a regulation or of a directive.

Regulations and directives come into being through the complex interplay of the EIs, four of which are especially relevant. First comes the European Commission (EC), which is in charge of the executive branch of power in the EU. The EC, governed by a College of Commissioners, each of them in charge of a specific policy area,[16] both adopts new legislative proposals (power of policy initiative) and monitors the implementation of the existing EU legislative corpus (guardian of the treaties). The Council of the European Union, that is, MS represented by their respective policy Ministers, and the European Parliament, that is, the Assembly of directly elected representatives of the EU citizens, are the two co-legislators that amend and adopt regulations and directives proposed by the Commission.[17] Possible disagreements among

MS and the EIs are brought for resolution in front of the Court of Justice of the European Union.

Basel III principles are reflected in the so-called Single Banking Rulebook, which sets up a common bank regulatory framework in the EU. Four major regulations and directives set up the foundation of that Single Rulebook—the Capital Requirements Regulation (CRR, Regulation (EU) No 575/2013, amended in some aspects by CRR II, Regulation (EU) 2019/876), the Capital Requirements Directive (CRD IV, Directive 2013/36/EU, amended in some aspects by CRD V, Directive (EU) 2019/878), the Bank Recovery and Resolution Directive (BRRD, Directive 2014/59/EU, amended in some aspects by BRRD II, Directive (EU) 2019/879), and the Deposit Guarantee Schemes Directive (DGSD, Directive 2014/49/EU).[18] Many other financial services–related legal instruments add to this banks-specific framework, such as the Payments Services Directive, the Mortgage Credit Directive, the Consumer Credit Directive, and the Anti-Money Laundering Directive.[19] The Single Rulebook is the foundation of the Banking Union in the EU, which was designed on three pillars—the Single Supervisory Mechanism (SSM, entered into force in November 2014), the Single Resolution Mechanism (SRM, entered into force in August 2014), and the European Deposit Insurance Scheme (EDIS, not yet in force).

This Single Rulebook applies to both credit institutions and investment firms. A credit institution is defined as "an undertaking the business of which is to take deposits or other repayable funds from the public and to grant credits for its own account" (CRR, Article 4). This legal definition corresponds to the economic definition of a fractional-reserve bank. An investment firm is "any legal person whose regular occupation or business is the provision of one or more investment services to third parties and/or the performance of one or more investment activities on a professional basis" (Directive 2004/39/EC, Article 4). This legal definition corresponds to the economic definition of a financial intermediary.

The goal of the Single Rulebook is to establish a fully harmonized regulatory framework for banks in the EU. Thus, it removes general national options and discretions, while allowing for institution-specific discretionary decisions in the context of the annual supervisory cycle. As it harmonizes fully the set of banking rules, the Single Rulebook naturally relies on the EU passport, which implies that host MS could not require authorization for subsidiaries or endowment capital for branches of credit institutions already authorized in another, home, MS. In that way, access to the banking industry is regulated equally throughout the EU. There is a minimum initial capital requirement of EUR 5 million for a credit institution (with an option for EUR 1 million, after notification to the Commission and the European Banking Authority) and of EUR 730,000 for an investment firm (reduced to EUR 125,000 if no dealings for its own account). It is further required that at least two persons effectively direct the business and that both shareholders and managers should pass a fit-and-proper assessment. This is meant to ensure that owners and managers are of sufficiently good repute and possess sufficient knowledge, skills, and experience. The start of activities is subject to prior authorization that the Competent Authority (CA) in charge of supervision in the MS of incorporation should grant or refuse within a twelve-month period.[20]

The Single Rulebook also requests banks to put in place effective and prudent management practices. To avoid groupthink and to preserve a critical mindset, the management body is expected to be strongly involved and to effectively assess and challenge the decisions of the senior management. Remuneration policies should not promote excessive risk-taking, notably by limiting the variable component of the staff remunerations to 100 percent of the fixed component. Furthermore, significant institutions should set up both Nomination and Remuneration Committees.

Above all, the Single Rulebook sets the minimum capital and liquidity requirements that aim at ensuring the solvency and stability of banks.

2.3 CAPITAL REQUIREMENTS

In corporate accounting, capital refers to a company's liabilities that never fall due. This corresponds to the difference between the book value of assets and all outstanding debt obligations. In other words, capital is the net book value. For traded companies, the market value of shares offers a continuous reappraisal of the book capital. Based on investors' expectations and actual decisions to hold or sell the shares, the market value might be above or below the book value. Nontraded companies get their capital book value tested at the time of selling part or all of it. Given that capital is never redeemed or reimbursed, but could only be sold to another owner, it represents the "own funds" of the company.

The economic role of the own funds is to provide a cushion against future expected and unexpected losses, and thus to ensure that the company can continue its operations on a "going-concern" basis, that is, without being restructured. Own funds are there to absorb the negative fluctuations in the value of assets, so that all repayable liabilities remain fully covered by net assets. If the own funds are not large enough to absorb current or future losses, the company's net value of capital becomes negative. This implies the company's insolvency, in which case some of the debts will remain wholly or partially unpaid. Expectations about possible insolvency might either trigger debtholders' anticipated requests for early redemption or increase the cost of debt refinancing (rollover). Both scenarios could lead to the company's temporary illiquidity or even effective and permanent insolvency.

Applied to banking, a minimum requirement of own funds ultimately aims at guaranteeing the protection of customers' deposits, which are banks' main redeemable liabilities. The different arguments that have been put forward in favor of government regulation of banks' capital adequacy are rooted in the perceived misbehavior of banks' owners and managers, if left to themselves. (Dowd 1997, 96–99). First, in the pursuit of ever-higher returns on investment to shareholders, bankers would engage in a race to the bottom, which would result in a capital level that is too low for an adequate protection of depositors. Second, aware of the availability of deposit insurance, banks are not incentivized to build up sufficiently high levels of capital on their own and choose to operate with higher leverage. Third, the financially unsophisticated and potentially ill-informed small depositors would be unable to judge whether a bank has a level of capital that is sufficient to make its balance sheet robust enough. Such instances of perceived market failure would result in banks' undercapitalization, and hence insufficient protection of depositors. This would make the case for a corrective action by the authorities in the form of imposing a minimum required level of capital.

The actual determination of these minimum capital requirements adheres to the notion of risk-based capital adequacy, according to which the adequate capitalization of a bank should consider the degree of risk associated to its assets. The first three subsections present respectively the capital instruments that are eligible to count as components of banks' own funds, the notion of total risk exposure, and the capital adequacy requirements themselves. The fourth subsection highlights an important macro-economic implication of the risk-based approach to banks' capital requirements. The last subsection develops a broader economic assessment of the minimum capital adequacy regulation, with a special focus on the search for the optimal level of banks' own funds.

2.3.1 Banks' Own Funds

Three broad categories of capital instruments are eligible to qualify as banks' own funds. First, the Common Equity Tier 1 (CET1) instruments, which are perpetual and fully paid up, are capital par excellence. In practice, they correspond primarily to ordinary shares, but also include the amounts on share premium accounts, retained earnings, accumulated other comprehensive income,[21] and other reserves and funds for general banking risk. To qualify for CET1 items, the issued shares should neither be funded by the bank nor be subject to an actual or contingent obligation to be repurchased by the bank. In the same way in which retained earnings or accumulated other comprehensive income boost CET1 capital, losses and accrued negative income erode it. Thus, the annual result from the profit and loss account reflects directly on the bank's end-of-year CET1 capital. Furthermore, the issued CET1 capital instruments are subject to prudential filters and adjustments, the most important of which are the provisions for impaired assets (known as general and specific credit risk adjustments). The values of the intangible assets and of the significant investments in a financial sector entity—both of which might be subject to high volatility, especially in times of financial distress—are also part of the prudential deductions.

Second, the Additional Tier 1 (AT1) capital, which is also perpetual and fully paid up, includes such capital instruments and the share premium accounts related to them that are not ordinary shares. In practice, this category of capital instruments refers to preferred shares and primarily to contingent convertible (CoCos) securities. AT1 instruments, which rank above CET1 instruments in insolvency but below holders of Tier 2 instruments, senior creditors and depositors, do not absorb losses automatically. Rather, they are subject to a trigger either for conversion into common equity or for an immediate write-down. To qualify for AT1 instruments, the CoCos' trigger must be set at or above a CET1 ratio of 5.125 percent. This means that if losses are large enough to reduce the bank's CET1 capital below that trigger level, then the AT1 instruments become loss-absorbing, either through a write-down or through their conversion in ordinary shares. In that way, the AT1 capital instruments contribute to preserve the bank's CET1 capital at least at the level of the minimum trigger.

Third, the Tier 2 capital instruments are those items that, even though fully paid up, are much less efficient in absorbing losses. To be admitted as own funds, these Tier 2 instruments must have a minimum original maturity of five years. In practice, they refer essentially to subordinated debt and to hybrid capital instruments. Most importantly, the provisions for losses, which are a standard deduction from CET1, are eligible for inclusion into Tier 2 capital, within some limits. This is justified by the likelihood that the bank could reverse some of these provisions in the future, namely if the expected losses do not materialize.

A bank's own funds correspond to the sum of the Tier 1 and Tier 2 capital instruments reported on the liabilities side of its balance sheet. Tier 1 capital is the sum of CET1 capital, adjusted for loss provisions and other prudential deductions, and of AT1 capital. The actual on-balance sheet amount of own funds and its distribution along CET1, AT1 and Tier 2 instruments must exceed the target levels as determined by the minimum regulatory requirements. These requirements are expressed in terms of minimum risk-weighted capital ratios. This brings us to the notion of risk-weighted assets (RWAs).

2.3.2 Risk-Weighted Assets (RWAs) or Total Risk Exposure

There are at least two reasons why the total risk exposure, rather than the total nominal exposure, has become the standard metrics for determining banks' capital needs. First, the weighing of each balance sheet asset item by an assigned risk-weight between 0 percent and 100 percent recognizes the fact that only the riskiest assets (weight of 100 percent, or even above) could result in a total loss, while other assets (weight below 100 percent, or even of 0 percent) are unlikely to ever produce a loss. As, by design, most risk weights are below 100 percent, a bank's total RWAs are smaller than its total nominal assets.

The different likelihood of loss contribution depends both on the asset class and on the evolving characteristics of the specific asset over time. For instance, deposits with central banks and euro-area government debt holdings are deemed as objectively less risky than household mortgages, themselves less risky than commercial mortgages, and so on. However, a specific asset in any of these categories might become riskier over time if the debtor's default likelihood increases or the asset becomes nonperforming, namely after missing payments for ninety days. A good example is the 2012 restructuring of the Greek government debt, known as the private sector involvement (PSI). It implied a haircut by 50 percent that resulted in a debt relief for the Greek government of about EUR 100 billion, which affected adversely many European banks.[22] This triggered a readjustment of the risk weights attached to holdings of Greek public sector securities. Second, the concept of total risk exposure allows for the inclusion of off-balance sheet items, such as guarantees or derivatives, when assessing the total risks that could drive future losses. Thus, the focus on RWAs, instead of nominal assets, as a basis for determining banks' capital adequacy requirements would also allow to account for risks that are not visible on a banks' balance sheet.

Conceptually, the RWAs are meant to capture all bank business-related risks that contribute to the credit institution's total risk exposure—credit risk, market risk, foreign exchange risk, interest rate risk, counterparty risk, operational risk, etc. In practice, as of the second quarter of 2022, total RWAs of euro-area significant banks amounted to EUR 8.7 trillion, or 32.4 percent of these banks' total unweighted assets (ECB 2022, 58 and 80). Credit risk contributed for EUR 7.3 trillion, or 84 percent of the total risk exposure. The remaining RWAs of EUR 1.4 trillion resulted above all from operational risk (EUR 0.8 trillion) and market risk (EUR 0.4 trillion). Hence, despite the complex though rational and seemingly convincing justification of the concept of total risk exposure, the classical credit risk, which stems from banks' standard loan-granting activity, remains the overwhelmingly most relevant driving factor of total RWAs.

This brings us to the crucial question about how the risk weights attached to the various asset classes are determined. There are two different paradigms—the standardized approach (SA) and the internal ratings-based approach (IRBA). When applying the SA, a bank takes for granted the fixed predetermined risk weights as laid down in the CRR. Tables 2.1 and 2.2 provide a snapshot of these risk weights, depending on the availability or not of external credit ratings. When applying the IRBA, a bank uses its own risk model-based estimates of Probabilities of Default (PDs) and of Losses Given Default (LGDs) to determine its RWAs. Basel III incentivizes the use of the IRBA in order to both reduce reliance on external credit ratings, which proved to be unreliable in the GFC, and to support banks in developing their own capacity to better assess, and therefore understand, their own risks. However, the IRBA remains reserved for banks that have developed internal ratings models for at least three years, thereby proving that they have built up sufficient technical expertise. Banks' internal ratings models are subject to supervisory benchmarking to ensure that they do not lead to standardization, preferred methods or herd behavior that might ultimately underestimate risks and jeopardize the primary objective of better grasping the institution's risk profile.

In practice, the larger banks with more complex business models follow the IRBA. For the 111 significant institutions under the direct supervision of the ECB, the risk-weighted credit exposure amounted to EUR 7.3 trillion as of mid-2022. The SA contributed EUR 2.9 trillion, while the IRBA accounted for EUR 4.3 trillion, the remaining contribution of EUR 0.1 trillion coming from securitization positions (ECB 2022, 63). The IRBA provides much lower risk weights than the SA, except for exposures to other banks (see Table 2.3).[23] Although a better inner understanding of the bank's own business model might explain this apparent risk underestimation, the data suggests that the widespread use of the IRBA by large banks might come

Table 2.1 Credit Risk Weights on Exposures to Rated Entities, Standardized Approach

Credit quality step	1	2	3	4	5	6
Central governments or central banks	0 percent	20 percent	50 percent	100 percent	100 percent	150 percent
Rated banks	20 percent	50 percent	50 percent	100 percent	100 percent	150 percent
Rated corporations	20 percent	50 percent	100 percent	100 percent	150 percent	150 percent

Source: CRR II, Articles 114–120.

Table 2.2 Credit Risk Weights on Unrated Exposures, Standardized Approach

Unrated corporations	100 percent
Retail exposures	75 percent
Secured by mortgages on commercial property	50 percent
Secured by mortgages on residential property	35 percent
Exposures to MS governments, Eurosystem, the Union, IMF, BIS, EFSF, ESM, multilateral development banks	0 percent

Source: CRR II, Articles 121–126.

Table 2.3 Credit Risk Weights, SA versus IRBA

Mid-2022	SA	IRBA
Exposures to banks	15.11 percent	18.61 percent
Exposures to corporations	86.00 percent	45.26 percent
Unsecured retail exposures	69.06 percent	27.89 percent
Retail exposures secured by real estate	39.91 percent	13.72 percent

Source: ECB (2022, 63).

with the significant drawback of artificially lowering banks' own estimates of their credit risk.[24]

The 2021 findings of the Targeted Review of Internal Models (TRIM) project, launched by the ECB in 2016 and covering 65 significant institutions, corroborate the thesis of a systematic under-estimation of credit risk when the IRBA is applied.[25] The TRIM found out that the RWAs under review were under-estimated by 12 percent, or EUR 275 billion given the amounts under investigation (ECB 2021, 7). The ECB issued 253 supervisory corrective decisions and limitations, with an expected average impact on the CET1 ratio of around 60 basis points.

In an attempt to prevent this expected adverse effect of the IRBA, the CRR introduces minimum floors for the banks' estimates of PDs and LGDs. For instance, in the case of exposures to corporates, the PD should not be lower than 0.03 percent and the LGDs should be at least 45 percent and 75 percent respectively for senior and subordinated exposures that are not guaranteed by eligible collateral. Given that the gap to the credit risk weights under the SA remains wide nevertheless, CRR II also introduces an IRBA output floor of 72.5 percent of the RWAs implied by the alternative SA, to be phased in over five years by 2028. Yet, while this target minimum floor might correct some of the well-identified cases of risk under-estimation, it remains short of fully absorbing a gap that is set to remain persistent.

2.3.3   Minimum Capital Adequacy Ratios and Additional Capital Buffers

Banks' requirement of own funds is determined based on their RWAs, to which a minimum capital adequacy ratio is applied. Banks are also requested to build up additional capital buffers on top of this basic capital requirement.

The three minimum capital adequacy ratios (CARs) are a CET1 ratio of 4.5 percent (of the RWAs), an AT1 ratio of 1.5 percent and a Tier 2 ratio of 2 percent. This implies a minimum own funds requirement, Tier 1 and Tier 2 combined, of 8 percent of the RWAs. Better quality capital can always substitute to lower quality capital. Hence, banks need not keep AT1 or Tier 2 capital instruments to the extent that they provide for these respectively allowed minima, or even beyond, with CET1 capital. A breach of the individual and combined minimum capital adequacy ratios implies the insolvency of the institution and its resolution, leading to a possible withdrawal of its license.

The additional capital buffers are all requested in CET1 capital exclusively. This further reflects the intention of Basel III to strengthen the actual capacity of banks' own funds to absorb losses effectively. The capital conservation buffer of 2.5 percent is mandatory and provides an extra cushion of capital at all times. The countercyclical capital buffer, set in steps of 0.25 percent up to 2.5 percent, requests banks to build up extra capital in times of booms and allows them to release capital during busts. It aims at smoothening the credit cycle. The global systemically important institutions (G-SIIs) buffer is a mandatory surcharge between 1 percent and 3.5 percent, depending on the global systemic importance of the institution.[26] The other systemically important institutions (O-SIIs) buffer of up to 2 percent follows the same logic with respect to systemic institutions of domestic relevance in the EU.[27] Finally, the systemic risk buffer, with no maximum limit, may vary across institutions or subsets of exposures, and addresses systemic risks that are not covered by the G-SIIs and O-SIIs buffers.[28] On top of this combined buffer, which could go as high as or even above 10 percent of RWAs, and based on its annual supervisory review findings, the supervisor can request an extra bank-specific capital add-on (Pillar 2 Requirement) or issue a further capital recommendation (Pillar 2 Guidance).

These additional buffers aim to ensure that unforeseen losses do not reduce a bank's own funds below its minimum capital adequacy requirement. The buffers act as preventive cushions against insolvency. A breach of the combined buffer triggers the submission of a capital conservation plan within five working days and possible corrective supervisory measures if the bank failed to submit and implement that plan. Until the buffer is restored, the Maximum Distributable Amount (MDA) enters into force and limits the bank's capacity to distribute profits. Indeed, retained earnings are the most straightforward means for a bank to replenish its own funds, save for issuing additional common equity. Overall, the capital buffers result in effectively higher amounts of own funds and provide flexibility to both the bank and the supervisor for finding an early solution in the event of actual capital erosion.

Since the CRR and the CRD IV entered into force, the own funds of euro area banks have increased notably from less than EUR 1.4 trillion in 2011 and 2012 to almost EUR 1.9 trillion at the end of 2021 (see Figure 2.1). More importantly, the share of Tier 1 capital into total own funds increased from 77 percent in 2008 to 88 percent in 2021. CET1 accounts for 93 percent of Tier 1 capital. During the same period, under the combined effect of writing off nonperforming loans, de-risking and overall balance sheet stagnation, the RWAs of euro area banks shrank from EUR 11.9 trillion to EUR 10 trillion. The declining RWAs and the growing own funds resulted in a notable improvement of banks' capital adequacy ratios. The total own funds ratio and the Tier 1 ratio increased from 11.5 percent and 8.4 percent in 2008 to respectively 19.0 percent and 16.6 percent in 2021. From that perspective, Basel III definitely contributed to both boosting the quantity and improving the quality of euro area banks' own funds, thereby effectively strengthening their loss-absorption capacity.

In addition to the strict numerical capital adequacy ratios, banks are required to develop and monitor a forward-looking Internal Capital Adequacy

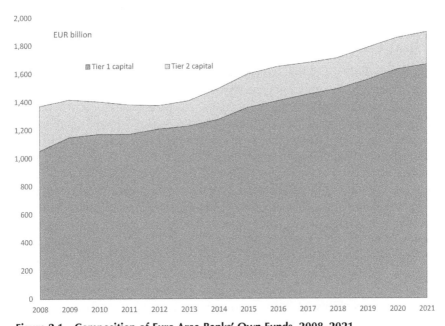

Figure 2.1   Composition of Euro Area Banks' Own Funds, 2008–2021.
Source: ECB Statistical Data Warehouse, https://sdw.ecb.europa.eu/browse.do?node=9689373.

Assessment Process (ICAAP), that is, to "have in place sound, effective and comprehensive strategies and processes to assess and maintain on an ongoing basis the amounts, types and distribution of internal capital that they consider adequate to cover the nature and level of the risks to which they are or might be exposed" (CRD IV, Art. 73). They must also disclose, by application of the Pillar 3 principle, a simple nonweighted leverage ratio between the Tier 1 capital and their total unweighted exposure, including off-balance sheet items.[29]

Another important capital-related requirement addresses concentration risk, that is, the potentially very strong impact of the default of a single large borrower on a bank's capital. A "large exposure," defined as exceeding 10 percent of Tier 1 capital, should be capped at 25 percent of Tier 1 capital, at the lender-consolidated level and with reference to all ultimate beneficiary owners at the borrower level.[30] The large exposure limit would have been of particular relevance for the zero risk-weight exposures, against which banks are de facto not required to build up any capital at all. Despite relevant discussions in that direction, sovereign and sovereign-guaranteed exposures, as well as exposures to international institutions and central banks, have remained exempt from this concentration limit.

This important observation brings us to the broader question of how the regulatory capital adequacy requirements influence banks' credit activities.

2.3.4 The Influence of the Capital Adequacy Regulation on Bank Credit

To illustrate how the risk-based capital adequacy regulation influences bank credit expansion, it is appropriate to start with a hypothetical, though not unrealistic, numerical example. Let us imagine two banks with total loan books of equal size (see Table 2.4). Both banks apply the standardized approach to determine their RWAs. Bank Innovent has lent out a thousand monetary units (for reasons of simplicity, one million EUR is assumed to be the relevant monetary unit, m.u.) across four segments: 65 percent to SMEs, 25 percent to farmers, 5 percent to governments in emerging markets and 5 percent to a partner bank in Africa. This distribution of assets reflects a business strategy of lending to private sector entrepreneurs and to the developing world, as suggested by the very name of the bank, a contraction of INNOVation and ENTrepreneurship. Bank Govbrick has granted loans for exactly the same amounts, but across four very different segments: 65 percent to households for house purchases, 25 percent to businesses to buy real estate, 5 percent to the European Stability Mechanism to support the Greek government and 5 percent to the French government, to build additional hospitals. This distribution of assets reflects a business strategy that ultimately supports households

Table 2.4 Assets of Banks Innovent and Govbrick

Bank Innovent	Exposure, EUR million	Risk weights, SA	Total risk exposure, EUR million
Loans to SMEs	650	75 percent	487.5
Agricultural loans	250	100 percent	250
EM Government bonds, rated 3	50	50 percent	25
African institution, rated 4	50	100 percent	50
TOTAL	1,000	81.25 percent	812.5

Bank Govbrick	Exposure, EUR million	Risk weights, SA	Total risk exposure, EUR million
Loans for house purchases	650	35 percent	227.5
Commercial real estate	250	50 percent	125
ESM bonds, to help Greece	50	0 percent	0
French bonds, to build hospitals	50	0 percent	0
TOTAL	1,000	35.25 percent	352.5

Source: own calculations.

and euro area governments. Hence, the name Govbrick, a contraction of GOVernment and BRICKs.

The fixed risk weights that the standardized approach assigns to each asset segment also determine the contribution of each nominal exposure to the total risk exposure. Thus, the 650 m.u. of SME loans result in a risk exposure of 487.5 m.u. for Innovent, while the same m.u. lent to households imply a risk exposure of 227.5 m.u. for Govbrick. Similarly, the 250 m.u. lent to farmers imply an equal risk exposure for Innovent, while in the case of Govbrick the risk exposure of the commercial real estate loans is halved to 125 m.u. The remaining nominal exposure of 100 m.u. to non-euro area governments and financial institutions imply a contribution to Innovent's total RWAs of 75 m.u. For Govbrick, the contribution of similar loans to euro-area governments and financial institutions is nil. Overall, the SA implies RWAs of 812.5 m.u. for Innovent and 352.5 m.u. for Govbrick. This corresponds to average implied risk weights of 81.25 percent and 35.25 percent of total assets respectively.

These RWAs determine the banks' respective capital needs (see Table 2.5). For simplicity, we can further assume that both banks comply with their total own funds requirement exclusively with CET1 capital, and that they are subject to the same combined buffer of 7 percent and a supervisory add-on of 1 percent. Thus, both institutions must keep a total (minimum and additional) capital adequacy ratio (CAR) of 16 percent. For Innovent, this 16-percent own funds requirement, when applied to its RWAs of 812.5 m.u., results into

Table 2.5 Capital Needs of Banks Innovent and Govbrick

EUR million	Innovent	Govbrick
Minimum CET 1, 4.5 percent	36.6	15.9
Minimum AT 1, 1.5 percent	12.2	5.3
Minimum Tier 2, 2 percent	16.3	7.1
Combined buffer (CET1), 7 percent	56.9	24.7
Supervisory add-on (CET 1), 1 percent	8.1	3.5
Total "Own funds requirement," 16 percent	*130.0*	*56.4*
Implied leverage ratio	13.0 percent	5.6 percent

Source: Own calculations.

capital needs of 130 m.u. For Govbrick, the capital needs are 56.4 m.u. only, as the 16-percent requirement applies to the much lower RWAs of 352.5 m.u.

To hold its portfolio of 1 000 m.u., Innovent needs to raise, accumulate and keep capital of 130 m.u. It owes other liabilities of 870 m.u. to bondholders (if it has issued marketable debt), institutional creditors (the central bank or other banks) and to depositors. To hold the same aggregate nominal portfolio, of admittedly different sectoral distribution, Govbrick needs to raise, accumulate and keep capital of 56.4 m.u. only. Its other liabilities can reach 943.6 m.u. To the extent that capital is the riskiest and hence most expensive source of funding, the average cost of capital of Innovent would then be higher than that of Govbrick. This regulatory advantage for Govbrick is a direct consequence of the fact that the standardized approach assigns higher risk weights to loans to the productive and entrepreneurial part of the economy than to more secure loans guaranteed by real estate or by the government.

Let us now put aside considerations about the average cost of funding and further assume that both banks have managed to raise and keep equal amounts of capital of 200 m.u. With a higher implied leverage ratio of 13 percent, 200 m.u. of own funds allow Innovent to originate and hold a loan portfolio of 1,538.5 m.u. With a lower implied leverage ratio of 5.6 percent, the same amount of capital allows Govbrick to originate and hold a loan portfolio of 3,546.1 m.u. Due to its lower average risk weight, with the same amount of capital Govbrick can expand its balance sheet significantly more than Innovent. Against this backdrop, a new entrant in the banking sector would tend to adopt Govbrick's business model, as it allows a quicker and greater growth of its balance sheet, and hence of its prospective market share.

The aggregate macroeconomic implication of the risk-weighted capital adequacy regulation appears straightforward. Banks are incentivized to expand credit primarily to those segments of the economy to which the regulation assigns lower risk weights. Under these conditions, investments in real estate and in domestic government securities become preferred to business and corporate loans, as they result in a lower requirements for own funds.

This further implies that households, real-estate promoters and governments enjoy a de facto privileged access to bank loans, at the expense of entrepreneurs and producers. Indeed, as the former tend, on average, to be among the first receivers of the new bank loans, and hence of the additional fiduciary media of exchange, they benefit from the Cantillon redistribution effects, at the expense of the latter. Thus, the risk-weighted capital adequacy regulation drives banks to finance relatively less productive activities, toward which scarce resources are directed at the expense of relatively more productive investment areas. The end-result is a lower growth potential for the economy as a whole.[31]

The conclusion that bank capital requirements based on differentiated risk weights by asset classes affect aggregate output negatively must be put in the context of the broader discussion of how central bank policy impacts the economy. The theory of the monetary transmission mechanism has identified several specific channels, and the concrete conditions for their operation, through which policy-induced changes in the money supply affect the real economy.[32] The domestic interest rate channel, the open-economy exchange rate channel, induced changes in the relative cost between new and old capital investments (Tobin's q ratio), the asset prices channel (including Modigliani's life-cycle consumption), as well as two distinct credit channels[33] have been advanced as standard causes for monetary nonneutrality (Ireland 2005). Any of these channels tends to justify a positive relation between an expansionary monetary policy and real economic activity.

Zukauskas and Hülsmann (2019) develop a broader framework for analyzing the monetary transmission mechanism that allows to factor in the effects of unconventional monetary policy. Starting from the observation that none of the standard monetary transmission channels explains successfully the stylized fact that financial asset prices have been growing relatively quicker than consumer prices, the authors propose to adopt the stock-based "total demand" approach to determining the monetary equilibrium.[34] This approach integrates individuals' subjective valuations of money, in particular, relative to financial assets as its closer substitutes, in the analysis of the consequences of monetary policy. Thus, perceived changes in the quality of money, and notably of its deterioration due to unconventional policy measures, account on their own for the growing relative gap between asset prices and consumer prices. In addition to providing an explanation for an otherwise unaccounted stylized fact, this broader framework emphasizes the relevance of qualitative factors, beyond the aggregate supply of money, for a more complete grasp of the monetary transmission mechanism.[35] Our finding that bank capital regulation, and especially its differentiated risk weights, privileges investments in real estate and in government bonds reinforces the point that monetary transmission is not only a matter of aggregate quantities.

In justification of these differentiated risk weights, it could be pointed out that loans to riskier economic activities, because they could lead to objectively higher losses, should indeed result in banks' better preparedness to absorb such losses, that is, in higher associated capital needs. After all, this is the very reason why different risk weights are applied to different types of loans. However, there are two fundamental issues with this view, which indeed underpins the very concept of total risk exposure.

First, the entrepreneurial decisions on investment and production are not subject to an objective risk quantification. Rather, they call for a subjective uncertainty assessment. No standard exists that could decree that real estate and government bond investments, everywhere and always, are systematically leading to lower losses than industrial or agricultural investments. The actual losses on investments depend on the capitalist-entrepreneurs' failure to anticipate the future state of market conditions better than their competitors. Moreover, the fractional-reserve banking activity itself affects adversely entrepreneurs' capacity to form correct judgments about the future state of the market. As already mentioned, a bank credit expansion leads to an artificial boom and to clusters of investment errors.

The point that could not be emphasized enough is that these bank credit-driven entrepreneurial errors occur precisely in the sectors where the credit expansion allowed the start of new investments that entrepreneurs have been discarding so far because of their insufficient expected profitability at the previously higher interest rates. This most essential finding of the monetary business cycle theory implies that the lower credit risk weights are bound to structurally underestimate the economic risk of bank credit-financed investments, due to the unavoidable malinvestments they bring about. The so-called subprime real estate crisis of 2008 in the US and the sovereign debt crisis of 2011–2012 in the euro area are two outstanding examples.

Second, the mechanical assignment of regulatory risk weights substitutes the flexible market discipline by rigid administrative decisions. As with other businesses, it belongs to investors in banks' shares and bonds to appreciate the risk profile of the related portfolio exposures, namely through the required return on investment. By demanding a specific minimum remuneration, shareholders and bondholders effectively differentiate between various loan portfolios and drive the bank-specific cost of capital. This market-driven process could involve significantly deeper balance sheet analysis than currently implied by the mechanical assignment of predetermined or of model-given risk weights. Although investors might not always be right, they have all the incentives to err seldom, as they are risking their own money. Yet, the empirical question of who errs more—the market participants or the market regulator—is beside the point. The key observation, rather, is that a standardization of the assessment of the risk associated to bank assets is unnecessary because the market can develop an institution-specific, rather than a one-fits-all, solution to circumscribing credit risk. If anything, the risk weights-based capital adequacy regulation prevents the development of a superior market-based alternative.[36]

2.3.5 Controversies around the Risk-Based Capital Requirements

The impact of the differentiated credit risk weights on the direction of bank credit expansion and the resulting redistribution of scarce resources toward less productive uses in the economy is only one of the controversies that surround the capital adequacy regulation. Researchers have raised other issues, starting from objections of principle. Dowd (1997) questions the very grounds for a capital adequacy regulation, namely perceived market failures, such as depositors' incapacity to judge banks' financial health, shareholders' inclination toward riskier, and hence less robust, balance sheets, or finally the moral hazard created by public safety-nets such as deposit insurance or the lender of last resort. Furthermore, the author points out that the capital adequacy regulation has moral hazard implications of its own, in terms of circumvention and avoidance strategies that ultimately compromise the regulator's general goal of banks' maintaining a sufficiently high level of capital. Bank capital adequacy regulation based on specific risk weights is found to present additional weaknesses, e.g., the arbitrariness of the risk categories and of the respective assigned risk values, the assumption of equal risk for all assets of the same category, or finally the resulting objectification of the relative riskiness between categories. Moreover, Dowd (1997, 104–105) emphasizes the role of the portfolio effects and of balance sheet relations in general on risk evaluation. Due to the correlation between assets and to the opportunity cost of their funding, the expected net value and returns of a single asset depend on both the aggregate portfolio composition and the funding structure of that portfolio. Subsequently, a more holistic approach to risk and capital adequacy should be preferred to the Basel framework, which appears inadequately fragmented to capture true risk fully.[37]

Hellwig (1995) makes the same argument, though generalized at the level of the aggregate economy, by pointing out that individual banks' uncoordinated management of the undiversifiable risk of assets does not allow for a proper assessment of the risk exposure of the system as a whole. Thus, bank capital regulation would be lacking both an important foundation and a satisfactory strategy for addressing systemic risk. With respect to the latter point, Hellwig (1995, 731–735) points out three specific weaknesses of the capital adequacy regulation. First, the benefits of higher capital requirements have been demonstrated in a one-shot scenario only. Their effect in the longer term, including in terms of dynamic incentives, has not been established with certainty.[38] Second, the independence of the capital requirements from the macro-economic conditions implies a pro-cyclicality in bank credit that exacerbates the effects of an original negative shock to aggregate demand.[39] Third, capital requirements do not address the problem of excessive risk-taking, as they are only rough and imperfect substitutes for the far more efficient continuous risk-monitoring strategies, whether by creditors and investors or by supervisors.

In a more recent stocktaking assessment of the experience with capital adequacy regulation, Haldane (2014) draws a very critical picture, especially of the implications from the widespread adoption of the internal risk-rating models. First, the intention to entrust banks with a more responsible self-regulatory behavior resulted into a historical decline in the attributed risk weights and precipitated a race to the bottom, which is the exact opposite of the policy goal. Second, the complexity of the risk-weights-based approach leads to opacity, regulatory capture and avoidance, while standard nonweighted leverage ratios appear to perform as well, if not even better. Third, the higher risk weights of the standardized approach result in higher capital requirements for the banks that follow this approach, namely the smaller banks. This turns out to be an effective barrier to entry that contradicts the objective of setting up a level-playing field. The unfortunate eventual outcome is a less competitive environment and under-provisioned risks. Altogether, these deficiencies would call for a fundamental revision of the capital adequacy regulation as it is applied nowadays.

The weakness of bank capital regulation as regards these very specific and technical aspects should be put in the perspective of micro-prudential regulation's primary objective, namely to ensure that banks have enough capital to withstand future losses stemming from the uncertain value of their assets. This broader perspective raises a most fundamental question. Irrespective of their manifold weaknesses, as detailed above, are capital adequacy requirements nevertheless broadly properly calibrated? In other words, are they sufficiently high? If that were not the case, the micro-prudential regulation would have failed at its most basic objective. The economic literature has studied this question from the angle of the optimal level of bank capital. It has followed two very different approaches in the quest of that optimality.

The utilitarian approach views the optimal level of capital as the result of a comparison between the benefits and costs associated with an increase in banks' own funds. The benefits, which are marginally declining, stem from the lower probability and the lower cost of a banking crisis that higher levels of capitalization make less likely and less impactful. Together, the lower probability and the lower cost result into a lower expected banking crisis-induced loss of GDP. The costs, which are marginally increasing, consist in higher interest rate spreads on new loans. The latter translate into a higher cost of capital for the nonfinancial part of the economy and therefore reduced economic growth. In this intellectual framework, the optimal bank capital level, and hence capital adequacy requirement, is determined at the point where the marginal benefits of additional own funds equal the marginal costs. Put differently, the optimal level of capital is such that there would be no net gain, in terms of aggregate GDP, from going beyond it.

Several studies, initiated by the BCBS in 2010, have calibrated this optimal level of bank capital on the basis of historical estimates of the likelihood and costs of bank crises and of the interest pass-through on the cost of capital for businesses. The results vary significantly. One study finds that the optimal CET1 ratio would be between 12 percent and 14 percent, thereby suggesting that the Basel III minimum 8 percent requirement is significantly sub-optimal (Cline 2016). Other studies conclude at a wider range or at a significantly higher optimal requirement of around 25 percent (BCBS 2019, 4). While all empirical results suggest that the minimum capital requirement appears insufficient, it has to be acknowledged nevertheless that the effective aggregate CET1 ratio in the EA, including the effect of the combined buffer, falls within the suggested optimality boundary.

The second approach goes beyond detailed calibrated models and utility calculations and focuses instead on the very essence of banking. Admati and Hellwig (2013) have promoted, prominently and vocally, this essentialist view. In their opinion, banks are not different from other corporations, and equity is not a costlier form of funding than debt. It follows that banks should be subject to the same equity requirement of around 30 percent of total assets, as practiced by other businesses on a nonmandatory basis.[40] Assuming an average risk weight of 50 percent, this would translate into a minimum risk weights-based capital requirement of around 60 percent, which is almost eight times higher than the current minimum. The implied degree of sub-optimality would be so significant that it is worthwhile quoting the authors' conclusion: "Requiring that banks' equity be at least on the order of 20–30 percent of their total assets would make the financial system *substantially safer and healthier*. At such levels of equity, *most* banks would *usually* be able to cope on their own and require *no more than occasional liquidity support*" (Admati et al. 2013, 179; our emphasis).

This conclusion is most puzzling. Even today, at levels of capital that the authors would consider much lower than the suggested optimum, most banks manage liquidity pressures on their own, save for occasional, though admittedly regular, liquidity support from the central banks. In what sense, then, would much higher levels of capital be a game-changer and make banks "substantially safer and healthier"? Unfortunately, Admati and Hellwig do not address this question straight. The reason for the missing answer probably lies in the incompleteness of their essentialist approach. Indeed, it is not enough to consider banks similar to any other corporations. In fact, due to their fractional-reserve privilege, modern banks are *fundamentally different* from any other industry—they can increase their balance sheet on their own by a multiple of any net liquidity inflow. Banks' capacity to finance the acquisition of new assets on the economy, in the form of additional bank loans, through an increase in the fiduciary media of exchange issued by them is limited only by their clients' readiness to withdraw their retail or wholesale deposits. But, as rightly perceived by Admati and Hellwig, if banks' safety and health are ultimately an issue of *liquidity*, then the real question is to find out the optimal level of own funds that would promote the stability of banks' liquidity condition.

The straightforward answer to this question consists in stating the obvious—the optimal level of capital is the one that minimizes the likelihood of a bank run. Depositors and bank investors demonstrate that optimal level by the very fact they remain depositors and investors in the bank. Bank managers have to discover that optimal level, which is specific to each institution and evolves with both the objective changes in its balance sheet and how depositors and investors perceive them subjectively. From that perspective, the reason for setting up minimum capital adequacy requirements, whatever their specific magnitude, lies in their capacity to act as *confidence-building tools*. Most importantly, no specific technical aspect of the operation of banks can determine, through an unequivocal causal relationship, a specifically optimal level for their own funds. The historical fact that banks have operated at very different levels of capital, without any noticeable link to the frequency or gravity of bank crises, best illustrates this conclusion.[41]

To conclude the discussion of the controversies around capital adequacy regulation, let us push this essentialist approach further. In particular, the very notion of an optimal level of capital, which would be determined based on objective and external factors, deserves to be questioned. To begin with, let us reiterate again that the credit-granting activity of fractional-reserve banks has a direct impact on the money supply in the broader sense. The additional media of exchange finance economic transactions that would not have occurred otherwise, *including the acquisition of existing and newly issued shares in bank equity*. This implies that the very same process by which banks expand their own balance sheets helps them alter, to their own advantage, the external conditions under which they can finance an increase of their own capital. This is the case because, as the marginal utility of holding extra media of exchange is necessarily decreasing, any addition to individual cash holdings must lead to conditions that are more favorable to the sellers of other present and future goods, including shares in bank equity. In other words, modern banks, in comparison to the companies in any other sector of the economy, have a structural advantage in meeting any minimum capital requirement, thanks to the fractional-reserve principle.

The sequential changes in the consolidated balance sheet of the aggregate banking system illustrate this point easily in accounting terms. In the first period, credit expansion implies that both loans (on the assets side of the T-account) and deposits (on the liabilities side) increase by the same amount ($\Delta L = \Delta D$). In the second period, a portion k ($0<k<1$) of the newly created deposits ($k.\Delta D$) is used to acquire extra capital (ΔE), thereby implying a substitution between equity and deposits on the liabilities side of the T-account. At the end of the second period, the expansion in assets (ΔL) is matched by both an equity expansion ($k.\Delta L$) and an increase in the money supply in the broader sense (($1-k$).ΔL). As long as banks manage to keep k sufficiently high relative to the minimum own funds requirement, the sector can easily comply with the regulation.

The crucial point to emphasize is that, as banks themselves create new media of exchange, part of which could be used to finance an increase of their own capital, no minimum capital requirement could be considered as objectively and externally binding. The prohibition of direct financing of shares in bank equity with loans from the same bank and the deduction from banks' own funds of direct holdings in other banks' equity de facto recognize this conclusion. However, banks are capable of circumventing the prohibition of direct self-financing or of cross-financing of a capital increase. To achieve that, they only need to convince a sufficiently large number of depositors, not even necessarily those who hold the fiduciary media of exchange issued by them, in the attractiveness of their shares, that is, to engineer a favorable change of depositors' preferences.[42] This would suggest that the optimality of bank capital is ultimately determined by the market. If, in fine, market discipline is anyway over-ruling any capital adequacy regulation, the raison d'être of distinct micro-prudential capital requirements becomes questionable, even more so as fractional-reserve banks have the structural advantage of being able to influence that market discipline to their favor.

2.4 LIQUIDITY REQUIREMENTS

The original Basel Accords were concerned exclusively with banks' capital as the main driver and guarantor of their solvency. Liquidity issues, that is, the capacity of a bank to pay back its maturing liabilities and to redeem its deposits upon demand, were not subject to international regulation. Two factors might explain this original neglect by the BCBS for issues related to liquidity. First, as shown in the first chapter, liquidity-based regulation and liquidity management by banks is an integral part of central banks' monetary control of the banking sector. Hence, from that point of view, liquidity issues were covered already. Second, improved solvency itself contributes to better liquidity as it strengthens customers' confidence and naturally deters liquidity outflows. From that perspective too, an explicit micro-prudential regulation of banks' liquidity would appear redundant.[43]

However, after the acute bank runs in Iceland, Ireland, the USA and the UK in 2007, followed by similar adverse events in Spain, Austria, Portugal, Greece and Cyprus in the following years, the Basel III reform could no longer avoid including specific regulatory provisions on liquidity.

2.4.1 Liquidity Ratios

Liquidity requirements aim at ensuring consistency between the maturity profiles of assets and liabilities on banks' balance sheets. They draw their inspiration from the standard *Loan-To-Deposit* (LTD) ratio, which a prudent institution necessarily keeps below 100 percent. A higher-than-100- percent LTD suggests that a bank has over-expanded credit and hence the size of its balance sheet, relative to its competitors. The resulting comparatively stronger liquidity outflows cause its deposit market share to shrink below its loan market share. On the opposite, an under-expanding bank retains liquidity better and manages to keep more deposits than it has granted loans, which results in an LTD ratio below 100 percent. At the same time, the lower the LTD ratio is, the higher is the coverage of deposits by more liquid nonloan assets. This makes the bank more resistant to deposit withdrawals, whether by retail depositors or by peers in the interbank market. The basic LTD ratio provides the inspiration for the two liquidity requirements that Basel III has introduced.

The Single Banking Rulebook implemented the first of these two liquidity ratios in the EU as from January 2018, following a three-year transition period. The Liquidity Coverage Ratio (LCR) requests banks to maintain sufficiently liquid assets to cover any imbalance between liquidity inflows and outflows over 30 days under stressed conditions. In other words, the stock of unencumbered High Quality Liquid Assets (HQLA) should be enough to sustain liquidity outflows, under stressed conditions as determined by the supervisor, over the next thirty days. In light of the various assets' different degree of liquidity and of liabilities' varying degree of stability, the banks must apply corrective haircut and run-off factors respectively when computing their LCR. If the LCR falls below 100 percent, the concerned bank must submit and implement a liquidity restoration plan. The significant institutions in the euro area held a liquidity buffer of EUR 5.2 trillion as of mid-2022, for an expected net liquidity outflow of EUR 3.2 trillion, resulting in an aggregate LCR of 164.4 percent (ECB 2022, 110). The LCR has been increasing significantly and reached this high level due to the massive liquidity injections by the Eurosystem, especially in the aftermath of the COVID-19 crisis. While at the end of 2019 two out of the 105 significant institutions missed the LCR of 100 percent, all 111 institutions complied with the requirement as of mid-2022, with eighty-nine institutions showing an LCR above 150 percent.

Following the adoption of the CRR II in 2019, the second liquidity requirement introduced by Basel III, the net stable funding ratio (NSFR), became binding in the EU as of July 1, 2021. The objective of this ratio is to ensure that enough longer-term liabilities, considered to be stable resources, correspond to, or fund, banks' longer-term assets. Respect for this metrics guarantees that the time profiles of both sides of banks' balance sheets are adequate with respect to each other, from a longer-term perspective. The ratio requests banks to cover their required stable funding (RSF) by at least 100 percent of available stable funding (ASF). The ASF includes, by default, all own funds and all liabilities with a remaining maturity above a year. All other liabilities receive weighting factors, depending on their type and maturity.[44] The RSF derives from the size and maturity structure of assets and off-balance sheet items, also based on weighting factors.[45] Banks are expected to fund their balance sheets by at least as many stable resources as required by the structure of their assets, and therefore to meet an NSFR, calculated as the ratio between the ASF and RSF, of at least 100 percent.

2.4.2 Controversies around the Liquidity Requirements

The inclusion of these two liquidity requirements in the micro-prudential toolkit raised questions that also account for the delayed implementation of the NSFR. Above all, is not one of the ratios superfluous? If liquid assets cover short-term liabilities fully (the LCR is above 100 percent), then the accounting identity between total assets and liabilities implies that the remaining longer-term liabilities also fund the remaining less-liquid assets completely (the NSFR is then necessarily above 100 percent). If one of the ratios is met, then the other one is respected too.[46] Hence, one ratio is redundant. Critics could rightly retort that the LCR is not a static ratio between balance sheet items, but that instead it involves the dynamic notion of expected net liquidity outflows. Yet, putting aside such technical details, if a bank can sustain a net liquidity drain under some conditions over a certain period, then at that point its balance sheet has to be considered funded in a stable way. Thus, conceptually, liquidity implies stability, which in turn suggests that a single ratio should be sufficient to capture banks' liquidity condition. Other critics have pointed out the excessive computational complexity of the ratios, which invites substantial regulatory discretion.[47] Finally, it must be pointed out that the liquidity requirements apply only at the highest level of consolidation.

Hence, they do not guarantee automatically that any single branch or subsidiary of a banking group is liquid enough on a standalone basis, even within the meaning of these same requirements. Pockets of illiquidity could then persist, even when the requirements seem to be respected.

More importantly, the micro-prudential liquidity requirements contribute to spread two related modern misconceptions about banking. The first misconception relates to the idea that banks must attract actual resources from the wholesale (financial) and retail (depositor) markets in order to fund their assets, primarily loans. This view, which rationalizes the NSFR based on the notions of available and required funding, applies correctly to any economic actor, who needs to first attract resources before starting production or consumption. However, this does not apply to fractional-reserve banks. As modern banks are involved in the production of fiduciary media of exchange, which themselves are liquid means to finance any economic activity, they need not attract resources prior to acquiring assets. Fractional-reserve banks create these resources themselves, through the process of expanding bank credit.

The fundamental problem that banks face, as shown in the first chapter, is one of limiting liquidity outflows and retaining enough money in reserves to finance (redeem) the residual liquidity outflows (redemption requests). This is definitely not a problem of funding assets, as implied especially by the NSFR. By reversing the causal relation between bank assets and liabilities, the liquidity requirements obfuscate the true nature of fractional-reserve banks. The introduction of this misconception contributes to legitimize, and hence perpetuate, a banking system that is structurally unstable because of its main feature, namely its fractional reserve. Hence, to the extent that by its very design the NSFR preserves the most destabilizing element of modern banks, it can hardly be considered as having achieved its purported goal to improve the soundness and safety of banks.

The second misconception behind the prudential liquidity requirements reflects the old economic fallacy of objective value. The requirements consider liquidity as a measurable, objective attribute of financial assets, like their size, maturity, or contractual return. This objective view of liquidity is, however, highly questionable. The liquidity of an asset depends on market participants' willingness to hold it. Thus, liquidity is a purely subjective quality that is determined by individuals' perception and ownership decisions. Even the persistently higher liquidity of some assets, for example, money itself or shorter-term Treasury bonds, is not in-built and needs daily reconfirmation. Asset owners reexamine continuously their expectations about future liquidity conditions, and good liquidity management always allows for contingency planning based on extra buffers and guarantee arrangements. The prudential liquidity requirements convey a very different perspective.

They hypothesize on the immediate salability of assets and on the redemption likelihood of liabilities in a mechanical fashion, based on an objective categorization of assets and liabilities and the application of uniformly standardized coefficients. The prudential liquidity regulation assumes that such an administrative approach, informed by past evidence at best, if not by arbitrary conventions, is fit enough to guarantee banks' ability to meet future redemption requests. This propagates false certainty and promotes a culture of blind respect for arbitrary rules rather than of alert preparedness.

In short, the prudential liquidity regulation endorses the notion of an optimal level of liquidity that a wise composition of assets and liabilities could achieve. It pays no attention to the very nature of deposits as redeemable fiduciary media of exchange and ignores that banks could function differently, namely on the basis of a hundred- percent reserve. This approach to the liquidity problem of banks mutes the conclusion that no fractional-reserve banking system is immune to bank runs and that its survival ultimately relies on a lender of last resort. From that perspective, rather than ensuring the banking system's stability, liquidity regulation merely circumscribes the prior conditions for gaining access to that lender of last resort, in terms of minimum holdings of specific assets that would be eligible as collateral for borrowing from the central bank, should the need arise.

2.5 BANKING SUPERVISION

The original concern and focus of banking supervision has been to enforce the prevailing micro-prudential rules. To achieve this goal, the supervisory authority has to monitor various aspects of banks' activity, especially as reflected in their balance sheets and profit and loss accounts. The results of such a compliance-based approach to supervision can be summarized in a synthetic ranking across several criteria. The best known such ranking system is certainly the CAMELS, in use by the US supervisory authorities since 1979. The CAMELS ranking (where 1 is the best score while 5 is the worst) provides an average snapshot of a bank's overall financial health based on its Capital adequacy, Asset quality, Management, Earnings, Liquidity, and Sensitivity to market risk, added in 1995 to the original CAMEL. The annual note on each of these criteria derives from the results of both on-site examinations and off-site inspections.[48]

Presently, in the aftermath of the GFC, banking supervision has adopted an approach that is much more risk oriented. The forward-looking identification of specific balance sheet weaknesses and of broader vulnerabilities related to banks' overall business model has become the core of banking supervision. Accordingly, supervision has evolved from the passive monitoring of historical compliance with rules toward a proactive understanding of each bank's activities and the related risks. This future-oriented approach is more holistic and results in addressing supervisory measures, that is, instructions and recommendations, to a bank that is deemed insufficiently prepared to address the identified risks.

In the EU, each MS sets up a national Competent Authority (CA) in charge of banking supervision. In practice, the national central bank assumes the tasks of the CA. In the EA, as the first leg of the Banking Union (BU), the Single Supervisory Mechanism (SSM) assumed its responsibilities in November 2014. Within the SSM, the ECB holds the ultimate responsibility for licensing and supervising all banks in the EA. The ECB exercises the related duties directly for the so-called significant institutions.[49] As of November 2022, the regularly updated list of significant institutions included 113 banks, accounting for more than 80 percent of all bank assets in the EA. The national CAs supervise directly all remaining less significant institutions (LSIs). The ECB carries out its direct supervisory functions through joint supervisory teams (JSTs) that include staff from both the ECB and the NCAs. These JSTs disseminate best practices and equal standards across all national CAs, thereby ensuring a level playing field and uniform implementation in all countries and across all banks. For the EA member states of the EU, participation in the SSM is mandatory. The non-EA member states of the EU can join the SSM through a close cooperation arrangement, in particular, if they prepare for euro adoption.[50]

2.5.1 The Supervisory Review and Evaluation Process

The annual exercise of assessing banks' preparedness to cope with risks takes place within the Supervisory Review and Evaluation Process (SREP). The JSTs run the SREP based on a common methodology and a wide set of quantitative data and qualitative information, for example, common reporting (COREP) and financial reporting (FINREP) published by the supervised banks, macro-economic data, central creditor registers data, banks' internal estimates, market views, and external reports. This first phase of orderly data gathering is followed by the phase of evaluation, that is, of assessing risk elements from both quantitative (risk level) and qualitative (risk control) perspectives. The last phase of the SREP results in a bank-specific decision, which the Governing Council adopts based on a proposal by the SSM Supervisory Board and addresses to the supervised entity. The SREP decision has three main elements. First, it contains the own funds requirements, composed of the Pillar 1 minimum requirements, the combined buffer requirement, and the additional Pillar 2 requirement (P2R). Second, the decision includes institution-specific quantitative liquidity requirements, such as a higher-than-the-minimum LCR. Third, it comprises the Pillar 2 guidance (P2G)[51] expressed as a CET1 ratio add-on and other supervisory measures, for example, restriction or limitation of business, restriction on dividend distribution, and imposition of further reporting obligations.

This annual review of the "arrangements, strategies, processes and mechanisms" implemented by the supervised banks has four distinctive elements, each of them covering a separate area of analytical investigation. The first element is an assessment of the bank's business model and profitability. Both viability, that is, the bank's capacity to generate acceptable returns over the next year, and sustainability, that is, its capacity to maintain sufficient profitability over the next three years and across the economic cycle, are examined. This overall business model assessment looks for key vulnerabilities and sets the stage for the other three elements that compose the SREP.

The second element deals with the internal governance and risk management practices of the bank. This includes the internal governance framework (the organizational structure, outsourcing, management practices, internal audit function, risk management and compliance function, etc.), the risk appetite framework and risk culture, and the risk infrastructure, including data aggregation and reporting. In short, this second element of the SREP evaluates the intended structure and the actual operation of all internal processes, from the point of view of their contribution to managing or amplifying risks. Based on this second element, the SREP decision might direct to needed changes of the bank functional organization and management.

The SREP's third element evaluates the risks to bank capital. First, the JSTs assess each of the four capital-related risks: credit risk, market risk, operational risk, and interest rate risk in the banking book. Second, the JSTs challenge the institution's internal assessment of its capital risks, as conducted in its ICAAP. The third phase challenges the bank's own stressed capital estimates. These three blocks of the capital risks evaluation conclude at a final capital adequacy assessment that contrasts the actual amount of own funds with the minimum own funds requirement. The fourth element applies this same approach—independent assessment, challenge of the bank's own assessment, and review of the bank's stressed estimates—to risks to the liquidity condition. Both the short-term liquidity risk and the funding sustainability risk are evaluated.

At the end of this holistic approach to banks' viability, the SREP assigns a numerical score from 1 (strong control of risks) to 4 (inadequate control). The JSTs have the capacity to apply constrained judgment by modifying the overall SREP score by +2/−1 notches, based on their knowledge of the institution, peer comparisons, the macroeconomic environment, future capital, and liquidity planning by the bank and the SSM's own risk tolerance. A qualitative rationale accompanies this numerical score.

The ECB carries out each SREP against the backdrop of concrete priorities and specific risks that it identifies for each annual exercise and that could lead to ad hoc thematic reviews. In light of the GFC legacy, asset quality and non-performing loans have been a continuous object of interest. Given the impact of the COVID-19–related crisis, the 2021 supervisory priorities focused on credit risk management, capital strength, business model sustainability, and governance. The SSM risk map for 2021 included such events as a correction in real estate markets, repricing in financial markets, increase in NPLs, cyber-crime, and disruptive digital innovation, among others. The priorities for the SREP in the 2022–2024 also include climate and environmental risks. The risk map concludes at the most prominent vulnerabilities that might threaten banks' safety. Banks are expected to address their internal vulnerabilities, such as weaknesses in management and coverage of credit risk, structurally low profitability, IT deficiencies, weak governance, and lingering cost inefficiencies. External vulnerabilities, for instance, high levels of public and private debt or overcapacities in banking and fragmentation in the regulatory and legal framework, further describe the environment in which banks operate and qualify the JSTs' assessment.

Out of all the elements that inform the SREP, one supervisory tool has become the epitome of the new forward-looking approach to identifying banks' risks and their capacity to cope with them—the stress tests (STs). In the context of the SSM, STs are part of a broader diagnostic exercise, known as the comprehensive review.

2.5.2 The Comprehensive Review

Prior to coming under the direct supervision of the ECB, including at the very start of the SSM in 2014, any significant bank undergoes a comprehensive review (CR), which has two components—the asset quality review (AQR) and the stress test (ST).

The purpose of the AQR is to check whether the bank's balance sheet reflects the true economic value of its assets. With the help of a large team of external evaluators, independent from the bank, the supervisor first selects specific asset (loan) portfolios. The second phase of the AQR consists in the review itself, subdivided in concrete steps, such as examination of the policies, processes and accounting (PPA), data integrity validation of the loan tape (DIV), loan sampling for each portfolio, credit file review of the sample based on updated collateral valuations, extrapolation of the findings from the sample to the entire portfolio, and review of the fair value exposures.[52] The AQR of a bank mobilizes tens, if not hundreds, of external auditors and might last several months. This very intrusive exercise forces the bank to open its books for a most detailed scrutiny by the supervisor.

The primary goal of the AQR is to identify cases of overvaluation of assets, based on too optimistic assumptions of expected loan loss recovery or of the collateral valuations. Consequently, the AQR typically results in downside adjustments to the book value of assets through additional loan loss provisions, which directly correct the bank's own funds. On an ongoing basis, outside the context of an AQR, banks following the standardized approach adjust the value of their nonperforming loans by means of specific and general provisions.[53] While both are deducted from the CET1 capital, through the profit and loss account, the amount of general provisions is eligible for Tier 2 capital, up to 1.25 percent of RWAs. The likelihood of being able to reverse the provisions, in case the expected losses do not materialize, explains this allowance. Banks following the IRB approach calibrate their provisions based on expected lifetime losses, as determined by the PDs and LGDs. If a positive difference is found between the accounting provisions and the model-determined expected losses, it is eligible for Tier 2 capital, up to 0.6 percent of RWAs. If that difference is found to be negative, further provisions must be built up, with a negative impact on CET1 capital.

The AQR findings trigger an adjustment to the CET1 capital that, in the supervisor's opinion, reflects more faithfully the actual quality of assets. It corrects the value of assets that are deemed over-estimated and thus attempts to offer a realistically objective picture of the net value of the bank, as reflected in its AQR-adjusted capital level. Even though primarily concerned with the adequacy of the provisions for expected losses, the AQR is essentially a backward-looking exercise. Its main focus is to ensure that banks' balance sheets, as they stand today, return a fair picture of the latest state of affairs. Finally, the AQR ensures that banks' capital adequacy ratios are comparable to each other.[54]

The stress test (ST), which is the second component of the comprehensive review, is very different in nature. Forward-looking, the ST is concerned with the bank's resilience to future shocks over the medium-term, typically the next three years. Under the assumption of a static balance sheet, the ST projects the impact of a variety of shocks—decline in GDP, rising unemployment and contracting incomes, rising interest rates, correction in the real estate prices, and so on—on the bank's assets and income, and hence on its capital level at the end of the three-year period.[55] A hurdle capital adequacy rate indicates the minimum CAR that the bank should maintain after the combined impact of all shocks. Under a baseline scenario, the shocks are assumed milder, and the bank is requested to keep a higher hurdle CAR, typically of 8 percent. Under an adverse scenario, the shocks are assumed stronger, and the bank is allowed to reach a lower hurdle CAR, typically of 5.5 percent. Based on the hypothetical results of the ST, the supervisor requires the bank to identify and implement remedial actions for the highest shortfall between the hurdle (target) CAR and the end-of-period CAR as projected under the two adverse and baseline scenarios.

In the EU, the use of the STs has proliferated. The ECB performs a ST on the banks under its direct supervision at least once per year, the results of which are an important input to the SREP. The European Banking Authority (EBA), in cooperation with the European Systemic Risk Board (ESRB) and the EC, has been coordinating an EU-wide ST every two years since 2014. The 2020 EU-wide ST, postponed to 2021 due to the COVID-19 pandemic, covered fifty banks, out of which thirty-eight from the EA represented more than 70 percent of total assets.[56] Finally, the ECB also conducts thematic STs, on a specific risk or for general financial stability purposes.[57]

The novelty of stress testing, which has introduced a major change in the supervisory approach since the GFC, consists in requesting banks to build up an actual cushion of capital today to withstand hypothetical shocks in the future. That extra level of capital, which goes beyond the regulatory minimum and the combined capital buffer and informs the P2R and P2G, is supposed to ensure banks' capacity to absorb future losses implied by these likely shocks, if ever they were to occur. The STs require banks to be ready, as of today, to cope with capital-adverse future events that might never happen. De facto, and based on the degree of adversity of their assumptions, the STs represent another layer of effective prudential capital requirement, beyond the static backward-looking micro-prudential ratios. From that perspective, and also because they contribute to enhancing confidence in the banks through the transparent disclosure of a significant amount of data and information, the supervisors have made a systematic use of the STs in their standard toolbox since the GFC.

2.5.3 Supervisory Measures

Based on the results of its supervisory review, broadly understood, the ECB has the power to request remedial actions from the banks. The failure of a bank to meet micro-prudential requirements or the CA's evidence-informed judgment that a breach of these requirements is likely within the next twelve months trigger supervisory measures. To protect financial stability, the CA might take any precautionary measure, including the suspension of payments (bank holiday) and the withdrawal of license. However, most supervisory measures function as *early intervention tools* and aim to avoid bank closure. The most important of these measures include i) the request to increase own funds; ii) the reinforcement of the internal strategies and arrangements, and of the recovery and resolution plans; iii) the application of a specific provisioning policy; iv) the restriction of operations or the divestment from specific risky activities; v) other risk-reduction requirements; vi) a limit on variable payments; vii) a restriction or prohibition on dividend distributions or interest payments; viii) enhanced reporting requirements; and ix) the request of additional disclosures. In short, the CA has the power to request the bank to amend its business model and to restructure its balance sheet as it sees fit.

Moreover, the CA may impose administrative penalties, up to 10 percent of the annual net turnover for legal persons and up to EUR 5 million for natural persons, or twice the amount of the benefit from the breach, if identified. Such penalties apply to any area of infringement, such as own funds requirements, large exposures limits, liquidity requirements, reporting and public disclosure, or anti–money laundering. While such penalties operate as strong individual deterrents, their aggregate macro-economic impact has been questioned. The Financial Stability Board (FSB) estimated in 2017 that had the resources paid in fines been retained in capital, they would have supported up to USD 5 trillion in loans to the private sector (Mishra 2019, 77).

This brings us to the important link between supervisory measures and bank credit. By releasing or strengthening the capital and liquidity requirements on banks, supervision directly influences banks' capacity to provide new loans. Thus, supervisory action goes far beyond the strict enforcement and monitoring of compliance with rules. It is a powerful and effective complement to regulation itself, which it reinforces or loosens, depending on the prevailing circumstances and political choices. The ECB supervisory response to the COVID-19 crisis best illustrates this often underestimated potential of supervision. In March 2020, the ECB allowed banks, on a temporary basis until the end of 2020, to deplete their capital conservation buffer, to operate below the P2G buffer, and to use non-CET1 capital instruments, frontloading the application of CRD V, to comply with the P2R. The combined effect of these measures was expected to result in a capital relief of EUR 120 billion that could be used either to absorb losses without triggering a supervisory response or to support new lending for about EUR 1.8 trillion. The ECB also invited the macro-prudential authorities to relax the countercyclical capital buffers and advised banks to delay and limit dividend distributions, to suspend share buybacks and to limit variable remunerations. Furthermore, to alleviate the possible negative impact of the COVID-19–related crisis on banks' capital, the ECB introduced supervisory flexibility with respect to loan loss provisioning and classification of debtors as unlikely to pay if covered by public guarantees or if related to COVID-19 moratoria.

The patently far-ranging powers of banking supervision call for a critical discussion of its underlying principles and its impact on the banking sector.

2.5.4 Principles and Consequences of Banking Supervision

The trained economist could easily identify objective value as the single most important principle that underpins banking supervision. This, indeed, is the fundamental assumption of AQRs and of any other value-adjusting exercises that purport to ensure an alignment of banks' balance sheets with a fair valuation of their assets. Accounting, of course, should reflect reality as closely as possible, if it were to be a useful guide for decision-making. However, banking supervision is rooted in the much stronger claim that banks' own—subjective—assessment of the economic value of their assets could not be trusted. Accordingly, that assessment should be checked, on a regular basis and following uniform classes-of-assets-related rules, against an external valuation. This approach makes sense only under the assumption that this external valuation is superior and unassailable, that is, within the intellectual paradigm of objective value. From that perspective, banking supervision is at odds with modern economic science as it has evolved since the late nineteenth century marginalist revolution that was started by Carl Menger and Stanley Jevons.[58]

The supervisory approach to future risks is not free either from the underlying influence of the assumption of objective value. First, the supervisors imply that the likely impact of these risks is exactly identifiable and hence knowable in advance.[59] Second, the impact is assumed quantifiable based on past experiences that could be summarized in numerical probabilities of default and loss given default for broad classes of assets. However, why should future defaults and losses follow past paths? What is the exact link between projected macroeconomic variables and these probabilities, often admittedly likened to a "black box"? In fact, such an approach rules out uncertainty and the need for genuine entrepreneurial action to deal with it. It portrays banks as responding exclusively to determinate risks, the future impact of which could be accounted for already at the present moment. In this intellectual framework, banks' actual profits or losses could be benchmarked, which implies that supervisors could have an informed opinion on whether a bank is sufficiently or acceptably profitable. This objectivist view of the banking business rationalizes all supervisory prescriptions and recommendations and has implications of its own on the banking system itself.

First, and foremost, bank supervisors act as de facto co-managers of the banks, as revealed by their wide powers to request banks to take specific actions. This situation, which is foreign to any other industry, considers that desk analysts and onsite examiners know as well as, if not even better than, the bank employees how the financial assets originated by the bank will evolve in the future. Why should external observers know better than the bank's own credit analysts, which presumably would have developed a more intimate knowledge of their clients' financial prospects?[60] This presumption of better external knowledge brings about a bureaucratic mentality that does not promote the individual responsibility of bank shareholders and the managers appointed by them.[61] Moreover, the very intrusive nature of supervision is at the origin of irreducible moral hazard that structurally involves the supervisors' responsibility in any bank failure. Under these circumstances, any banking crisis, rather than questioning the fundamentals of modern banking, gives rise to calls for a reform of the prevailing supervisory practices through the political mechanisms. As a result, political considerations become more and more influential in shaping the banking sector.

Second, the strong regulatory and supervisory involvement, originally meant to ensure a level-playing field in the sector, leads to a relative uniformity across banks. While some differences in the funding models and in the investment strategies might be perceptible, depositors tend to view banks equally, once the supervisor has granted its seal of approval. Thus, depositors become less alert to the condition of individual institutions, especially as revealed by changes in their financial indicators. Such a situation does not incentivize consumers to develop their own financial literacy. Moreover, it creates an environment that shields banks from competitive pressures to improve their business model or to develop innovative solutions to emerging problems. Hence, even without explicit coordination or tacit agreement, the banking sector evolves toward further uniformity and cartelization.[62]

In light of these structural pitfalls, it has become increasingly evident that micro-prudential regulation and the related supervision could not, alone, guarantee financial stability. It could even be argued that, because of their intellectual validation and de facto legal protection of the fractional-reserve principle of banking, they are ultimately responsible for the structurally entrenched financial instability of modern banking. Without going that far, both analysts and regulators have recognized the insufficiency of the micro-prudential approach. This precisely explains the recent focus on macro-prudential regulation as a necessary complement, notably to deal with the systemic risk and to ensure the stability of the system as a whole.

2.6 CONCLUSION

This chapter offered an analytical presentation of the micro-prudential banking regulation, in particular, as applied in the EU. It described the main capital adequacy and liquidity requirements, and the essential building blocks of banking supervision. It also highlighted some major consequences of that regulation, both on the banking sector itself and on the broader economy, as well as outstanding controversies. In summary, the discussion crystallizes three main conclusions.

First, micro-prudential policy became prominent since the mid-seventies, which coincides with the demise of the Bretton Woods agreements. Since then, it has evolved into a complex nexus of a myriad of overencompassing requirements that concern practically any single balance sheet item or aspect of the banking activity. International cooperation has played a central role in this ongoing process. Beyond adapting to financial innovation, micro-prudential regulation has evolved, above all, through attempts to address its own failures to prevent financial sector crises. The latest paramount example is the GFC of 2007–2008, which brought about a significant strengthening of the regulatory environment and a major revision of perspective as regards supervision. There is little doubt that the regulatory corpus, as we know it, is awaiting its next amendment at the occasion of the next major financial crisis.

Second, irrespective of its continuous complex refinements, micro-prudential policy is bound to miss its goal of containing bank default risks. Its foundational premises of objective value and of historically determined risk necessarily imply a disconnection from reality, where the future state of the market is driven by noncalculable uncertainty and the subjective valuations of the acting individuals. To correct for this built-in discrepancy and permanent tension, intrusive and forward-looking supervision must complement the regulatory rules. The end-result is a situation in which the public authorities become de facto co-managers of the banks, almost on a daily basis, thereby engaging their own responsibility in case of adverse events.

Third, the objective value bias of both the risk-based capital adequacy and liquidity requirements bring about adverse effects on the system as a whole. In addition to contributing to divert scarce resources toward less productive sectors in the economy, for example, the government budget or investments in real estate, the capital adequacy regulation exposes banks' own funds to unavoidable erosion through the malinvestments that bank credit expansion, unmatched by an increase in savings, triggers. The recent introduction of additional capital buffers and of an extra capital cushion derived from the results of stress tests only confirms this unsurmountable problem and illustrates the arbitrariness of any minimum capital requirement on banks. Similarly, the liquidity requirements ensure that banks remain afloat only as long as their assets, on top of possessing an adequate structure in relation to the liabilities, are themselves sufficiently liquid. This is to say that the actual success of micro-prudential regulation does not depend on its own rules, their rigorous calibration and their strict enforcement. Rather, it depends on the general conditions in the financial sector and the broader economy.

NOTES

1. The lender of last resort, here, is understood in a very broad sense and includes also all interventions that address the ex-post occurrence of default risk, that is, deposit guarantee schemes, asset support mechanisms, and so on. The stronger the moral hazard implied by the lender of last resort, the more stringent the other two tools must be, to compensate for its adverse effect. The literature on this optimal mix of prudential tools, according to its main proponent, is in its infancy (Calomiris 2012, 41).

2. The macro-prudential regulation, which aims at mitigating risks to the financial system as a whole, is discussed in the next chapter.

3. For details on membership, cf. https://www.bis.org/bcbs/membership.htm.

4. The introduction to the 1983 Principles for the Supervision of Banks' Foreign Establishments is very clear: "The principles set out in the report are not necessarily embodied in the laws of the countries represented on the Committee. Rather they are recommended guidelines of best practices in this area, which all members have undertaken to work toward implementing, according to the means available to them" (BCBS 1983, 1).

5. For a short description of the event, within its broader international context, see Jeffs (2008, 264–65).

6. Schenk (2014) argues convincingly that two other bank failures from the summer of 1974, namely the Lloyds Lugano and the Israel-British Bank, drove the early agenda of the BCBS, which focused more on problems of responsibility and governance in the supervision of international banks rather than on issues with information exchange, as exemplified by the Herstatt incident.

7. Branches, which have no capital of their own, are subject only to liquidity requirements.

8. These four minimum standards are i) the consolidated supervision of international banks by the home supervisor, ii) the joint prior authorization of both home and host supervisors for cross-border banking establishments, iii) the right for the home supervisor to gather information from the cross-border establishments and iv) the right for the host supervisor to impose restrictive measures or withdraw the authorization if it considers that the first three prudential standards are not met (enforcement mechanism).

9. An upgrade to the Basel III set of rules, indistinctly referred to as either Basel IV or Basel 3.1, was negotiated in 2017 and began implementation in January 2022, with phase-in periods of up to five years with respect to some rules. EBF (2019) provides a clear summary of the envisaged amendments and estimates that this upgrade of Basel III, when finalized eventually, would increase European banks' minimum capital requirements by 16.7 percent. It is estimated that banks in the United States would experience no increase in their capital requirements.

10. At the time, it was widely admitted that the dominant position of Japanese banks in international lending (a market share above one-third, with eight out of the ten largest institutions) was due to a favourable funding cost that ultimately could be traced back to a less-demanding capital requirement. From that perspective, Basel I

was perceived as restoring a level-playing field for the American and European banks. Wagster (1996) challenges this view, by documenting significant cumulative wealth effects for Japanese bank shareholders after the introduction of Basel I rules.

11. Many of these upgrades only took stock of amendments that have been taking place gradually.

12. In contrast, Basel I has been associated with the phenomenon of regulatory arbitrage, whereby the regulated entity readjusts its business model to escape the impact of regulations, which brings about an outcome that is not aligned with the objectives of the intended regulation.

13. For convincing arguments on the crucial role played by monetary policy, government housing policies, various instances of regulatory failure in the financial sector, institutional privileges enjoyed by rating agencies and the influence of economic misconceptions, cf. in particular, Acharya and Richardsom (2009), Wallison (2009), Jablecki and Machaj (2009), White (2009), and Acemoglu (2009).

14. Subsequently, the revised framework was further expanded to include margin requirements for noncentrally cleared derivatives and capital requirements for banks' equity in funds (2013), a standardized approach for measuring counterparty credit risk exposures (2014), capital requirements for securitizations and the introduction of large exposure limits (2014), and a revision to the market risk framework (2016).

15. The latest version of the TFEU is the result of successive versions of consolidated amendments that reflect the evolution of the European project, the most important of which are known as the Treaty of Rome (1957, establishing the European Economic Community based on the four freedoms), the Treaty of Maastricht (1992, establishing the European Union and the monetary union), and the Treaty of Lisbon (2007, consolidating the Union's prerogatives).

16. Each Commissioner is assisted by a directorate general that provides the necessary administrative support. For instance, DG FISMA (financial services, financial stability, and capital markets union) carries out the analytical and legislative work of the Commission in the area of financial services.

17. The European Council, which gathers the heads of state or government of the EU MS, its own president and the president of the European Commission, should not be confused with the Council of the EU. The role of the European Council is to determine the Union's general political direction and strategic priorities.

18. The 2019 amendments introduce Basel IV into the Single Rulebook.

19. The full regulatory framework for financial services, institutions and infrastructures in the EU includes a much broader set of legislative pieces, the most prominent of which are the Solvency Directive on insurance companies, the EMIR (European Market Infrastructure Regulation) on derivatives and central counterparties, and the MIFID (Markets in Financial Instruments Directive) on financial instruments, firms and markets.

20. In the MS that are part of the Banking Union, the ECB itself is in charge of licensing.

21. The other comprehensive income corresponds to revenues, expenses, gains or losses that have not materialized yet. The most common items that drive the other

comprehensive income are the gains or losses from available-for-sale (AFS) investments and foreign currency exchange fluctuations.

22. The losses from the PSI on the Greek public debt were a major driving factor of the subsequent banking sector crisis in Cyprus.

23. The higher average IRBA-produced risk weight for exposures to banks implies that the larger, more sophisticated banks that apply the IRBA method consider inter-bank loans riskier than the smaller, less sophisticated banks that apply the SA method.

24. Haldane (2014, 17) documents an average decline in the aggregate risk weights of seventeen major international banks by 2 percentage points per year, from over 70 percent in 1993 to below 40 percent in 2011.

25. The fact that it took the ECB five years to complete this review is also a proof of the degree of complexity of the internal ratings models.

26. The BCBS (2018) presents the updated methodology for assessing the global systemic importance of a banking group, originally developed around five criteria: size of the group, its interconnectedness to the financial system, its complexity, its cross-border activity, and the substitutability of the services provided by its infrastructure. The Financial Stability Board publishes the list of the thirty global systemically important banks, distributed in five buckets, since November 2011. In addition to the requirement for an additional capital buffer, the G-SIIs are also subject to stronger preparedness for resolvability and to higher supervisory expectations.

27. The EBA (2014) has clarified the methodology for identifying the O-SIIs in the European context around four main criteria: size of the institution, its importance for the financial system infrastructure, complexity and cross-border activity and its interconnectedness. The latest 2021 list includes 175 European banks.

28. Strictly speaking, the countercyclical capital buffer and the systemic risk buffer are instruments of macro-prudential regulation. Yet, they are addressed in this chapter for the sake of completing the presentation of the capital buffers.

29. As part of the Basel IV or 3.1, the CRR II eventually introduced a binding minimum leverage ratio of 3 percent in 2019.

30. Moreover, banks are also required to disclose their twenty largest exposures, even if they fall short of the 10 percent trigger in the official definition of a large exposure (Pillar 3 requirement on disclosure and transparency).

31. A recent BIS research paper comes very close to a similar conclusion, though within a different theoretical framework. Agénor et al. (2018) examine the impact of prudential regulation on economic growth through four very different channels: i) the effect on risk-taking and borrowing/lending, ii) the effect on bank intermediation costs, iii) the effect on the size of the financial sector, and iv) a broader effect through income and wealth redistribution. As these channels do not operate in the same direction, the final impact of prudential regulation on economic growth is theoretically ambiguous. More precisely, the overall effect is positive if regulation succeeds in mitigating risk-taking. The authors conclude that, from a growth perspective, prudential regulation should be formulated within the broader context of structural policies that foster financial development and integration.

32. The monetary transmission mechanisms put a special focus on "an accurate assessment of the timing and effect" of monetary policy on the economy (Mishkin

1995, 4). The concept has gained wide popularity since the *Journal of Economic Per-spectives* published a dedicated symposium, featuring Bernanke and Gertler (1995) on the credit channel, among the other seminal contributions by Taylor, Meltzer, and Obstfeld and Rogoff.

33. The first credit channel (bank lending channel) clarifies that a tighter mon-etary policy implies tighter liquidity conditions for banks. Hence, banks cut back on their credits. The reduced credit availability, which impacts especially the relatively smaller companies that rely on bank lending instead of market funding, leads to a contraction of aggregate output. The second credit channel (corporate balance sheet channel) refers to the direct (cost of funding) and indirect (lower value of assets) impact of a tighter monetary policy on companies' net equity, which in turn reduces access to bank lending and contracts investment.

34. Total demand refers to the sum between the reservation demand, that is, goods kept in stock by their owners, and the standard flow demand via exchanges. The advantage of the total demand approach for the theory of price determination is that it avoids any interrelatedness between the transactional notions of supply and demand and identifies two independent causes of price determination: the total supply (stock) of the good and its overall demand (to hold it and to acquire it through exchanges), itself determined by subjective valuations. This approach shows that transaction volumes do not cause prices; rather, they are implied by the initial distribution of the supply and by changes in subjective preferences.

35. Zukauskas (2021) develops further the quality of money as a separate channel for the transmission of monetary policy and constructs a statistical index, which docu-ments a persistent decline in the perceived quality of the euro.

36. This finding suggests a fundamental tension between regulation and market discipline as constitutive pillars of the Basel framework.

37. Admittedly, the now popular asset quality reviews and stress tests, which have become standard supervisory tools, aim to address this very same weakness of the capital adequacy regulation.

38. The very first contribution by Kahane (1977) on the analysis of capital adequacy regulation makes already the point that higher capital requirements might incentivize banks to take more risk. The question about the possible adverse effects from more stringent capital requirements is further discussed in the very broad literature review on bank capital regulation in banking theory by Santos (2000).

39. Hellwig and Blum (1995) point out the amplification effect of rigid capital adequacy requirements, which lead banks to cut on lending at times when their capital gets eroded because of some borrowers' insolvency that a negative demand distur-bance is causing. This implication of bank capital regulation suggests that additional capital buffers, which increase the flexibility of the overall capital requirement, would then have a distinct macro-economic benefit. Admittedly, this is one of the rationales of the macro-prudential regulation, presented in the next chapter.

40. The authors also point out, and rightly so, that the principle of the double liabil-ity, whereby shareholders were liable for their obligations also on their own wealth for as much as their equity stake, historically has implied effective capital levels of

close to 100 percent of total assets (Admati and Hellwig 2013, 30). On the history and principle of the double liability, see Macey and Miller (1992) and Bodenhorn (2015).

41. For a comprehensive historical summary of bank crises since the nineteenth century, see Reinhart and Rogoff (2009, 343–92).

42. Notice also that the exchange of a portion of the newly issued media of exchange for new shares in bank capital has a sterilizing impact on the monetary consequences of the bank credit expansion, as in the case of loans securitization.

43. Lately, liquidity regulation has been rationalised as an efficient policy response to banks' tendency to over-invest in risky assets and under-invest in liquid assets in the presence of fire sale externalities (Kara and Ozsoy 2020). The authors suggest that liquidity regulation, instead of being redundant, is complementary and even necessary to correct for the fact that tighter capital requirements imposed by the regulator incentivize banks to keep lower liquidity buffers. From that perspective, the liquidity requirements under Basel III are an outgrowth of the same concern for systemic financial stability that justifies macro-prudential regulation.

44. For instance, the weighting is 95 percent for fixed-term deposits with a remaining liability below a year and sight deposits considered as stable, 90 percent for the same deposits considered as retail, 50 percent for operational deposits and other liabilities with a maturity between six months and a year, and 0 percent for liabilities without maturity or with a remaining maturity below six months.

45. For instance, the weighting factor for cash reserves, accounts with central banks and Level 1 assets is 0 percent. It is between 12 percent and 55 percent for Level 2 assets and dues with a remaining maturity below a year, 65 percent for loans with a risk weight of up to 35 percent, 85 percent for loans with a risk weight above 35 percent, and 100 percent for all other assets and derivatives with a positive market value.

46. Cecchetti and Schoenholtz (2017, 6–9) demonstrate this point based on simple balance sheet identities.

47. Calomiris (2012, 40–41) argues in that direction and suggests that a simple cash requirement, such as 20 percent of assets, would be much preferable. Notice that a cash requirement relative to total assets, rather than relative to deposits, contributes to obfuscate the economic nature of banks' deposits as fiduciary media of exchange with a promise of redeemability into money.

48. Onsite examiners visit the premises of the bank and go through the various processes together with the bank employees. Such examinations, admittedly very intrusive, take place at least once every three years and may last several months. Offsite inspections refer to the daily desk monitoring of various balance sheet items and the related prudential ratios.

49. Euro area banks' significance, and hence their direct supervision by the ECB, is determined based on the fulfilment of at least one of the following four criteria: i) size (total assets above EUR 30 billion); ii) economic importance for the country or the EU economy (three largest banks); iii) cross-border activities (total assets above EUR 5 billion and cross-border assets/liabilities in another MS above 20 percent of total assets/liabilities); and iv) direct public financial assistance (the bank has requested and/or received direct assistance from the European Stability Mechanism).

50. The Banking Union can be seen as the major post-GFC reform of the European Monetary Union. The application of Bulgaria and Croatia to join the euro area naturally raised the question of how, and when, to organize their membership in the BU. The adopted solution, namely their joining the SSM in 2020, suggests that single banking supervision (and regulation) has now become a constituent element of the single currency, and hence an effective prerequisite for euro adoption.

51. Unlike the P2R, the P2G is not mandatory. However, banks can afford to ignore this recommendation only at the cost of accepting a higher degree of scrutiny from the supervisor.

52. Details on the various steps of the AQR can be found in the updated guidance addressed to external valuators and auditors (ECB 2018b).

53. A good rule of thumb requires banks to cover their stock of nonperforming loans by 60 percent of provisions. If this coverage ratio is lower, the bank is suspected of having under-provisioned its future losses, which implies an overestimation of its capitalization.

54. Indeed, capital adequacy is comparable across banks only to the extent that their coverage ratios (of NPLs by provisions) are deemed sufficient, and themselves comparable for banks operating in the same economic environment.

55. Details on the methodology of conducting stress tests can be found in EBA (2019).

56. The EU-wide ST no longer includes hurdle rates under the baseline and adverse scenarios, which makes it a solvency exercise without "pass or fail" thresholds. The 2021 methodological notes and final results can be found here: https://www.eba .europa.eu/risk-analysis-and-data/eu-wide-stress-testing.

57. For instance, in January 2022 the ECB announced the launch of a climate risk stress test, as a learning exercise to assess banks' climate-risk preparedness.

58. Economic analysis in terms of marginal units, which are the actual objects of acting individuals' subjective valuations, is considered as "nothing less than a Copernican revolution in social science" (Mises 2003, 163).

59. This is not to say that new risks, for example, related to climate change, to green finance or to the digital transition, do not appear. The point is that the impact of these risks is assumed to be assessable in a finite and objective way.

60. Note that this is precisely the assumption that underpins the introduction of the internal risk-ratings models since Basel II.

61. Mises (1983) provides an in-depth economic analysis of the inefficiencies of bureaucratic management as an alternative to profit management based on private property, and of its social, political and psychological consequences.

62. Other analysts of the regulatory reform since the GFC arrive at a similar conclusion: "In closing, we note a series of concerns about our current approach to regulation and how it is influencing the financial system. First, by placing such a large number of complex constraints on intermediaries' activities, we may be pushing them to become more and more similar. [. . .]. To the extent that regulation makes the financial system more homogenous, it creates, rather than reduces, systemic risk" (Cecchetti and Schoenholtz 2017, 19).

Chapter 3

Macro-Prudential Regulation and Financial Stability

The previous chapter examined banks' individual capital and liquidity requirements. Putting aside their own merits and weaknesses, the sufficiency of such a single institution-focused approach is doubtful in itself. Indeed, all banks are interconnected, inter alia through the interbank market, and even beyond the national borders. Their operations are influenced by the same, often abrupt, changes in economic conditions, to which they themselves contribute. Banks expand or contract credit more or less synchronously. These observations suggest that financial stability is a systemic issue that would then need a broader solution, one that goes beyond considering banks in isolation from each other. Such a wider view of banks' safety and soundness must then look into potential systemic threats to the sector's stability. Once diagnosed, systemic risk must be contained through adequate policy instruments. In a nutshell, this is the ambitious promise of the macro-prudential approach to banking regulation.

The term macro-prudential seems to have been coined in 1979 by a Bank of England official (Turner 2018, 19), at a meeting of the Cooke Committee, the forerunner of the BCBS (Clement 2010, 59). Its initial use reflected a concern for the macro-economic implications of institution-specific regulatory issues, in particular in the contemporary context of rapidly growing international bank lending. Thus, originally, macro-prudential policy was primarily concerned with limiting and mitigating the potentially destabilizing effects of international capital flows, especially from the perspective of the emerging market economies. In practice, it consisted in regulatory tools, for instance restrictions on foreign currency deposits and loans, which aimed at insulating the domestic banking sector from "hot" liquidity coming from abroad.[1]

The notion of macro-prudential policy and regulation gained true notoriety, to the point of becoming almost a buzzword, only after the GFC and the accompanying significant asset price deflation. The catalyst for that popularity was the 2009 report by the High-Level Group in Financial Supervision in the EU, known as *De Larosière Report*, which emphasized the need for setting up an EU-wide macro-prudential authority that would ensure the safety and soundness of the financial system as a whole. Thus, the realization that some systemic factors, beyond the solvency or liquidity situation of any individual institution, were among the contributing causes of the GFC led to a renewed interest in the very meaning of the macro-prudential concept. It increasingly referred to policies, regulations and tools designed to ensure the stability of the financial system as a whole, and hence to limit or mitigate the impact of systemic risk.

Under the impetus of the international financial institutions, both academics and practitioners started paying accrued attention to this renewed concept. The Bank for International Settlements dedicated two important international conferences to the new policy (BIS 2011, 2016). The International Monetary Fund issued a policy paper that serves, even today, as a vade-mecum on how to calibrate and operationalize the appropriate macro-prudential tools (IMF 2013). The very first book on macroprudential policy acknowledged that the topic, still in its infancy, is influenced heavily by practitioners' experience and noted much confusion about the theory and little agreement on the practice. The remaining open questions would concern such basic issues as the measurement of systemic risk, the interaction between monetary and macro-prudential policies or the unintended consequences of banks-focused regulation on diverting risk to other parts of the financial system (Freixas et al. 2015). Lately, at the occasion of the first decade after the *De Larosière Report*, there was a noticeable analytical effort to take stock of progress in the area (Aikman et al. 2019; Mishra 2019; Mizen et al. 2020).

The macro-prudential regulation consists in the introduction of systemwide requirements that aim to smoothen bank credit through the cycle and to limit contagion from systemically important institutions. It includes such tools as counter-cyclical capital buffers, systemic risk buffers, loan-to-value and loan-to-income limits, collateral haircuts, dynamic provisioning and taxes on some "hot" liabilities, among others.[2] Our economic approach here will focus primarily on understanding the rationale for macro-prudential regulation. The first section, which is mostly conceptual and analytical, will present the standard case for macro-prudential policy, in particular, by investigating the underlying concept of systemic risk. It also discusses the relation between macro-prudential and monetary policies and some implications for understanding financial stability. The second section, which is mostly descriptive, presents the institutional architecture of the macro-prudential oversight of banks in the EU and the content of the available toolkit.

3.1 THE CASE FOR MACRO-PRUDENTIAL POLICY

The rationale for a broad systemwide regulation of the banking sector is rooted in the observation that bank credit is procyclical.[3] During the boom stage of the cycle, credit expansion contributes to the funding of new investments and of aggregate demand, thereby boosting the indicators of economic growth, such as GDP figures. During the bust stage of the cycle, credit contraction contributes to exacerbate, or amplify, the underlying economic contraction. Two aspects of this procyclicality deserve special attention. First, all banks participate together in these waves of expansion and contraction. This common behavior calls for a systemic explanation, which is rooted precisely in the specific concept of systemic risk. Second, the amplification effect on the real economy of the credit contraction in the bust, including its negative welfare implications, justifies a dedicated preventive or mitigating policy.

This is the particular mandate of macro-prudential policy, namely, to avoid a generalized credit contraction, or to smooth the credit cycle, in order to insulate the real economy from the destabilizing financial factors. According to an early definition, "In the simplest terms, one can characterize the macro-prudential approach to financial regulations as an effort to control the social costs associated with excessive balance sheet shrinkage on the part of multiple financial institutions hit with a common shock" (Hanson et al. 2011, 5). More recent analyses describe the macro-prudential regulation as "aiming at ensuring that the financial system does not create shocks that trigger recessions or amplify other shocks to make recessions materially worse" (Aikman et al. 2019, 108). A sharper statement asserts, "Macroprudential policies seek to address the debilitating impact of deleveraging following credit booms" (Mishra 2019, 131).

Thus, at the heart of macro-prudential policy lies a concern for the real economy. This link between the financial sector and the wider economy is also a distinctive mark of how systemic financial stability is being defined. Before engaging into a broader discussion, let us first examine the concept of systemic risk, which macro-prudential regulation aims to contain.

3.1.1 FINANCIAL SECTOR VULNERABILITIES AND SYSTEMIC RISK

From the very outset, the notion of systemic risk brings about a certain degree of uneasiness. According to the official definition, "systemic risk means a risk of disruption in the financial system with the potential to have serious negative consequences for the financial system and the real economy" (CRD

IV, Art. 3). Neither the rather vague notion of "disruption" nor the reference to "potential" serious consequences help identify the feared adverse event behind systemic risk. Moreover, what is the specific factor that would cause this adverse event? A more analytical definition clarifies that "systemic risk arises when shocks are amplified and inflict significant *damage* on the broader financial system and broader economy" (Liang 2013, 130; our emphasis). Systemic risk monitoring distinguishes then between difficult-to-predict external shocks and systemic vulnerabilities, which transmit and amplify these shocks throughout the system. The specificity of systemic risk lies in that it is not determined by the summation of individual risks, but rather by the interactions of financial institutions and markets.

Rochet and Tirole (1996) emphasize this interactional aspect: "Systemic risk refers to the propagation of an agent's economic distress to other agents linked to that agent through financial transactions" (733).[4] Allen and Carletti (2013) identify four areas of systemic risk, depending on the type of interactions: panics, banking crises due to asset price falls, contagion and foreign exchange mismatches. Freixas et al. (2015) insist upon the real economic implications of systemic risk: "Systemic risk is not simply financial instability but an unusual financial shock that causes strong negative shocks to the real economy: aggregate output, employment, and welfare" (13). Its endogenous nature and the negative consequences on the broader economy would then be the two distinctive features of systemic risk.

While these definitional efforts clarify many aspects of systemic risk, the notion of *damage* to the system definitely remains vague. Moreover, the driving factor that contributes to the actual realization of systemic risk remains unspecified. It is symptomatic that no such lack of clarity arises, for instance, in a discussion of liquidity, credit, market, or any of the other individual, non-systemic risks. Without any need for an official definition, the specific adverse situation in which the realization of a concrete risk factor negatively impacts a bank's balance sheet is clear even intuitively. The notion of systemic risk lacks this advantage of being intuitively understandable and hence appears as categorically different from those individual risks that micro-prudential policy purports to address.[5]

To grasp the real-world expression and thus the implied meaning of systemic risk, one should first identify the specific vulnerabilities of the banking sector. The literature on systemic risk suggests that these vulnerabilities result from a collective action problem, that is, from some form of market failure due to negative externalities. De Nicolo et al. (2012) identifies three broad types of externalities leading to systemic risk. First come externalities related to strategic complementarities and interactions between banks that result in the build-up of common vulnerabilities during the expansionary phase of the financial cycle. A prima facie case would be a generalized credit expansion in the same types of assets, for instance household mortgages, mortgage-backed securities or public debt instruments.[6] This case would justify corrective "lean against the wind" policies that prevent the build-up of common exposures and hence alleviate the risk of causing widespread losses during the bust.

The second type of externalities refer to the generalized sell-off or amortization of financial assets in the contractionary phase of the cycle. Fire sales, in the case of marketable securities, or a credit crunch, in the case of nonmarketable loans, would cause asset prices to decline and banks' balance sheets to contract, thereby further deteriorating the conditions for economic growth. This case would justify supportive policies during the bust that would contain the asset price deflation and the balance sheet compression, so that banks would not be constrained in their regular and ongoing credit provision to the economy.

The third type of externalities derive from bank interconnectedness through cross-institution exposures, which propagate a negative shock from one financial institution, in particular, systemically important, to the rest of the system. Both liquidity and solvency constraints might be responsible for the transmission of the original shock beyond the single balance sheet of the originally affected bank, which cannot absorb it alone due to these constraints. In a nutshell, systemic risk would boil down to the risk of contagion between financial intermediaries.[7] This case would rationalize the continuous monitoring, through multiple indicators, of developments in the financial sector, with additional liquidity and capital requirements imposed especially on the systemic institutions, with a view of ensuring their balance sheets can absorb shocks on their own, without propagating them further.

To some extent, the first and third sources of systemic vulnerabilities do not exemplify a systemic risk aspect that would be specific to the banking sector or even to the broader financial system. The likelihood of a generalized herd behavior, as in common asset exposures, is not unique to banks or to financial investments. It is actually a very common feature of human action, as illustrated for instance by mass production of many standardized goods. As an actual outcome, herd behavior finds its justification in the very close similarity between market participants' preferences. More fundamentally, and going beyond the effects of fade, imitation, or virtue signaling, the emergence of general or common patterns in human choices and actions is a rational response to the need to economize on resources, that is, to scarcity itself. Finally, in the specific case of banking, common exposures are not an issue in themselves as they need not imply a higher risk of losses. Losses stem from malinvestments, the failure of which is not rooted in the commonness of choice, but in the commonness of error. A fuller account of systemic risk due to herd behavior would then require the additional explanation of how clusters of investment errors are formed.

As regards the propagation of a shock between institutions, the case of contagion seems to be specific neither to banks nor to the financial sector. Losses due to cross exposures between creditors and debtors in default, due to illiquidity or to insolvency, are characteristic also of the real economy, where the bankruptcy of a supplier or of a client can disturb the whole chain of production. A fuller account of systemic risk due to interbank contagion would then require an additional explanation of the uniqueness of the linkages between banks. This would also make the fractional-reserve nature of modern banks, to which the interbank market can be shown to be foundational, an integral part of the analysis of systemic risk.

Thus, the strong standard case for systemic risk in the banking sector rests on the two instances of fire sales of securities and of bank credit crunch. Indeed, they are both perceived as resulting from and representing the costs of "generalized asset shrinkage" (Hanson et al. 2011, 5). At the end, our discussion eventually brought us to the more distilled understanding of systemic risk as the risk of generalized balance sheet contraction, the two main expressions of which would be asset fire sales and a credit crunch.

3.1.2 Deleveraging, Fire Sales, and Credit Crunch

The starting point of this generalized balance sheet contraction is the sudden need for banks to deleverage, to reduce their reliance on borrowed funds, due to two related yet independent factors. First, banks might be liquidity-constrained, in the sense that disproportionately high short-term debt is funding long-term assets inadequately. To respond to the lack of available liquidity, and of market funding given the generalized nature of the liquidity constraint, banks must liquidate assets to repay their maturing short-term debt. The resulting fire sales, defined as the liquidation of portfolio holdings "at below fundamental values in bad times," are due to the simultaneous debt overhang in the banking system (Shleifer and Vishny 2010, 307). The fire sales are described as banks' rational profit-maximizing response to an assets-liabilities mismatch that imposes economic losses on the liquidity-constrained banks during the bust stage of the cycle. The fire sales then erode the amount of own funds, which thereby become insufficient to support the provision of new loans to the real economy. In addition, the underpricing of outstanding securities creates expectations for future capital gains that make them a preferred investment option in comparison to new exposures to the real economy.[8] The combined result of capital erosion and investment in underpriced securities is a marked procyclicality of bank credit, which amplifies the economic recession during the bust.

The second general cause of balance sheet deleveraging lies in the insufficiency of banks' own funds to absorb losses on loans and securities. Rather than raising additional capital, which appears challenging during the downturn, these capital-constrained banks respond to their eroded capital levels by reducing their risk-weighted assets. The easiest means to achieve that reduction and to deleverage the balance sheet consists in not renewing maturing loans. This natural amortization of the loan book leads to a credit crunch for the real economy. The theory of the credit crunch[9] emphasizes that the subsequent additional credit constraints on borrowers worsen their repayment capacity and thus further amplify the initial shock on banks' capital. This reinforces credit constraints, which engender further asset sales and price corrections, very similar to the Fisherian debt-deflation mechanism (Gersbach and Rochet 2012, 74).[10]

While the theory of the fire sales justifies credit procyclicality on the ground of generalized liquidity constraints, the theory of the credit crunch focuses on insufficient capital to absorb losses on assets. Irrespective of the concrete liquidity- or capital-driven vulnerability that triggers the systemic risk, the implied procyclical banking sector contraction in the bust (following its expansion in the boom) further compresses aggregate demand, and hence aggravates the economic recession. From that perspective, macro-prudential policy is justified by its unique objective to avoid such exaggerated swings in bank credit activity or to smoothen the provision of credit by banks. In short, the macro-prudential objective is to "maintain credit creation during recessions" (Hanson et al. 2011, 8).

This admittedly very distilled, yet accurate, description of the goal of macro-prudential policy clarifies in which sense analysts perceive systemic risk as a threat to financial stability. The latter is defined as "the ability of the financial system to *consistently supply the credit* intermediation and payment services that are needed in the real economy *if it is to continue on its growth path*" (Rosengren 2011, 2; our emphasis). Defined as it is, financial stability implies the need for an uninterrupted flow of bank credit. Moreover, that continuous flow of credit is deemed necessary for real economic growth. Hence, for all its analytical sophistication, the standard explanation of systemic risk boils down to the likelihood of a feared sudden stop in bank credit. When materialized, a systemic risk event brings about financial instability.[11]

Thus, from the outset, the analytical discussion of systemic risk, financial stability and macro-prudential policy presents an undeniable bias toward continuous bank credit expansion. It is true that the literature admits the need to dampen the expansion during the boom, lest it becomes unsustainable and is reversed. After all, the whole point of the "lead against the wind" policies is, precisely, to recognize the fact that credit expansion should be kept under control. However, the macro-prudential literature never explains why a continuous bank credit flow would be a desirable social outcome or how exactly it exerts its positive contribution to real economic growth.[12] Consequently, the literature never gets to the very relevant question of how to determine that limit on credit expansion that would make it sustainable and irreversible during the bust. Moreover, there is no discussion of the very nature of bank credit provided by modern fractional-reserve banks, and hence of its essentially destabilizing effect due to the illusion it creates of additional real resources. The monetary business cycle theory clearly demonstrates that a bank credit expansion leads to a misallocation of capital investments that is structurally unsustainable. Thus, credit expansion by modern banks hampers economic growth, while the misallocation of real resources necessarily implies financial losses and hence a credit contraction. An analysis that integrates these insights would espouse a very different, not to say diametrically opposite, view of which conditions would be conducive to financial stability. Suffice it to say here that the continuity of bank credit expansion would not be among the relevant factors.

Given this procredit expansion bias, how credible are the two main instances of systemic risk, on their own ground? Two critical assumptions underpin the theory of fire sales. First, each asset is characterized by a fundamental value, assumed or determined within a mathematical model. To the extent that such modelling techniques rely extensively on cardinal formalistic language, the concept of fundamental value employed by these models could not possibly reflect the distinctive ordinality of subjective preferences. Rather, these models must rely on objective factors as the ultimate determinants of assets' fundamental value. Thus, the starting position of the theory of fire sales is, in practice, a normative view of what asset prices should be, under normal circumstances.

This normative bias naturally raises a second difficulty for the theory of asset fire sales, namely, the identification of actual fire sales in reality. The question would have been easily solved if a method for finding out the fundamental value existed. Then, major discrepancies between the latter and the actual market prices would point to a case of fire sales. However, without such a method, the identification of a fire sale remains a delicate, if not unresolvable, matter. At this stage, the second critical assumption comes to the rescue. The market pricing mechanism is deemed to have failed to discover the fundamental value. This failure would be attributable to an information asymmetry among the buyers or to temporary liquidity constraints that would force sellers to neglect both the objective factors behind fundamental value and their own, true, preferences. However, this assumption does not contribute to a more elaborate and realistic cause-to-effect explanation of actual fire sales. It merely makes them an analytical concept or a postulate akin to the market failure argument. It is revealing to point out that the theory of fire sales assumes the market pricing mechanism to fail only downward, never upward. Indeed, why are "rocket" purchases never mentioned as another, equally plausible, source of systemic risk?

The identification of a credit crunch encounters a similar problem. For a credit crunch to develop, it is not enough that loan expansion stops; the deleveraging must be caused by a systemic capital insufficiency due to a generalized loss-driven capital erosion or to another system-wide factor. Yet, what is the criterion for determining that fresh capital has become too expensive so that banks objectively cannot raise more own funds, which would then leave them with the single option, which appears to be forced upon them, to contract their balance sheet? Again, which objective criteria would be determining the fundamental, fair or just price for banks' new equity and why would this alleged mispricing occur in the downturn only?

This critical discussion of the concepts of fire sales and of credit crunch as the specific causes of systemic risk fundamentally questions their link to reality. To the extent that standard explanations of systemic risk eventually make it a purely analytical concept, all attempts to measure or describe it should prove extremely difficult. This is exactly what the International Monetary Fund has acknowledged explicitly: "Systemic risk is a term that is widely used, but *is difficult to define and quantify*. Indeed, it is often viewed as a phenomenon that is there 'when we see it,' reflecting a sense of a broad-based breakdown in the functioning of the financial system, which is normally realized, ex post, by a large number of failures of FIs (usually banks). Similarly, a systemic episode may simply be seen as an extremely acute case of financial instability, even though the degree and severity of financial stress *has proven difficult, if not impossible, to measure*." (IMF 2009, 113; our emphasis). The quest for a real phenomenon that would describe the systemic risk led the authors of the report to propose several measures, such as the return-on-assets rate, the rate of non-performing assets, the capital ratio, probability-of-default options, equity options, currency swaps, etc. However, these variables are standard indicators that characterize individual financial institutions and market volatility. The lack of a realistic account of systemic risk, as opposed to an explanation that relies on conceptual models only, naturally results in significant difficulties with identifying a specific quantitative indicator.[13]

In the absence of a specific indicator of systemic risk, probabilistic measures of the impact of likely shocks, such as the conditional value at risk or the expected marginal shortfall of capital, have gained wide popularity. On that basis, Allen et al. (2012) develop a macro-index that has been successful in forecasting economic downturns six months before they occurred. However, it is widely acknowledged that such indexes are unfit to guide policy choices. Löffler and Paupach (2018) show that the aggregate risk in the system might be increasing while, according to individual measures, banks' own contributions to systemic risk are decreasing. The authors conclude that institutions-based measures of systemic risk can lead to wrong regulatory decisions. Moreover, the tested measures fail to capture the ambiguous effect of bank size and remain prone to estimation errors. Danielsson et al. (2016) focus on the critical issue of estimation errors and find out that, whatever the concrete technique for estimating systemic risk, it does not pass even a standard test of reliability. This implies that macro-prudential policy lacks an ex ante guidepost and must operate in the dark.

To go beyond the purely conceptual description of systemic risk and the related identification and measurement problems, one needs to inquire into its actual driving factors. As shown above, the standard explanation of systemic risk occurrence is rooted in banks' liquidity and capital constraints that act as effective triggers of the generalized balance sheet deleveraging. But then, are we not back to those same individual funding and credit risks that micro-prudential regulation purports to address? Ultimately, the missing account of systemic risk's unique specificity implies that either micro-prudential regulation has failed to prevent the individual risks or that macro-prudential regulation lacks a solid rationale of its own. After all, the standard reason for macro-prudential regulation boils down to the point that standalone bank-specific regulatory requirements are unfit to address some structural aspects of the banking sector. If these structural aspects themselves are not convincingly articulated, the rationale for macro-prudential regulation remains incomplete.

In fact, the issue with the standard explanations of systemic risk is that they themselves are not systemic enough. Indeed, due to their bias for continuous bank credit expansion, they look only at possible causes of the credit contraction in the downturn. A more complete approach should strive to provide a unified explanation of both credit expansion and contraction, that is, of the two stages of the credit procyclicality.

3.1.3 Macro-Prudential Policy in the Context of Present-Day Monetary Policy

As highlighted in the first chapter, banks' credit activity is subject to the liquidity-based regulation of the central bank in charge of fiat money production. A generalized bank credit expansion is driven by an expansionary monetary policy that offers banks more liquidity (central bank money) at a lower interest rate. The credit expansion necessarily unfolds into a subsequent, cyclical, credit contraction due to the generalized clusters of entrepreneurial investment errors that it itself induces. The loan losses and the asset price declines in the downturn result from and reveal these investment errors, in particular the inadequacy between the structure of production and consumers' intertemporal preferences. These losses and price corrections signal the need for and make possible the necessary restructuring and reallocation of factors of production. Indeed, at the higher credit-inflated prices, alternative investment projects could not become profitable, and the necessary aggregate restructuring of entrepreneurial decisions could not take place. The welfare cost of this boom-bust cycle consists in the foregone consumer preferences that could not be satisfied and in the unfitness of some of the inconvertible capital that has been produced but lacks ultimate economic use. Against this backdrop, both the procyclicality of bank credit and its debilitating impact on the real economy are due to the expansionist monetary policy. From that perspective, monetary policy itself is the true cause of systemic risk.

This radical approach to explaining the origin of systemic risk has at least three advantages. First, it is truly realistic as it refers to one of the objective characteristics of the contemporary monetary order.[14] It is also truly systemic, as it focuses on a key aspect of the monetary and banking system itself. Second, it elucidates the procyclicality of bank credit in its totality, while successfully describing all stages of the cycle as a necessary implication of the credit expansion. Third, it provides a unified account of all standard hints at instances of systemic interconnectedness and externalities between banks. For instance, the build-up of common, erroneous, exposures reveals itself as a necessary feature of the boom where all banks operate under the same monetary policy conditions. The systemic interconnectedness through the interbank market and the appearance of very large (systemically important) institutions are a consequence of the moral hazard created by the very existence of a lender of last resort. Finally, developments that are perceived as instances of fire sales or of a credit crunch come into being only because extra liquidity injections have inflated banks' balance sheets and asset prices in the first place. Had it not been for that original expansion of bank credit and asset prices, effectively fueled by the central bank's monetary injections, there would be no ground and actual possibility for a subsequent contraction. Thus, monetary policy and its effects on banks in the current monetary regime provide a holistic explanation of systemic risk, and thus a solid rationale for macro-prudential policy.

This alternative view rationalizes macro-prudential policy as a corrective response to bank vulnerabilities that are induced by the very operation of the present-day monetary regime. The most widespread framework for both the strategic and daily conduct of monetary policy since the 1990s, namely, inflation-targeting, strengthens this view further. Inflation-targeting aims at producing a continuous moderate inflation, defined exclusively as a definite numerical change in an index of consumer prices. By design, this monetary policy framework nourishes expectations about an irreversible and never-ending depreciation of money's purchasing power. In such an environment, to preserve their wealth and savings, money users tend to privilege investments in financial and real estate assets, often financed with debt. The result is an asset prices inflation that, in addition to not being sustainable, could discredit monetary policy itself. From that point of view, the raison d'être of macro-prudential policy is to complement monetary policy itself, by mitigating its undesired consequences.

The changes in the conduct of monetary policy since the GFC reinforce this conclusion. While keeping their inflation-targeting objective, monetary authorities have embarked also upon stabilizing the prices of specific categories of assets, most notably government and mortgage-backed securities. As highlighted in the first chapter, the expansion in central banks' balance sheets through the massive acquisition of assets has produced a situation of systemic excess liquidity in the banking system. The pursuit of this new goal of stabilizing the prices of financial assets, which arguably can be considered as the pursuit of financial stability, ties central banks' actions and reduces their independence as regards the other final or intermediate objectives, namely, inflation-targeting or control of bank credit expansion. To solve this conflict, which ultimately is rooted in the impossibility to reach two policy goals with a single instrument, financial stability must become the specific mandate of a new standalone regulatory policy so that monetary policy remains focused on its own objective.[15] This explains the rising focus on macro-prudential regulation of banks in the last decade.[16]

Even though it might have started as a fancy buzzword, macro-prudential regulation has evolved into a developed subject of studies in banking regulation and policy-making. After a decade of experience, the latest research has evolved away from the conceptual justification toward an emphasis on the efficiency of macro-prudential regulation and even its impact on the real economy. Many empirical studies confirm that macro-prudential tools have been efficient in smoothening the credit cycle (Belkhir et al. 2020, 7). Outstanding among the country-specific studies, Bruno and Shin (2014) show that the measures undertaken by the Korean authorities in 2010, that is, a leverage cap on the notional value of foreign exchange derivative contracts and a levy of twenty basis points on wholesale foreign exchange liabilities of banks, successfully reduced the sensitivity of capital flows to global factors. Acharya et al. (2020) find out that the introduction in 2015 of loan-to-value (LTV) and loan-to-income (LTI) limits in Ireland reallocated bank credit from the "hot" urban market to the "cooler" rural areas, thereby slowing down house price growth and curbing the feedback loop between collateral values and mortgage credit expansion. Furthermore, Belkhir et al. (2020) discuss the overall effectiveness toward financial stability of macro-prudential policies by identifying and quantifying a possible destabilizing effect due to the policies' negative impact on economic growth. The authors conclude that the direct effect on lowering the probability of banking crises dominates the indirect effect on depressed economic growth. Irrespective of their structural assumptions, parameters and empirical findings, these studies tend to reinforce the case for macro-prudential regulation on the ground of its efficiency.

Our economic approach suggests that macro-prudential policy is an outgrowth of the present-day monetary regime. Inflationary fiat money policies and fractional-reserve banks' reliance on an unconstrained lender of last resort are in-built features of the current monetary system that account for the unsustainable credit expansions and asset bubbles, followed by generalized crises and contractions. Hence, the resulting banks' vulnerabilities and risk of systemic breakdown are not an odd behavioral contingency that the right incentives could fix. Instead, they are structural consequences of the foundational principles on which modern banks operate, namely, fractional reserves and fiat paper money. In this approach, systemic risk is implied by the very nature of modern banking, which has the advantage of providing a more realistic explanation. The policy aiming at its prevention appears then as a response to the natural impotency of the other forms of banking regulation.

3.2 THE INSTITUTIONS AND TOOLS OF MACRO-PRUDENTIAL REGULATION IN THE EU

Since the GFC, macro-prudential policy has become an entrenched aspect of the updated regulatory framework and financial landscape through newly created institutions charged with the mandate to implement it and the specific tools they have been granted.[17] In the EU, the institutional setup involves supranational entities, namely, the European Systemic Risk Board (ESRB) and the ECB, and dedicated national authorities. The coexistence of two distinct legal bases for granting powers and responsibilities to the national authorities further complicates this organizational setup.

3.2.1 The Institutional Setup of Macro-Prudential Policy in the EU[18]

The ESRB started its operation in 2010 as a central element of the newly established structure for financial supervision known as the European System of Financial Supervision (ESFS). At the same time, in line with the recommendations of the *De Larosière Report*, three other European Supervisory Authorities (ESAs) were created, that is, the European Banking Authority (EBA), the European Securities and Markets Authority (ESMA), and the European Insurance and Occupational Pension Authority (EIOPA). All three ESAs rely on high-level professional experts from the respective sectors who draft the detailed regulatory and technical standards in their respective areas.

These standards provide the detailed rules for calculating the various ratios through which prudential regulation is applied in practice. Because they serve as repositories of expert knowledge, the ESAs also provide advice and assistance to the respective national supervisors.

The ESRB is in charge of i) the macro-prudential oversight of the financial system in the European Union and ii) the coordination of EU policies for financial stability. It exercises its role primarily by issuing nonbinding warnings and recommendations, by providing opinions on macro-prudential measures, and by collecting, publishing and analyzing data with respect to systemic risk. Even though the warnings and recommendations, which could be addressed to the Union, to member states or to any supervisory authority, are nonbinding, the ESRB can apply moral suasion, notably through the "comply or explain" procedure. To provide its opinions on whether a specific measure is necessary, effective and proportionate, the ESRB develops a macroeconomic framework through the build-up of inside expertise, while also admitting the validity of external counsel.[19] The continuous collection and dissemination of relevant data, namely, through the quarterly publication of the ESRB Risk Dashboard,[20] further supports the analytical work.

The general board, chaired by the ECB president, and comprising the ECB vice presidents, the governors of the NCBs, the chairpersons of the ESAs, and one representative of the European Commission, is the decision-making body of the ESRB. A steering committee, an advisory scientific committee, and an advisory technical committee support its quarterly meetings. The ESRB is endowed with a permanent secretariat, hosted at the ECB. This organizational structure and the related administrative setup both show a very close cooperation between the ESRB on the one hand and the ECB and the NCBs on the other hand. This strong institutional influence of central banks in the EU on the ESRB confirms our finding that macro-prudential policy is an outgrowth of the present-day monetary regime. Based on its broad mandate of oversight and coordination, the ESRB itself appears as a promoter of expertise within the EU, a repository for EU and national data, and a forum for high-level policy dialogue.

The actual policy formulation and implementation is in the hands of the national authorities and the ECB. The so-called National Macro-Prudential Authorities (NMAs) are established following the ESRB Recommendation ESRB/2011/3 to conduct macro-prudential policy and to define and pursue intermediate macroprudential objectives, such as the mitigation of excessive credit growth, of leverage, of maturity mismatch, and of market illiquidity; the limitation of direct and indirect exposure concentrations; and strengthening the resilience of financial infrastructures. The NMAs must develop and operationalize an overall national policy strategy, conduct in-depth analysis, and exchange their assessments with the ESRB.

The implementation of the macroprudential measures under the CRD IV and the CRR requires MS to designate a responsible body. This distinct second legal basis gave birth to the national designated authorities (NDAs). Several candidate institutions are eligible, in principle, to perform the functions of an NDA: the newly set-up NMAs, the existing micro-prudential supervisors, or a newly set-up separate institution. In the context of the SSM, and for the banks under its direct supervision, the ECB also acts as the responsible NDA. The selection, calibration, activation and de-activation of macro-prudential measures always falls into the remit of the NMAs. The NDAs, which might or might not be the NMAs, perform the follow-up on the effective implementation of these measures. Very diverse institutional models coexist across the EU.[21]

The advantage of entrusting the ECB with the macro-prudential powers of an NDA for the banks under its supervision resides in the synergies stemming from a common analytical framework and common access to information. Furthermore, these additional supervisory responsibilities allow the ECB to address the challenge arising from the significant overlap between the nature of the capital instruments used within both the micro- and the macro-prudential perspectives.[22] The ECB Governing Council is the ultimate decision-making body. It takes decisions on the basis of analyses and assessments produced by the Supervisory Board, together with which it forms the Macroprudential Forum. The Financial Stability Committee provides analytical and technical support on macro-prudential policy. The overarching strategy of the ECB for containing systemic risk is delivered through three operational objectives: prevent the excessive build-up of risk to smoothen the financial cycle (time dimension); limit contagion and increase the resilience of the sector (cross-country dimension); promote a systemwide perspective to create the right incentives (structural dimension). In addition to its duties as NDA for the banks under its remit, the ECB has a "top-up power," according to which it can impose a stricter macro-prudential requirement, but only after an NMA has activated a specific measure. The ECB has no corresponding "scale-down power."

In summary, multiple actors, at both the national and EU levels, share the responsibility for defining and implementing macro-prudential policy, regulation, and supervision in the EU. The resulting complexity in the distribution of powers and interactions is hardly conducive to a proactive and transparent decision-making process. A similar type of complexity characterizes the set of available policy instruments.

3.2.2 The Macro-Prudential Toolbox in the EU[23]

The macro-prudential measures fall in two broad categories, depending on whether they affect the behavior of lenders or of borrowers. A more detailed classification by the ECB, based on the use of the specific financial instrument, refers to four types of tools: capital-based, liquidity-based, borrower-based, and others (see Table 3.1). The macro-prudential tools that find their legal basis in CRD IV and CRR are available for use by both the national authorities and the ECB. National legislation-based tools can be used only by the national authorities. The fact that macro-prudential policy is decided primarily at the national level poses a risk to the level playing field in the banking sector in the EU. The principle of reciprocation, that is, the replication by one MS of the macro-prudential measures implemented by another MS, attempts to provide a solution to this problem.[24] To ensure a further alignment between the national macro-prudential policies, the ESRB has set up a framework of notifications, which allows the NMAs and the ECB to exchange assessments and views and to improve policy consistency across the EU. The choice of the

Table 3.1 Classification of Macro-Prudential Instruments in the EU

	Can be used by the national authorities and the ECB		*For use by national authorities only*
	CRD IV Tools	CRR Tools	Other Tools
Capital-based	Counter-cyclical capital buffer (CCyB) Systemic risk buffer (SRB) G-SII & O-SII capital buffer	Risk weights Capital conservation buffer (CCB) Own funds level	Leverage ratio
Liquidity-based		Liquidity requirements Large exposure limits	
Borrower-based			Loan-to-Value (LTV) ratio caps Loan-to-Income (LTCI) ratio caps Debt-Service-to-Income (DSTI) ratio caps Debt-to-Income (DTI) ratio caps
Other measures		Large exposure limits Disclosure requirements	Margin and haircut requirements

Created by the author using data from Constancio (2019).

macro-prudential tool involves a cost-benefit analysis that weighs the instrument's effectiveness toward the intermediate objective with the potential social costs due to the implied restriction of activity. The ESRB identifies five intermediate objectives: i) credit growth and leverage, ii) maturity mismatch and market liquidity, iii) exposure concentration, iv) misaligned incentives, and v) resilience of the financial infrastructures.

The presentation of the macro-prudential toolbox is further complicated by the fact that many of the instruments are also commonly used tools available for the purposes of micro-prudential regulation and supervision. The CRR grants a non-negligible degree of flexibility to the NMAs to "activate" these same tools for macro-prudential purposes, that is, to make them more stringent than under the EU micro-prudential framework. These so-called "national flexibility measures" include i) own funds requirements, ii) liquidity requirements, iii) large exposure requirements, iv) risk weights, including LGDs, v) capital conservation buffer, vi) disclosure requirements, and vii) intrasectoral exposures. The activation of these national flexibility measures involves a complex multilevel procedure, which explains why only five countries had decided to apply them by 2018.[25] Lately, two more NMAs have notified the ESRB of their intention to activate national flexibility measures (the Netherlands on a minimum average risk weight for residential mortgages and Norway on stricter risk weights for targeting asset bubbles in residential and commercial property).[26]

The capital-based instruments include the different metrics of own funds under Pillar 1 and Pillar 2 and the various buffers (capital conservation, countercyclical and the systemic risk, G-SII, and O-SII, of which the largest applies).[27] This same "pecking order" clarifies the sequence in which the buffers are stacked, activated for macro-prudential purposes and hence built up or alternatively consummated by the banks. The countercyclical capital buffer epitomizes how macro-prudential policy is expected to work. A higher buffer during the boom requires banks to build up additional capital, which slows down credit expansion. Conversely, a lower buffer requirement during the bust allows banks to become more expansionist, given that the accumulated capital released from the buffer adds to the available own funds, which can then support a larger volume of loans.

While the counter-cyclical buffer is the par excellence example of a macro-prudential tool that dampens the procyclicality of credit, all other capital-based measures operate in the same way. Higher risk weights, often used as national flexibility measures, result in higher calculated risk-weighted assets, and therefore in a higher overall capital adequacy requirement. This makes them a very efficient tool for slowing down a credit expansion that is concentrated in a specific class of assets. Indeed, the relative changes in the risk weights applied to the different asset classes efficiently divert credit from one sector to another. A more stringent leverage ratio has only an aggregate effect on credit expansion in general. In all circumstances, banks are capable of avoiding, at least partially, the effect of the macro-prudential tools by moving credits off-balance sheet, for instance, through securitization.

The liquidity-based measures address risks that could originate from a maturity or funding mismatch between assets and liabilities. In addition to imposing more stringent LCRs and NSFRs, the NMAs could introduce a standard loan-to-deposit (LTD) limit,[28] which also has a braking effect on the granting of new loans. Even though large exposure restrictions are not concerned directly with funding, they reduce the risk of illiquidity by limiting the exposure to large debtors. Levies increase the cost, and thus reduce the attractiveness, of types of liabilities that are deemed as too unstable, such as nonresident deposits or foreign-currency liabilities. They incentivize banks to prefer more stable resources, and thus contribute to reducing the risk of a "sudden stop" of funding. In order to eliminate a possible fiscal bias in the choice and calibration of the levy, which is a type of a (Pigouvian) tax, the tax proceeds can be collected in a special escrow account at the central bank, thereby avoiding entering the general government budget.

The borrower-based measures aim at reducing the demand for bank loans, by rendering access to credit more complicated and costly for potential borrowers. A lower LTV ratio limits the size of a prospective loan to a smaller percentage of the assessed value of the property for acquisition, which implies that the borrower must provide more own funds upfront. As savings take time, credit demand is postponed, in addition to being constrained in size. The other borrower-based metrics, including collateral haircuts requirements, loan amortization requirements and maturity limitations, aim at bringing about the same effect. The lack of harmonized legal basis for these measures leads to very different application rules and multiple grey areas. How is the value of the property to be assessed? In particular, could the lender increase upward the allegedly independent external valuation by the expected appreciation due to renovations and extensions? Could additional collateral, such as other financial and nonfinancial assets held by the borrower, be included too? If the loan has two parts, one for the acquisition and another one for future improvements, are both parts subject to the LTV cap, or does the limitation concern only the part for initial acquisition? These very simple, yet numerous, questions suggest that banks and borrowers could find easy ways to circumvent the effective application of the borrower-based measures thanks to the high degree of definitional ambiguity.

In summary, the macro-prudential toolbox in the EU offers multiple options to policy-makers and regulators.[29] However, this great degree of flexibility comes at the cost of high complexity, which is rooted in the legal basis, nature, scope and even definitions of the macro-prudential instruments. Their actual implementation is also subject to heavy notification and coordination procedures. This state of play naturally raises questions about the timeliness of their activation and ultimately about their effectiveness.

3.3 CONCLUSION

Macro-prudential policy has acquired an outstanding and firmly established position in the financial sector regulatory debate and actual landscape. Beyond the strong intellectual interest for the subject, one real-world proof of the overwhelming prevalence of macro-prudential policy in the last decade is its very imposing institutional setup and the diversity of the associated toolbox. However, the sheer number of institutions and instruments involved, at least in the EU, leads to a high degree of complexity, likely difficult coordination and possible confusion that only insiders and highly qualified experts could stay clear of. The efficiency of macro-prudential decisions could also suffer from a slow and intertwined decision-making process. Nevertheless, all countries in the EU have applied macro-prudential measures, which would suggest that macro-prudential regulation has been a success story so far, especially as the banking sector has not gone through another global crisis yet since the GFC. Based on this encouraging institution- and practice-based evidence, is it possible to conclude that macro-prudential regulation has solved the problem of financial stability?

The theoretical considerations presented in the first section of this chapter raise a serious question mark as regards such a definitive conclusion. The standard arguments in favor of macro-prudential regulation are deficient in two respects. First, the explanations of a possible systemic cause of instability are not rooted in a meticulous understanding of the economic and financial aspects of the modern banking sector as it is in reality. Rather, they derive from normative models of banking behavior that rely, in one way or another, on the questionable notion of objective or fundamental value. This approach, which considers and studies systemic risk as an abstract analytical concept, has great difficulties with describing, identifying and illustrating a corresponding real-world phenomenon. Second, the development of an impartial approach to financial stability is further complicated by an explicit bias toward the continuous and uninterrupted expansion of banks' balance sheets. This intellectual framework justifies the mandate of macro-prudential policy on the basis of an assumed need to prevent sudden stops in the availability of bank-created financial resources. Ultimately, this approach originates in an exaggerated dichotomy between the financial and the real sectors, which assumes that bank credit alone is sufficient to ensure the realization of all entrepreneurial projects.

This is not to say that systemic risk is not a real phenomenon. On the contrary, the discussion in this chapter argues that a change of perspective away from the narrow focus on bank credit deleveraging can offer a realistic account of systemic risk. The relation between a bank credit expansion triggered by an increase in the money supply and a focus on both stages of the boom-bust cycle offer a different perspective on financial stability. Moreover, this alternative approach sheds new light on the rise of macro-prudential policy in the post-GFC context of very accommodative monetary policies. The former appears then as an antidote to the unintended consequences of the latter. Yet, for all its achievements, macro-prudential policy leaves unaddressed the too-big-to-fail problem, for which other regulatory initiatives seek a solution.

NOTES

1. That original meaning, with its particular emphasis on emerging and developing economies, has not been lost completely to date. For instance, Jeanne (2016) examines the potential macro-prudential role of international reserves as a means for emerging market economies to protect themselves against the instability of the banking system in the advanced economies.

2. For a general overview of macro-prudential policy tools, see Claessens (2014) and the extensive literature referenced there.

3. One of the very first postcrisis foundational and institutional articles on the topic emphasizes this point very bluntly: "The financial system is inherently procyclical. The model, and common sense, tells us that delivering financial stability requires constraining financing during a boom" (Kashyap et al. 2011, 159).

4. The authors focus on extending the Diamond–Dybvig model, thereby suggesting that system risk is an equilibrium phenomenon that originates in decentralized interbank transactions. Government insurance of interbank claims or even centralized bank liquidity management would then be two regulatory means to prevent systemic risk. Freixas et al. (2000) provide another equilibrium model extension that also locates systemic risk in the functioning of the interbank market, with insolvency as the original shock. Eichberger and Summer (2005) further explore the link between bank capital and systemic risk and suggest that binding capital adequacy regulation has an ambiguous effect on financial stability as the interbank market transfers risk from banks with a weak equity base to other, seemingly stronger, institutions. Acharya (2009) also contributes to the modeling of systemic risk as an equilibrium phenomenon that results in an endogenously preferred inefficiently high level of correlation between bank asset returns.

5. The intuitive understanding of the non-systemic risks is due to their almost daily experience. The lack of intuitive understanding in the case of systemic risk suggests that, rather than referring to a concrete aspect of reality, it might correspond to a purely analytical concept, in quest for a plausible real-world manifestation.

6. Das and Uppal (2004) extend the common exposures argument to the case of strongly correlated returns on international equities. They suggest that the systemic risk stemming from the synchronous jumps in equity returns reduces the gains from portfolio diversification and penalizes levered investment positions, with the potential to imply full loss. This approach views systemic risk, defined as "the risk from infrequent events that are highly correlated across a large number of assets," as a case of high covariance.

7. The most elaborate theoretical account of systemic risk and of macroprudential policy concedes this point: "It is the spreading nature of the shock, namely the contagion effect, that distinguishes systemic risk from the idiosyncratic risk of individual financial institutions" (Freixas et al. 2015, 14).

8. As this conclusion emphasizes a fundamental dichotomy between financial sector investments and investments in the real economy, it is worthwhile quoting it in full: "As long as banks continue to hold, and can choose to invest in, undervalued securities, the lending mechanisms will be blocked or weakened by the banks' own choice. This is true so long as securities trade at prices below their fundamental values. Unlocking the lending channel requires an increase in security prices, so that trading can no longer compete as profitably with real lending" (Shleifer et al. 2010, 317). This finding provides a justification for quantitative easing and for direct central bank support to asset prices as the most suitable policy to stimulate bank lending to the real economy.

9. The notion of a credit crunch that takes its origin in a shortage of equity capital which limits banks' ability to grant loans comes from Bernanke and Lown (1991). The authors even suggest that it might have been preferable to call this phenomenon a "capital crunch." The original driving factor for this capital crunch, pushing banks to scale back their loans, would have been the introduction of the new regulatory standards of the Basel Accord.

10. The authors provide three reasons for the credit crunch: moral hazard (banks shirking on their monitoring of borrowers' activities), high exposure to aggregate shocks (positively correlated returns), and ease of capital reallocation between different lines of business.

11. Mainstream economics, in line with its dichotomy of analysis between monetary and financial factors, on one hand, and real economic phenomena, on the other hand, struggles to produce a convincing theory of financial stability. In his foundational essay, Crockett emphatically defines financial stability as "an absence of financial instability, and I shall define financial instability as a situation in which economic performance is potentially impaired by fluctuations in the price of financial assets or in the ability of financial intermediaries to meet their contractual obligations" (Crockett 1997, 2). He then proceeds with presenting a myriad of explanations, based on market-failure and imperfect information arguments, of asset prices' volatility and financial intermediaries' instability. Yet Crockett makes a good point when identifying contagion risk as the core reason for regulating the financial industry (ibid., 10) and excessive debt levels of both households and governments as the key factors for transmitting the effects of financial instability to the real economy (ibid., 14).

12. This bias can be explained by the very successful literature on "financial deepening," that is, on an assumed positive link between financial sector development and economic growth, as expounded for instance in the seminal summary by Levine (1997).

13. The failed construction of early warning indicators, meant to foretell the exact timing of the next financial sector crisis, is due to the same difficulties with defining and measuring systemic risk.

14. By the same token, it clarifies also why macro-prudential concerns emerged in the late 1970s, after the first experiences with generalized inflation in a world of independent fiat money producers.

15. Yet, given the long-term commitment of central banks to quantitative easing, monetary policy appears as captured by the objective to stabilize specific asset prices if not permanently, at least in the long run. One could then wonder whether macro-prudential policy, with its strong focus on bank credit developments, has not become the new monetary policy in this very specific present-day context.

16. Canuto and Cavallari (2013) also conclude at a complementary relationship, or as they call it "division of labour," between monetary policy, which should focus on macroeconomic goals, and macro-prudential policy, which would be in charge of financial stability exclusively. Without this division of labor, and given that "monetary policy tools are too blunt to curb asset price bubbles," attempts to address financial stability concerns through monetary policy tools would result in undesired consequences on the real economy (idem., 26). This is another way to say that monetary policy alone cannot pursue two goals and that another degree of freedom is needed in the menu of policy options.

17. For a very detailed presentation of the macro-prudential framework in the EU, including institutions, procedures and tools, see Constancio (2019).

18. Further information on the institutional set-up of macro-prudential policy in the EU can be found in Grigaite et al. (2020a).

19. This is the fundamental purpose of the various Assessment Teams (AT), comprising of thirteen permanent members and three permanent observers, namely, to foster the sharing and development of inside and outside expertise.

20. This quarterly publication (https://www.esrb.europa.eu/pub/rd/html/index.en .html) contains a wide set of quantitative and qualitative indicators of interlinkages in the EU financial system and composite measures of systemic risk, with a strong emphasis on the macroeconomic risk, credit risk, funding and liquidity, market risk, profitability and solvency, structural risk, and risk related to central counterparties. The ESRB Risk Dashboard is also part of the ECB Statistical Data Warehouse, https: //sdw.ecb.europa.eu/reports.do?node=1000003268. This specialized publication is to be read in conjunction with the Financial Stability Reports published by NCBs and the Global Financial Stability Report of the IMF, which focuses on current market conditions and access to finance by emerging market economies (https://www.imf .org/en/Publications/GFSR). The ECB publishes its Financial Stability Review on the euro area twice a year (https://www.ecb.europa.eu/pub/financial-stability/fsr/html /index.en.html).

21. The full list of NMAs and NDAs can be found here: https://www.esrb.europa .eu/national_policy/shared/pdf/esrb.191125_list_national%20_macroprudential _authorities_and_national_designated_authorities_in_EEA_Member_States.en.pdf.

22. In particular, this overlap strengthens the often referred to fallacy of composition when it comes to coordinating micro-pru with macro-pru. Indeed, in the boom stage of the cycle, micro-prudential regulation tends to release its requirements, while macro-prudential regulation tends to tighten them. The exact opposite happens during the bust stage of the cycle, when micro-prudential requirements typically become stricter, while the macro-prudential regulation is then more supportive of banks' credit activity.

23. Further information on the available macro-prudential tools can be found in Grigaite et al. (2020b). The ESRB publishes annual reviews of macro-prudential policy in the EU, with very detailed information on the latest state of play: https://www .esrb.europa.eu/pub/reports/review_macroprudential_policy/html/index.en.html.

24. Reciprocation is mandatory in the case of the countercyclical capital buffers, higher risk weights and higher LGDs. It is optional in the case of the systemic risk buffer and for national flexibility measures.

25. In a Special feature on the national flexibility measures in its Review of Macro-prudential policy in the EU in 2018, the ESRB refers to Belgium (risk-weight add-on of 5% for residential mortgage exposures, in 2014 and 2018), Finland (a risk-weight floor of 15% for residential mortgages, in 2017), Cyprus (an add-on on the liquidity coverage requirements, in 2017), France (a large exposure limit of 5% to highly indebted French non-financial companies, in 2018), and Sweden (a risk-weight floor of 25% for residential mortgages, in 2018).

26. See ESRB (2021, 96).

27. For further details on the buffers, see Subsection 3.3 of Chapter 2.

28. As a rule of thumb, an LTD of 85% is considered as sufficiently conservative, while any value above 100% is a clear sign of overexpansion.

29. For the latest table of activated macro-prudential measures, see https: //www.esrb.europa.eu/national_policy/html/index.en.html, and more specifically https://www.esrb.europa.eu/national_policy/shared/pdf/esrb.measures_overview _macroprudential_measures.xlsx.

Chapter 4

The Too-Big-to-Fail Issue and Its Regulatory Solutions

To some extent, the recurrent banking crises are an embarrassment for the prudential approach to banks' safety and soundness. The persistence of banking crises demonstrates that, for all their outreach and complexity, bank regulatory requirements have not succeeded in removing the likelihood of isolated bank failures and even full-blown systemic distress. It is true that the frequency of banking crises appears to have declined, and that arguably their nature might have changed too. On the one hand, the extensive safety nets and the evidence of past bank bailouts discourage alert preventive deposit withdrawals and contribute to build up a higher risk tolerance among bank customers. The relatively satisfactory track record of the current monetary regime, which has avoided hyperinflation despite the technical possibility for unlimited liquidity support and has even succeeded in getting slow continuous depreciation of money's purchasing power accepted as the norm, has also contributed to the lower frequency of bank runs. On the other hand, these same circumstances lead banks to adopt riskier investment strategies and to underprovision for future losses, which results in growing nonperforming loans and a higher likelihood of insolvency. The risk that toxic assets could deplete the bank's capital has replaced the old-fashioned bank run based on liquidity concerns.

Public authorities fear bank bankruptcies for several reasons. First, the failure of one bank could cause the failure of other institutions and evolve into a systemwide crisis, either due to sufficiently large direct cross-exposure losses or because of indirect reputational contagion. Second, the subsequent contraction of the stock of bank deposits, and hence of the money supply in the broader sense, has deflationary implications that might further aggravate the financial health of indebted corporations, while also compromising the general macroeconomic or public welfare policies. Third, to prevent the direct implications of an individual bank failure or its propagation to the system, the government might be tempted to come to the rescue through targeted bailouts or other support measures. Such rescue interventions often have a material fiscal impact with nontrivial implications on public-debt sustainability, that governments would have preferred to avoid.[1] For instance, in the aftermath of the GFC, total government support in terms of both capital and liquidity reached a peak of EUR 906 billion in 2009, which represented 8.6% of the 2009 EU GDP (EC 2013b).[2] Banks' anticipation of being bailed out creates moral hazard—knowing that the government will come to their rescue, banks invest and behave less prudently and grow their balance sheets at the expense of taxpayers' money and in an unsustainable manner. In turn, this moral hazard effectively brings about the objective conditions that would justify the public bailout. This self-fulfilling prophecy, generally known as the too-big-to-fail (TBTF) problem,[3] in addition to tying public authorities' hands and purse, has distortive effects of its own and affects negatively financial stability.[4]

The notion of TBTF originated in the 1984 rescue of Continental Illinois Bank, following the US authorities' public commitment to provide de facto total deposit insurance to the eleven largest banks in the country (Gorton and Tallman 2016). Among the first empirical studies, O'Hara and Shaw (1990) find out that positive wealth effects accrued to banks in the United States after their being announced as TBTF, thereby confirming that TBTF institutions benefit from subsidies that distort the market risk perceptions. The size and relevance of the phenomenon have been subject to some controversy. For instance, Mishkin (2006) argues that, though real and rooted in the authorities' lack of credibility in committing to *not* bail-out banks, the TBTF, which is therefore another example of public policy being time-inconsistent, is no longer a threat to financial stability thanks to the regulatory improvements in the '90s.[5] Strahan (2013) identifies four distortions that have become increasingly consensual among economists: i) the TBTF status leads to excessive leverage, due to the underpricing of debt liabilities; ii) it also implies excessive risk-taking, due to the abnormal leverage and because risk is not fully priced in; iii) financial firms grow inefficiently large, to capture the TBTF-related subsidy; and iv) smaller financial companies suffer from a competitive disadvantage.[6] Barth and Schnabel (2013) argue convincingly, and document empirically, that banks' size does not matter for bail-out expectations. Instead, the TBTF issue would be attributable to a bank's systemic importance, which goes beyond size and reflects its interconnectedness and correlation with the remaining banking sector, as well as the substitutability of its services.[7] Both the economic distortions triggered by the TBTF status and the high fiscal costs related to bank bailouts have incentivized authorities to address the TBTF issue and thus to break the banks-sovereign nexus.

Moreover, the actual materialization of the risks from this nexus during and after the GFC, with a negative feedback loop from the sovereign's worsened fiscal position and higher public debt yields to the banks' negatively revalued holdings of government securities, has further motivated a change of perspective in the analysis of the relation between government bank guarantees and financial stability. This strand of literature follows the rather critical empirical study by Demirgüç-Kunt and Detragiache (2002), which shows, based on evidence from 61 countries in the period 1980–1997, that deposit guarantee schemes, especially when funded and run by governments, tend to increase the likelihood of banking crises.[8] More recently, Keister (2016) builds a model where banks' expectations of bailouts distort incentives and lead them to become excessively illiquid, thereby increasing the system's financial fragility. Allen et al. (2017) and Leonello (2018) identify direct and indirect effects of public guarantees on banks and on the stability of public finances, which move in opposite directions. Hence, their combined aggregate effect on the overall economy is unknown upfront and could turn out either positive or negative. The authors conclude that alleviating distortions and minimizing the deposit guarantee costs are two legitimate policy goals. These studies represent a significant departure from the original Diamond–Dybvig framework (1983), which sees a government deposit guarantee scheme as an always optimal response to reduce the likelihood of a bank run.

From the outset, it should be clear that the direct and most natural solution to the TBTF issue is to remove the causes of moral hazard in banking. Above all, that would require understanding the origin and sources of moral hazard. Hülsmann (2006) argues convincingly that moral hazard originates in the systematic forced separation between ownership and control, that is, in government interventionism. By implication, unconditional respect for private property in banking, including the sheer removal of any government-sponsored guarantees and backstops, would appear as the most efficient response to the TBTF problem. By contrast, mainstream economic and financial theory maintains that moral hazard is a market-driven phenomenon,[9] essentially rooted in information asymmetries (Hülsmann 2017). This still dominant view is the rationale for incentives-changing reforms, deemed capable of alleviating the issue of moral hazard, and hence the TBTF problem.

The regulatory solutions offered to the TBTF issue since the GFC fall in two categories. First, the existing safety nets have been reformed, including through the addition of new backstops. The first section describes the overall contours of these reforms and comments on their effective contribution to limiting the problems of moral hazard and of perverse incentives. Second, the EU introduced a new framework for bank recovery and resolution with the specific goal to avoid an outright recourse to bailouts, while still not triggering the insolvency of a bank that is failing or about to fail. The second section presents and analyzes the features of this special regime for resolving problem banks.

4.1 BANKRUPTCY PREVENTION AND CRISIS MANAGEMENT: SAFETY NETS AND BACKSTOPS

When micro- and macro-prudential regulation and supervision have failed to avoid an adverse event in the banking sector, last-resort safety nets and backstops kick in to prevent a system-wide crisis propagation and to limit its potential impact. The two major safety nets, that is, deposit guarantee and state aid, function as *ex ante* instruments to boost confidence in the banking system. Thus, they aim at preventing bank runs and actual bankruptcies. Backstops are tools of *ex post* management and aim at circumventing the effects of a crisis, in particular, from a cross-country perspective.

4.1.1 Deposit Guarantee Schemes

The GFC revealed, among other things, significant insufficiencies with the deposit guarantee framework in the EU. Above all, the prevailing guarantees at the time failed to avert bank runs, namely, in Ireland (2008–2009), Greece (2010), and Cyprus (2012). The national deposit guarantee schemes offered different protection ceilings, often with lengthy repayment periods. Funded schemes in some EU countries coexisted with unfunded schemes in other countries. The conclusion that the deposit guarantee failed to strengthen confidence in the banking system motivated an EU-wide reform that entered into force in 2014, following the application of Directive 2014/49/EU.

The main features of the reform include the introduction of uniform rules with respect to the eligibility of covered deposits, the protection ceiling and the funded nature of the scheme. Deposit guarantee schemes (DGS) are mandatory in each MS, which has two implications. First, each MS must set up at least one DGS. Second, the requirement for credit institutions to participate in a DGS is a prerequisite for receiving a license, and hence its ability to attract deposits. Covered deposits, that is, deposits that are eligible for protection by the DGS, include retail deposits, which excludes i) deposits by other credit institutions; ii) deposits by financial institutions, investment firms, insurance undertakings, collective investment undertakings, pension and retirement funds, public authorities; and iii) deposits arising from money-laundering transactions. Deposits of personal and occupational pension schemes set up by SMEs and deposits of local authorities with an annual budget of up to EUR 500,000 can be considered as eligible for coverage by the DGS. In short, the protection by the DGS concerns deposits by households and small nonfinancial companies, who are deemed as lacking the sophisticated financial knowledge required to evaluate banks' riskiness.

The repayment of covered deposits kicks in only after their unavailability has been determined by the national competent authority (the supervisor) or following a court decision. Repayment coverage is set up at EUR 100,000 per depositor and per institution, irrespective of the number, type, location, or currency of the accounts.[10] The repayment period has been reduced to seven working days as of January 2024.[11] For branches of foreign institutions, the host DGS intervenes on behalf of the home DGS, which remains ultimately responsible for the repayment of covered deposits. Most importantly, the coverage limit of EUR 100,000 applies to the net eligible liabilities to depositors, after set-off with current dues to the institution.[12]

The national deposit guarantee funds (DGFs), which fund the DGSs, repay the covered deposits in the event of deposit unavailability. The affiliated institutions finance the DGFs with contributions that are meant to reach a minimum target level of 0.8% of covered deposits by July 2024.[13] The funds are encouraged to develop adequate alternative funding arrangements, with other DGFs, international financial institutions, or the public authorities, to secure contingent resources for the event where deposit repayments could exceed the collected resources. If the latter occurs, to replenish the depleted financial means of the fund, the affiliated institutions can be required to provide extraordinary annual contributions of up to 0.5% of covered deposits. In ordinary times, the DGFs invest their accumulated resources in low-risk assets in a sufficiently diversified manner. In addition to repaying unavailable covered deposits, the collected funds can be used also to finance the resolution of a credit institution, for alternative measures to prevent the failure of a credit institution (if these measures cost less than deposit repayment) and for measures to preserve the access to covered deposits during national insolvency proceedings (if the cost is lower).

This reformed deposit guarantee regime, as applicable currently in the EU, has several advantages relative to the previous national frameworks. The high level of coverage and the short repayment periods effectively deter deposit withdrawals, especially by smaller depositors, and hence are efficient in reducing the likelihood of bank runs. The fact that the credit institutions themselves fund the DGSs ensures that they have "skin in the game," which makes them collectively responsible for avoiding a deposit repayment event. This incentivizes banks to support each other to prevent the occurrence of a repayment event, which would deplete the fund and result in the request for further individual contributions, with negative implications for the banks' individual profitability. Thus, by design of the DGS and of the DGF funding arrangements, the affiliated institutions have fiduciary duties toward their peers.

These features and the incentives they imply have been construed to ensure that the reformed deposit guarantee framework successfully alleviates the moral hazard issue. In fact, under the DGS, banks provide deposit protection to each other, by means of an interinstitutional cooperation agreement that, prima facie, does not involve the public authorities and taxpayer money. Yet, despite this significant improvement that decouples the DGS from a blank guarantee based on the state budget, the question whether the moral hazard issue does not persist nevertheless remains valid.

First, participation in the DGS is mandatory and regulated by the national public authorities. This results into several limitations that reduce the efficiency of the guarantee. Banks do not have the freedom to join the guarantee scheme of their own choice. Rather, they are stuck in a forceful mutual collaboration agreement with what happen to be the other banks on a national basis. The arbitrariness of such an arrangement is further aggravated by the fixed relative size of the national DGF, which also appears so much limited that it could barely repay less than one percent of all covered deposits. Thus, by no means do the national DGFs have available resources to address an event of deposit unavailability at even a medium-sized bank. This significantly dents the credibility of the funded DGS in the EU and implies that the system relies on an implicit additional public guarantee. This implicit back-up aspect strengthens the TBTF problem and its moral hazard implications.

Second, there is an even stronger explicit connection between the DGS and the national public authorities. Governments are responsible for setting up the national DGS and DGF, to which they stand ready to provide additional ad hoc funding in the event the regular funding arrangements turn out insufficient to repay the covered unavailable deposits. Thus, the state continues to act as the ultimate guarantor, which means that the moral hazard issue remains largely unaddressed. Moreover, the DGFs invest their accumulated funds primarily in Treasury bills, perceived to be the most secure financial instruments. As a result, the liquidity of the resources available for deposit repayment depends on the liquidity of public debt. Hence, the reformed DGS does not severe this banking sector safety net from the possible adverse impact of a sovereign debt crisis.

Finally, the DGSs render all banks uniform from the point of view of the safety of deposits. This uniformity dampens all incentives for depositors to select their bank on the ground of a rational risk assessment analysis. In addition to not promoting financial literacy, the DGSs contribute to an effective cartelization of the banking sector, because individual institutions have no material reason to outcompete their peers with respect to deposit safety.[14] This fundamental lack of incentive for depositors to be selective is an equally important cause of moral hazard in banks' investment decisions.

This assessment of the post-GFC reform of deposit insurance in the EU suggests that it falls short of addressing the main drawbacks that economists have identified. A crucial missing element, part of the analytical consensus following the savings and loan crisis from the 1980s in the United States, seems to be the introduction of risk-based premia for calculating banks' deposit guarantee contributions. Insurance premia that vary with banks' portfolio risk, in the context of a credible commitment by the insurer to close all failing banks and to publicize banks' self-reported risk based on market values, are shown to theoretically remove the moral hazard (Pecchenino 1992).[15] High coverage limits and government involvement in the management of the guarantee have also been proven to exacerbate excessive risk-taking (Demirgüc-Kunt and Kane 2002). Accordingly, to avoid a negative overall outcome on financial stability, deposit guarantee schemes, if maintained, should be complemented by measures that strengthen depositors' and investors' monitoring of banking risk, and market discipline in general. The 2014 reform of the DGS in the EU reflects none of these important findings.[16]

The remaining structural weaknesses of the reformed DGSs also offer some insights into the usefulness of the European Deposit Insurance Scheme (EDIS), the unrealized third pillar of the Banking Union. In comparison to the current framework, the main addition of the EDIS would be to offer a supranational funding arrangement for the deposit guarantee. This aspect does not address any of the identified vulnerabilities and perverse incentives of the DGSs. While it removes the dependence of the DGFs on the liquidity of national public debt instruments, it escalates that same dependence at the level of a supranational financial liability. Such a transfer of responsibility with respect to the ultimate payer might have a positive impact in the short term, due to the de facto centralized refinancing that it offers. However, in the longer term, it contributes to a further dilution of accountability, which can only strengthen the underlying moral hazard issues.

4.1.2 Public Rescue of Banks

Direct public financial support to banks is another safety net, the intense recourse to which in the aftermath of the GFC showed a clear need for reform. Public rescue of banks, including through bailouts, falls in the category of state aid, which the EU law prohibits with a view to avoiding its distortionary impact on competition in the internal market. However, to preserve financial stability in a MS or in the EU, the European Commission could approve national state aid to banks in exceptional circumstances and if specific rules are respected. The Commission took close to sixty decisions on state aid to banks annually between 2009 and 2012, totaling more than EUR 1 trillion of capital-like aid instruments (ECA 2020, 10). To establish a single framework on state aid to banks, while providing clear guidance to MSs in the context of the latest regulatory advances, the Commission codified the principles of state aid to financial institutions in a series of communications, which ultimately led to the so-called "Banking Communication" from August 2013 (EC 2013a).

Three fundamental principles guide state aid to banks. First, state aid should be compatible with the internal market. This means that it should be i) exceptional only, "to remedy a serious disturbance in the economy of a MS," ii) limited to the minimum necessary and adequately remunerated, and iii) complementary to burden-sharing by both the owners of the bank (shareholders bear losses) and investors in hybrid and subordinate debt (sophisticated investors participate in funding an AQR-ST capital shortfall). Second, the institution receiving the aid should be able to regain viability "within a reasonable time frame and on a solid and lasting basis." If the viability analysis shows that this is not possible, the failing institution should be "wound down in an orderly manner." Third, state aid is subject to prior authorization by the European Commission, which needs to approve the restructuring plan submitted by the MS. In addition to proving the compatibility of the state aid and the viability of the institution, the restructuring plan should justify the feasibility of the proposed support measure and detail its expected impact on the market structure. In short, state aid to banks should be exceptional (rationale of the serious disturbance), limited (principle of the burden-sharing and of the adequate remuneration), reimbursed without delay (viability requirement) and nondistortional (compatibility requirement).

In practice, state aid to banks consists either in guarantees and liquidity support outside central bank liquidity provisions or in recapitalization-related measures. The guarantees and liquidity support measures can be either specific to an individual institution or part of a scheme, limited to six months and open to banks with no capital shortfall. Putting details aside, this liquidity-related public support is considered as *rescue aid*. The Commission approves rescue aid on a temporary basis, before the MS submits a restructuring plan within two months, "if such measures are required to preserve financial stability." In the case of capital-related measures, the MS could invoke this financial stability clause only for current capital shortfalls, that is, if the supervisor would have had to withdraw the bank's license. Given the emergency of such a situation, and as a matter of exception, ex-post burden-sharing arrangements are allowed. Another type of simplified state aid are the *schemes for small institutions*, restricted to banks with a total balance sheet of up to EUR 100 million and representing less than 1.5% of the country's aggregate banking system. Such schemes should have a clearly defined remit and be limited to a 6-month period.

The main form of state aid to banks consists in *recovery aid* for addressing an AQR/ST-identified capital shortfall. This form of state support to a bank with an estimated or expected capital shortfall happens either through direct government-funded *recapitalization* or through a government-funded impaired assets measure.[17] Before or as part of the restructuring plan, the MS submits a capital-raising plan, including a fair asset valuation (AQR) and a forward-looking capital adequacy assessment. State aid is limited only to the residual capital shortfall, after accounting for the effects of burden-sharing, of capital-raising measures, and of the likely safeguards put in place prior to the restructuring, in an attempt to prevent the outflow of funds and hence to restore the viability of the bank. The latter safeguards, which attempt to economize on capital, include a prohibition of the payment of dividends on shares and coupons on hybrid instruments, of share buybacks, of aggressive commercial practices, and of new acquisitions. Burden-sharing refers to the direct absorption of losses by equity and to the conversion into CET1, or the mere writing-down, of subordinate and hybrid debt. The capital-raising measures, to be achieved within 6 months, include the issue of new equity shares, the voluntary conversion of subordinate debt, other liability management exercises (LMEs), capital-generating sales of assets and the retention of earnings. State aid also leads to governance actions, such as the dismissal of the previous senior management and a remuneration cap of fifteen times the national average salary or ten times the average salary in the bank.

The general principles of state aid and the design of their practical implementation are based on the explicit recognition that "state aid can create moral hazard and undermine market discipline" (EC 2013a, 8). The Banking Communication is founded on the firm conviction that the principles of prior burden-sharing and of adequate remuneration for the state aid solve this moral hazard and promote market discipline. Yet, the fundamental rule of "adequate burden-sharing by those who invested in the bank" (ibid., 3) applies with the proviso that "fundamental rights are respected and financial stability is not put at risk" (ibid., 4). Moreover, burden-sharing should not lead to "disproportionate results," in which case the sequencing of measures to address the capital shortfall could be reconsidered (ibid., 8). In other words, while the post-2013 redesign of state aid to banks in the EU rules out blank bailouts, the real-world implementation of the rules is subject to a judgmental assessment of how they relate to financial stability. The introduction of this explicit degree of discretion seriously challenges the assertion that the updated post-2013 framework of public rescue of banks has succeeded in removing the implicit moral hazard linked to this safety net and rooted in the expectation that a bank would nevertheless be bailed out for reasons of preserving financial stability. In particular, as the large and systemically important institutions could expect the financial stability exception to apply to them almost by definition, it is doubtful that the reformed framework for state aid to banks is credible enough to address the TBTF problem.

Moreover, the very idea that state aid could be designed in a way that it does not distort market discipline is intrinsically questionable. Public rescue, as a safety net, intervenes precisely because no private investors were ready to fund the capital shortfall of the bank. Put differently, the market participants do not expect the bank to be viable. This *revealed* nonviability contrasts sharply with the *hypothetically planned* viability, which substantiates the restructuring plan and justifies the approval of the state aid. By the fact that private investors abstain from putting their money in the bank, they express their disagreement with the risk assessment of the restructuring plan. One immediate implication of this observation concerns the degree of adequacy of the remuneration for the state support. Typically, the public authorities calculate the interest rate required on the state-aid injection based on the latest market transactions, to which a small penalty add-on is applied. However, even though aligned with the market price of capital for the *other banks*, this approximation deviates seriously from the true counterfactual for the *rescued bank*, which has no access to the capital market. This genuine impossibility for the administratively calibrated remuneration of the state support to integrate a fair assessment of the public investment risk seriously questions its alleged adequacy.

It is therefore hard to escape the conclusion that, despite its sophisticated reform, the EU framework for public rescue of banks offers a clear nonmarket advantage to the recipient institution, and hence distorts competition. Moreover, the reformed state aid framework does not remove expectations, notably by the systemically important institutions, to be bailed out in the event of a capital shortfall. While the reform introduces some limits to the use of state aid, it also codifies the conditions under which it would not be refused. Finally, the very existence of such a standing safety net hampers banks' individual responsibility and induces moral hazard, thereby contributing to create the objective conditions for actual public rescues. The subsequent potentially nonnegligible fiscal implications could propagate a crisis from the banking sector to the public finances. As a solution to this problem, the euro area has set up an additional, supranational, backstop.

4.1.3 The European Stability Mechanism

The European Stability Mechanism (ESM) was the ultimate euro-area response to the widening sovereign debt spreads between the yields on government bonds issued by the core countries of the euro area (e.g., Germany and France) and by the periphery (e.g., Greece, Ireland, Portugal, and Cyprus). These widening spreads, which were reflecting major changes in investors' risk assessment and especially a much differentiated view about the default probabilities of the sovereign issuers within the euro area, fueled fears of a possible break-up of the European Monetary Union.[18] At the time, policy-makers did not have a specific instrument to support the financing of a euro area MS with such worsened conditions of access to capital markets. First, the balance-of-payments assistance instrument was available to non-euro area MSs only.[19] Second, the ECB could not intervene in the secondary bond market because the revised external ratings classified the peripheral sovereign debt as of too low quality (junk) to be acceptable for outright purchases or as collateral against liquidity-providing operations. For the specific case of Greece, pooled bilateral intergovernmental loans (the Greek Loan Facility) offered a partial ad hoc solution in May 2010, before the European Financial Stabilization Facility (EFSF) provided the legal tool for a temporary EU-level solution in June 2010. The permanent backstop for euro area governments that can no longer tap capital markets at acceptable terms came in October 2012 when the ESM was established.

The euro area MS established the ESM as an International Financial Institution (IFI), funded with its own paid-in capital of EUR 80 billion, subscribed by the euro area MS, and located in Luxembourg. The MS finance ministers act as its board of governors. The paid-in capital, which is invested in high-quality securities, allows the ESM to issue its own debt at preferable conditions. The collected funds are then passed on, after a small deduction of a service fee, to the MS with a worsened market access, thereby supporting its funding needs at significantly better interest rates than it would have managed on its own. Thus, the financial assistance effectively improves the current state and future prospects of the MS public finances in the short term, which restores investors' confidence. As a result, the distressed yields stabilize and even converge back to the yields on the sovereign debt issued by the core euro area MS. Thanks to this solidarity mechanism, the ESM contributes to a realignment between member states' borrowing costs, thereby strengthening the stability of the euro area in the immediate future.

The ESM has six intervention instruments in its toolkit, of which it has used only the first two so far. First, it can provide loans directly to the budget of a MS within a macro-economic adjustment program. Second, it can provide loans to a MS for indirect bank recapitalization or for funding an impaired assets measure. Third, it can recapitalize financial institutions directly. Fourth, it can acquire securities in the primary market. Fifth, it can make secondary market purchases. Sixth, it can provide a precautionary credit line.[20] Since its inception, and together with its temporary predecessor the EFSF, the ESM has provided a total of EUR 294.1 billion of macro-economic adjustment loans to five MS through a single or a number of successor programs, namely, to Greece (EUR 202.8 billion), Spain (EUR 41.3 billion), Portugal

(EUR 26 billion), Ireland (EUR 17.7 billion), and Cyprus (EUR 6.3 billion).[21] The Spanish program focused exclusively on supporting the restructuring of the banking sector through the indirect funding of SAREB, the Spanish bad bank. All the other country loans accompanied macroeconomic adjustment programs, which are the core and the main business of the ESM as a euro area backstop.

A macroeconomic adjustment program aims at removing the risks and addressing the structural weaknesses that have resulted from economic and fiscal imbalances. It consists in structural policy measures over a 3-year horizon that also serve as conditions for the sequential, typically quarterly, disbursements of the assistance. Thus, the loan disbursements are conditional upon the actual program implementation, thereby providing a strong incentive for fulfilling the policy commitments. This structural policy conditionality, which is also meant to address potential moral hazard issues triggered by the availability of cheaper institutional financing, is designed in three main areas.

First, fiscal consolidation aims to resorb short-term public deficits and to ensure the longer-term public debt sustainability through lower expenditure and higher taxes. Second, sectoral reforms aim at improving the flexibility of labor markets, the governance of state-owned enterprises, or the general conditions for doing business. Third, financial sector stabilization measures include bank recapitalization and restructuring, regulatory and supervisory reform, tackling the issue of nonperforming loans, and so on.[22] A memorandum of understanding details the specific policy actions and provides for quarterly onsite reviews. These reviews, which are carried out jointly with other involved IFIs, such as the IMF and the ECB, and the EC,[23] check implementation and maintain a continuous macroeconomic dialogue with the national authorities (ministry of finance, other ministries, central bank, regulatory agencies, etc.), as a result of which the policy conditionality could be redesigned.[24] These reviews continue even after the closure of the programs at the end of the 3-year implementation period in the context of a postprogram surveillance (PPS), and until the MS has repaid 70% of the assistance to the ESM.

The ESM, which copies the model of the IMF, assumes, as suggested by its very name, that these designed three-year programs are bringing about financial sector stability, either directly through their action on the banking sector or indirectly through their effect on public finances. While their immediate patchwork benefit could hardly be denied, the ESM programs face at least four major longer-term challenges. First, by offsetting the loss of market access at acceptable terms, the programs invalidate the market discipline that comes from higher public-sector funding costs. If the market funding of a public deficit is unacceptable or even impossible, and in the absence of institutional financing, no deficit could materialize. It might be a difficult administrative decision to identify the spending programs to cut. Yet the point is that the loss of market financing implies a consolidation of the public budget by means of an unavoidable contraction of expenditure, without the need to raise taxes. ESM programs counteract this dynamic, by allowing governments to reduce less or even maintain expenditure. Then fiscal consolidation, which is de facto impeded, must be "programmed" through a mixture of expenditure cuts and tax hikes. Thus, by necessity, the macroeconomic stabilization programs slow down the fiscal adjustment and contribute to a heavier fiscal burden on the economy.

Second, the bias toward higher taxes that is inherent to a "programmed" adjustment leads to internal contradictions between the three main policy areas: fiscal consolidation, economic stabilization and financial sector recovery. The heavier tax burden, especially in an economic downturn, worsens the prospects for economic recovery by hampering entrepreneurs' capacity to restructure their businesses. Thus, program-induced fiscal consolidation impairs the natural tendency of the market toward macroeconomic stabilization. Moreover, the reduced margins of businesses make debt repayment more difficult, thereby contributing to the problem of impaired assets within the banking sector. As a result, fiscal consolidation also conflicts with financial sector stabilization. Overall, the conflicts between the different policy objectives put additional pressure on some sectors and prolong their recovery unnecessarily, from an economic point of view, and often painfully, from a social point of view. These unavoidable contradictions suggest that the economic stabilization programs are a less-than-perfect substitute for the market-driven restructuring of public finances and of the broader economy.

Third, the short-term stabilization induced by the ESM-sponsored programs causes moral hazard and leads to longer-term instability. In the absence of a market-imposed limit on profligate public spending, the requirement to make socially and politically painful trade-offs no longer restrains the fiscally less responsible governments. Sovereign debt investors also factor in the backstop availability, which implies less likely losses and therefore lower funding costs for the public sector. Similarly, the very existence of a supranational backstop on public funding creates expectations about the guaranteed availability of resources needed to rescue failing banks. Hence, the ESM leads to perverse incentives for both governments and banks, thereby institutionalizing the banks-sovereign loop as a cause of twin crises.[25]

Fourth, analysts might have exaggerated the overall stabilization function of the ESM. After all, the recipient governments have repaid only slightly more than one-tenth of their EFSF and ESM loans, with remaining maturities extending until 2027 (Spain), 2031 (Cyprus), 2040 (Portugal), 2042 (Ireland), and even 2060 (Greece). From that perspective, the economic assistance programs are tantamount to an institutionalized long-term debt restructuring that de facto has bailed out private investors. It is premature to declare the involvement of the ESM a success story before the recipients have repaid the loans in full. Moreover, it is difficult to disentangle the short-term stabilization effect of the ESM on the peripheral sovereign debt yields from the broader role played by the ECB. Finding comfort in the ESM-sponsored programs, the ECB granted the beneficiary MS a special waiver, whereby their low-rated public debt securities were readmitted as acceptable collateral for accessing the liquidity-providing operations or as eligible asset for direct acquisition. It is true that the ESM programs provide a rational justification for this patent exception to the strict application of the standard risk management framework of the Eurosystem. Yet, it was the ECB special waiver and the subsequent strong demand for these MS public debt securities that brought about the narrowing of the spread between sovereign yields in the periphery and in the core of the euro area.[26] Had it not been for the ECB, its waiver and the subsequent policy of quantitative easing, the ESM-sponsored programs would not have had this short-term stabilization effect to that extent, or even not at all, on their own.

This intimate link between the ECB waiver and the stabilization effect of the ESM programs sheds new light on the ESM contribution to the stability of the monetary regime in the euro area. Decentralized fiscal policies are a risk factor for the single monetary policy, and hence for the very integrity of the euro area. As much as the ECB waiver contributes to the success of the ESM programs, these programs contribute to the continuation of the expansionary monetary policy of the ECB. In that sense, the ESM supports the inherent inflationary tendencies of the present-day monetary regime in the EU. This further fuels modern fractional reserve banks' expectations for continuous liquidity refinancing even when the quality of their eligible collateral would have deteriorated substantially. This independent source of moral hazard questions the overall contribution of the ESM to longer-term financial stability in the euro area.

Ultimately, the setup of the ESM as a supranational fiscal backstop in the euro area, especially as a direct response in a crisis context, acknowledges that the moral hazard implications of public guarantees and rescues of banks have materialized to the point where they significantly impair the sustainability of national public finances and even threaten the very integrity of the euro area. Our critical discussion of the reform of the safety nets and of the main features of the ESM suggests that the too-big-to-fail issue remains topical, as it is inherent to the very existence of state institutions with the explicit mandate to prevent or to manage bank bankruptcies-related crises. This finding also provides a rationale for the introduction of a special resolution regime for banks that would restrict the public sector involvement in a credible way, while still avoiding the unwanted consequences of bank closures. Indeed, this is the more radical approach that banking regulation has followed lately, through the introduction of a special regime for resolving banks.

4.2 MINIMIZING RECOURSE TO PUBLIC MONEY: BANK RECOVERY AND RESOLUTION

A special resolution regime exempts problem banks from the standard "end-of-life" insolvency proceedings. This bank-specific substitute to corporate bankruptcy law gives early intervention powers to the supervisor or to another public agency, which can then implement a resolution scheme before net equity has become negative. In addition to safeguarding problem banks' value, resolution has multiple rationales from a systemic perspective (Cihak and Nier 2014, 109–10). First, by preventing the outright bank closure, it protects depositors and avoids possible contagion to other parts of the financial system through the interbank market or other funding spillovers. Second, standard bankruptcy proceedings, which are lengthy and always affect bank debtors' discipline, thereby destroying most of the value of the wound-down entity, appear too disorderly when applied to banks.[27] Third, on top of having high fiscal costs, bailouts create perverse incentives that lead to smaller amounts of equity in banks, thus increasing the likelihood of their failure (Nier and Baumann 2006). Bank resolution offers a regime that minimizes the fiscal cost, relative to bailouts, and improves the systemic impact, relative to standard insolvency.

The EU introduced this special resolution regime for banks in 2014 through the adoption of the Bank Recovery and Resolution Directive (BRRD 2014/59/EC) and of the Single Resolution Mechanism Regulation (SRMR 2014/806). Next to the SSM, which it mimics in its institutional structure, the Single Resolution Mechanism (SRM) represents the second pillar of the Banking Union (BU) and is applicable in the euro area countries. The Single Resolution Board (SRB) is the resolution authority for all significant banks under the direct supervision of the ECB and for other cross-border groups in the BU. National Resolution Authorities (NRAs) are responsible for exercising resolution powers and applying resolution tools for all other banks. The main objective of the SRM is to introduce the principle of the bail-in of shareholders and of major bank creditors as a credible and viable alternative to public rescues.[28] This upfront change in banks' expectations aims to address the moral hazard linked to the TBTF issue and to restore market discipline. The ultimate goal of the SRM is, by credibly removing the bail-out expectations, to alleviate the moral hazard-induced excessive risk-taking and risk mispricing, and to thus introduce a sounder differentiation between stronger and weaker institutions.

4.2.1 Principles, Conditions, and Tools of the Resolution Framework

There are at least five general principles that should guide the design of a special bank resolution regime (Cihak and Nier 2014, 112). First, the resolution authority should have early intervention capacity through "official administration," that is, it should have the right to take control of a problem bank and to replace current managers and shareholders. Second, the law should provide for a wide enough intervention toolbox that would make it fit for a large variety of distress situations. These tools should be directly applicable, without the need to secure the prior consent of shareholders and creditors. Third, the resolution regime should also allow for the quick and efficient liquidation of the bank, as a last resort option. Fourth, the resolution framework should have clear objectives and means at its disposal, to avoid legal uncertainty and the risk of post-resolution litigation. Finally, all regulatory and supervisory agencies, especially if involved in cross-border cases, should cooperate, including through information exchange, and coordinate their actions.

The various features of the SRM reflect one or the other of these five general principles. According to the bail-in rule, which is the great novelty introduced by the BRRD, losses are absorbed first by shareholders, then followed by the creditors to the bank according to their ranking. The bail-in rule exemplifies the principle that current shareholders should not benefit from the special resolution regime and that the private creditors, rather than the State treasury, should replenish the bank's capital in the event of a shortfall. At the same time, the SRM guarantees that shareholders and creditors would not end up in a worse situation than in the case of ordinary insolvency. This is the very meaning of the No Creditor Worse Off (NCWO) rule, which applies to each category of creditors.[29] Moreover, creditors within the same class of liability should be treated equally, in line with the standard pari passu principle. If a bank is put in resolution, a special administrator replaces the current management, which remains nevertheless liable for its past actions and decisions in terms of civil and criminal responsibility. To reduce legal uncertainty and litigation risks, the bank's assets undergo independent valuation both before and after the resolution.

To operationalize these basic features of the resolution regime in the EU, the SRB and the NRAs have been endowed with great special powers. For instance, they can take control of any bank with the purpose of resolving it and exercise all rights and powers instead of the shareholders and managers. Moreover, they can convert or alter liabilities into new instruments or write them down. Finally, they can cancel shares, reduce their nominal amount, and transfer them to another entity, as well as transfer rights, assets, or liabilities. In a nutshell, these mighty resolution powers allow the public authorities to break up the balance sheet of a problem bank and to repackage it as seen expedient, with a view of protecting both depositors and the public funds.

To circumscribe the actual exercise of these extraordinary powers and to guarantee that they are not abused, three conditions must hold. First, the supervisor, that is, the SSM, must determine the institution as failing or likely to fail (FOLTF), on the back of one of four possible scenarios. The problem bank has incurred or is likely to incur losses that deplete all or a significant amount of its own funds (proven or expected insolvency). Its assets have become, or are objectively determined to become, less than its liabilities (proven or expected negative equity). Thirdly, the problem bank is, or is objectively determined to become, unable to pay its debts or other liabilities as they fall due (proven or expected illiquidity). Finally, the bank requires extraordinary public support, except to preserve financial stability or to remedy a serious disturbance in the economy of a single MS or of the EU. The second condition establishes that no alternative private solution or another supervisory measure can restore the bank's viability within a reasonable timespan. Put differently, resolution must come always as a last resort solution after all other options have been envisaged and exhausted. The last and third condition stipulates that resolution is warranted only if it is in the public interest.

Once these three conditions are found to be gathered, the specific resolution scheme consists in the application of one or more of four available tools. The bail-in tool is the resolution tool par excellence. It implies the write-down of equity and of liabilities, or the conversion of liabilities into equity, so that all current and expected future losses are absorbed and the post-resolution entity has sufficient capital. Indeed, in the absence of interest from external investors, and when recourse to public funds is ruled out, the bail-in tool is the most straightforward instrument for internal generation of capital by converting liabilities into equity. In essence, it is a form of a liabilities management exercise (LME). To respect prior contractual agreements and to limit contagion to other institutions, covered deposits, secured liabilities, clients' assets and liabilities arising from fiduciary relations and liabilities to other banks with a maturity below 7 days (interbank market funds) are excluded from bail-in.

The other three tools instrumentalize a broader restructuring of the problem bank's balance sheet, notably by involving its assets too. The sale of business achieves a total or partial disposal of assets and liabilities to a private purchaser. This "good bank out" approach assumes private interest in a viable portion of the bank, while the legacy entity is run down.[30] The bridge institution tool is very similar, with the difference that it replaces the private purchaser by a publicly controlled entity. The intervention of the bridge institution is meant to be temporary, until the bank becomes attractive enough for a private buyer. The asset separation tool takes the "bad bank out," through the transfer of the toxic assets to an asset management vehicle (AMV), owned wholly or partially by one or more public authorities. The transfer of the toxic assets helps remove uncertainty from the balance sheet of the remaining good bank and avoids their immediate liquidation, betting on their revaluation under improved future market conditions. The asset separation tool can be used only jointly with another tool.[31]

4.2.2 Factors of Resolvability

For resolution to be a credible policy option, banks must be resolvable first. Already prior to the setup of the SRM, analysts identified two key reforms precisely as prerequisites to ensure that problem banks could be resolved in case of need (Goodhart 2014, 98–99). First, banks should increase their total loss-absorbing capacity (TLAC), namely, through additional equity beyond the minimum requirement for own funds and through other loss-absorbing liabilities. Indeed, bail-in could not possibly take place if the amounts of bail-inable liabilities were insufficient. To that end, the FSB issued its final TLAC standard for the global systemically important banks (G-SIBs) in November 2015.[32] The second piece of reform refers to the sufficient degree of preparedness of both banks and the authorities for an adequate and efficient resolution. Accordingly, banks and authorities are now required to arrange advance recovery and resolution plans, which should be updated in the context of a regular annual cycle. These two prerequisites for resolvability—enough bail-inable liabilities and advance planning—are integral elements of the SRM.

The Banking Union has translated the TLAC concept into the minimum requirement (for own funds) and eligible liabilities (MREL), the detailed calculation policy of which has been developed by the SRB (2016a; 2021a). To be eligible for bail-in, and hence accounted in the composition of the MREL, the liability instruments must be i) issued and fully paid up; ii) not owned, secured, or guaranteed by the institution itself; iii) not funded directly or indirectly by the institution; iv) of remaining maturity exceeding one year; and v) not arising from a derivative contract. The complex calibration, based on the sum of a loss-absorption amount (LAA) and a recapitalization amount (RCA), becomes fully applicable for the banks in SRB's remit as from 2024. Intuitively, this approach to defining MREL boils down to ensuring that a bank that lost all its supervisory capital (LAA) is able to restore its required capital on its own through the bail-in of existing liabilities (RCA).[33] As of mid-2021, the average 2024 MREL target in the BU amounted to 22.73% of RWAs (26.04% if the combined buffer requirement is included) and varied significantly across countries (SRB 2021b, 2, 6).[34] In all circumstances, the MREL is subject to a floor equal to 8% of the bank's total assets, that is, its total liabilities, including own funds.

To strengthen the credibility of resolution within the BU, the legislators have endowed the SRM with its own backup facility—the Single Resolution Fund (SRF), which is formally owned by the SRB. Banks are building up the SRF through annual contributions, calculated pro-rata to the amount of their liabilities, excluding own funds and covered deposits, over a period of 8 years (2016–2023). Expected to reach at least 1% of the amount of all covered deposits in the BU, or around EUR 80 billion, the SRF stood at approximately EUR 66 billion by the end of 2022.[35] A resolution scheme to be implemented might have recourse to the SRF, as a last resort and only after bail-in, to ensure the effective application of the resolution tools.[36] The SRF should not be used to absorb the losses of a bank or to recapitalize it. However, in exceptional circumstances, where liabilities are excluded from write-down or conversion, the SRF can contribute financially to a bank under resolution if two conditions are met. First, the bail-in tool must have been applied already to absorb losses amounting to at least 8% of the bank's total assets. Effectively, this means that the SRF can intervene only after the bank has exhausted its own MREL capacity. Second, the contribution from the SRF should be limited to 5% of the bank's total assets. If the resolution scheme requires more funds, the national government remains a possible last resort provider.

The second prerequisite for resolvability of banks in the BU, namely, advance planning, is ensured through the regular drafting of recovery plans and resolution plans. Banks are required to draw up their own recovery plans and to update them annually in line with changes in their business models and in the economic environment. These plans focus on the suitable strategies to restore viability in the event of a crisis, assuming no extraordinary public support. The ECB reviews the plans produced by the significant banks before their submission to the SRB. Based on the findings in the plans, and after horizontal benchmarking, the supervisor might direct the institution to revise its business strategy, funding structure, risk profile or management practices. On their side, the resolution authorities prepare the resolution plans, which describe the preferred resolution strategy based on a comprehensive resolvability assessment.[37] The ultimate purpose of these plans, which also determine the bank-specific level of MREL, is to identify early enough and to remove any potential obstacles to resolvability (SRB 2016b).

In the event of a crisis, the actual implementation of the resolution scheme, based on the advance plans, follows an institutionally intricate, though quick, adoption procedure. After establishing that the conditions for resolution are met, the SRB adopts the proposed resolution scheme, which determines the tool to be applied and whether a contribution from the SRF is needed. The scheme enters into force if neither the EC nor the Council of the EU expresses an objection within 24 hours. If the EC endorses the scheme explicitly, it enters into force. If the EC objects to some discretionary elements, the SRB must introduce the requested amendments before the scheme enters into force. If the EC objects to the scheme on the ground of unjustified public interest or because of unjustified recourse to the SRF, the Council of the EU can overrule the EC opinion, in which case the scheme enters into force, or it can back the EC position, in which case the SRB modifies the scheme accordingly. The relevant NRAs carry out the actual implementation of the resolution scheme. If they fail to do so, the SRB can directly address executive orders to the bank under resolution (SRB 2016b, 15–16).

4.2.3 Effectiveness and Credibility of the Resolution Framework

The credibility of this newly introduced resolution framework has not passed the test of experience yet. Since its inception, the SRB has rejected the rationale for resolution in four of six examined cases. Banco Popular was resolved by means of selling its shares to Santander in the summer of 2017 (sale of business tool). This resolution scheme ensured that Banco Popular continued to operate under normal business conditions as a member of the Santander Group, thereby protecting depositors fully and containing the propagation of the risk. The shares of the Slovenian and Croatian subsidiaries of Sberbank Europe AG were sold respectively to the Croatian Postbank and to NLB Group in March 2022. In four other instances—the Italian banks Banca Popolare di Vicenza and Veneto Banca (2017), the Latvian and Luxembourgish banks ABLV (2018), the Latvian bank PNB (2019), and the Austrian parent of Sberbank Europe AG (2022)—the SRB did not find their resolution to be of public interest.[38] Rather, it argued that they did not provide critical functions to the economy and that consequently their failure was not expected to have an adverse impact on financial stability. Thus, the newly set-up resolution framework in the BU remains broadly untested, namely, in the case of serious shocks affecting large systemically important banks. Irrespective of this limited experience with real-world distress cases, a general reflection on the resolution framework's main features remains of interest for assessing its credibility and effectiveness, especially to address the TBTF issue.

From the outset, the adoption of single rules in the EU for resolving distressed banks is part of the setup of a level playing field that mitigates the build-up of pockets of risk across MS. Indeed, a plurality of national bank closure policies would incentivize banks to grow their balance sheets and concentrate their risks in the jurisdictions that are perceived to be more lenient. As the EU bank passport grants entry in any MS on equal footing, banks would tend to concentrate their risks in those MS that offer better exit conditions, irrespective of the actual economic origin of the risk. As a result, risks would accumulate asymmetrically in the MS with the less strict closure policy, which is a threat to financial stability. The single resolution framework, because it unifies the bank closure policy in the EU, avoids this moral hazard linked to the actual or perceived regulatory forbearance as regards bank closures. Thus, it removes one reason for banks' excessive growth in some EU countries, thereby making a clear contribution to financial stability. Moreover, by achieving this standardization of bank closure policy in the EU, the single bank resolution framework establishes what has been noted as a necessary pre-condition for a cross-country convergence of the capital adequacy requirements. Indeed, Acharya (2003) argues convincingly that unified cross-border capital adequacy requirements are desirable and optimal only if regulatory forbearance as regards bank closure policy is removed. Admittedly, this is exactly what the single bank resolution framework has achieved in the EU.

However, by design, the resolution framework in the EU relies on rules, assessments and procedures that are exclusively administrative. Given its goal to avoid standard insolvency, resolution discards the positive role that private arrangements, contracted before or after the event of a bank crisis, could play. Rather, it invests an external public agency with all powers to reformulate any such private arrangements, notably through forced transfers, sales, and purchases.[39] This bureaucratic financial re-engineering of a bank's balance sheet with the purpose of making it compliant with regulatory and supervisory requirements does not offer a market-based solution to instances of economic failure. In essence, resolution consists in a balance sheet restructuring, imposed from the outside, which in many cases is not different from an accounting trick.

While effectively avoiding an outright public rescue, bank resolution does not remove all perverse incentives that stem from the expectation of a likely bail-out. The possibility for a contribution by the resolution fund, which could even be supplemented by national public funds under exceptional circumstances, dilutes banks' own individual responsibility. In practice, the SRF limits the bail-in of shareholders and creditors to the 8%-of-assets intervention threshold. From the point of view of the individual investors, this backstop facility might turn out insufficient to prevent their own losses. However, from a broader institutional point of view, and given the average bank capital ratios, this safeguard clause is sufficient to create the expectation for collectivizing future and especially large losses, while keeping the distressed bank in business. The moral hazard implications, in terms of excessive risk-taking and growth of the balance sheet, are straightforward. They are even amplified by the dissociation between the contributors to the fund (the banks) and the decision-taker on the specific resolution tools (the SRB).

It is true that the larger amount of MREL operates as additional contingent capital. Hence, it provides an effective boost to banks' capacity to withstand losses. However, its formalistic determination, practically capping it at eight percent of the total balance sheet, is arbitrary and falls under the same criticism that applies to the calibration of the capital adequacy micro-prudential requirements. Moreover, the effectiveness of MREL for financial stability purposes is dependent on the economic position of the holders of the liabilities eligible for bail-in. If the conversion or write-down of the eligible liabilities leads to the propagation of losses to other banks or systemically important institutions,[40] MREL might fail to contain contagion. The larger the bank under resolution is, the more likely and the wider is the expected spread of losses and contagion throughout the financial system. This implies that the foundational principle of resolution, that is, the bail-in of private shareholders and bank creditors, is less effective in the case of larger banks. This conclusion questions the efficiency of the bank resolution framework in addressing the TBTF issue.

In addition, the high degrees of arbitrariness and subjectivity in fixing many of the resolution parameters question the credibility of the framework. While the failure of a bank can be objectively ascertained ex post, the determination of its ex ante likelihood to fail, and hence the appropriate timing of the resolution, is a clear matter of discretionary judgment. The external asset valuations that determine the required amount of bail-in are necessarily arbitrary, as by definition they concern problem assets with a limited or nonexistent market. The independence of the external financial advisors that produce these valuations does not make them more resilient to economic criticism or better protected from political influences.

Finally, the complexity of the decision process, especially when contributions by the SRF might be involved, introduces a high degree of uncertainty, and even arbitrariness, with respect to the preferred solution. This further contributes to a subjective perception of the framework by the banks themselves. Given that the various resolution tools and the respectively different ways to restructure and repackage the balance sheet of a FOLF bank bring about equally different patterns of loss distribution, the resolution framework in the EU does not anchor banks' expectations in a solid and unambiguous manner. In addition to undermining the credibility of resolution itself, the reality of multiple possible scenarios and outcomes is not conducive to strengthening banks' own responsibility in risk-taking and loss-absorption.

4.3 CONCLUSION

This chapter completes our analytical presentation of banking regulation in the EU with a description of those policy measures that aim to circumscribe an imminent bank failure, that is, when all other micro- and macro-prudential regulatory and supervisory requirements have failed to prevent an adverse event. Our review of the various safety nets, backstops, safeguards, and framework changes, notably as amended in light of the lessons learnt from the GFC, points to three conclusions.

First, the reforms successfully reduced the fiscal impact of all forms of public guarantees and rescues. Nowadays, the banking sector itself, instead of the national state treasuries, finances the intervention funds, whether they are national, as the DGFs, or supranational, such as the BU-wide SRF. Similarly, financial assistance in the context of ESM programs avoids the otherwise direct impact of state support measures on the national finances. Hence, from a purely national fiscal point of view, the reforms contributed to effectively breaking the sovereign/banking nexus.

Second, and notwithstanding this achievement, the reformed institutional setup of preventive guarantees and of crisis management does not address the more fundamental problem of moral hazard, especially as revealed in the TBTF issue. From the individual point of view of any single bank, the potential future costs entailed by its excessive risk-taking are still collectivized and distributed throughout the system thanks to the different safety nets and backstops. Hence, moral hazard and the related perverse incentives remain an integral part of the banking sector crisis prevention and management setup. From that perspective, the very same institutions that aim at limiting the impact of a bank failure appear as one of the driving factors of that same system risk that contributes to the likelihood of banking crises.

Finally, the failure of the reforms to remove the moral hazard and the TBTF issue is due to the lack of truly market-based solutions. Past a point where the sector-financed intervention funds of the various backstops and safety nets are exhausted, an explicit guarantee by the public authorities steps in. The prospect of, after all limited, bail-in in the case of bank resolution resembles more to an administrative restructuring than to an entrepreneurial turnaround. Ultimately, the proposed reformist solutions to the TBTF issue do not address its fundamental cause, namely, the legally protected operation of modern fractional-reserve banks. As long as this nonmarket privilege remains unchallenged, the structural vulnerabilities that invite public guarantees in the broad sense, and thus lead to the TBTF issue, will persist.

NOTES

1. Bailouts are always the result of the interplay between political factors. Different outcomes, always contingent and often contradictory, are possible, depending on the prevailing public opinion and the specific composition of the failing institution's balance sheet. A government might have the backing to bail-out a bank if its failure would affect retail depositors primarily. In other cases, it might lack public backing, in particular, if the bank failure would affect larger institutional or foreign investors. The public opinion about government interventions in general and the influence of special interest groups also play a role. This is to say that, while very relevant, the many political factors that drive the actual outcome of a bailout are a subject matter for sociological and historical studies.

2. This average hides significant extremes, such as Ireland (above 31% of 2014 GDP), Greece (22% of 2014 GDP), or Cyprus (19% of 2014 GDP). For a descriptive presentation of the fiscal impact of the very diverse financial sector support measures during the GFC, see ECB (2015). A less descriptive, model-based study that aims at capturing both direct and indirect fiscal costs suggests that, at the conditions prevailing in 2018, a potential banking crisis could lead to an average increase in public debt by as much as 40% of GDP (Borio et al. 2020).

3. While the TBTF issue refers, literally, to the larger systemically important institutions, and hence relates to the notion of systemic risk, it originates in the moral hazard embedded in the expectation of a public bailout. Thus, from a broader perspective, it concerns any institution that expects to be bailed-out by the government, irrespective of its size or the specifics of the public rescue (state recapitalization, guarantee on liabilities, liquidity support, regulatory forbearance, etc.).

4. The TBTF status, which implies "lack of exit" for distressed and unprofitable banks, and banks' own efforts to capture the related implicit subsidies by reaching this status provide plausible explanations for the well-document bank bias in Europe (Langfield et al. 2016, 86–88). The authors note that the bank bias, relative to market finance, makes its appearance in the late 1990s, but fail to establish a link to the introduction of the euro.

5. The 2007–2008 GFC and the subsequent massive bailouts do not corroborate this view.

6. Iyer et al. (2019) document, based on evidence from the Danish banking system, a TBTF distortive effect on the lending market. The de facto asymmetric deposit guarantee implies tighter funding conditions for non-TBTF banks, which leads them to cut on their credits. This leads to tougher credit conditions for SMEs, which rely primarily on bank credit.

7. The authors also argue that size alone could not define the TBTF issue, because some institutions grow TBTS (too-big-to-save). This pertinent observation highlights that the essence of the TBTF problems lies in the credible expectations of public bailouts and the related adverse incentives.

8. Historical studies of past experiences with deposit guarantee are notably critical. Calomiris (1990) reviews the early 19th-century experience with deposit guarantee in the United States and convincingly shows that government-controlled schemes

promoted excessive risk-taking instead of achieving financial stability. Instead, self-regulation and voluntary coinsurance of liabilities are demonstrated to have produced better results. While other studies of early experiences do not focus explicitly on the role of government, they systematically confirm the phenomenon of moral hazard. Wheelock and Wilson (1995) conclude that insured banks in Kansas during 1910–1928 tended to reduce their capital-to-asset ratios, which resulted in a higher probability of failure than noninsured banks. Grossman (1992) shows that following the introduction of deposit insurance in the 1930s, the originally less risky thrifts became riskier than their noninsured counterparts after 5 years. Cebula (1993) and Brewer and Mondschean (1994) also confirm the moral hazard of government deposit guarantee and document its role in the savings and loan failures of the 1980s in the United States.

9. One of the first discussions of moral hazard finds its cause in the "willingness of the insured to take greater risks on an uncertain outcome" and sees the phenomenon as "expected, economically rational behavior of persons confronted by the lowered price for a service" (Grubel 1971, 101–102). This analytical framework views moral hazard as a standard individual utility-optimizing response to changes in the market data. In that case government intervention, and especially compulsory insurance, might appear as capable of raising public welfare under certain circumstances.

10. This implies that, while all accounts in an institution are consolidated for determining the extent of the effective coverage, joint accounts are split among owners.

11. The reduction of the repayment period follows a prolonged phasing-in period of 20 days by the end of 2018, 15 days by the end of 2020, and 10 days by the end of 2013.

12. Let us assume two joint deposits A and B of two married couples, each standing at EUR 200,000. The first couple has no liability to the bank. The second couple has an outstanding mortgage for EUR 300,000. In the event of deposit unavailability, the DGS will repay the whole amount of EUR 200,000 to the first couple and nothing to the second couple. For the latter, the event of deposit unavailability has the effect of reducing its net liability to the bank to EUR 100,000.

13. Detailed comparable data on the national DGFs can be found here: https://www .eba.europa.eu/regulation-and-policy/recovery-and-resolution/deposit-guarantee -schemes-data.

14. The rule of offsetting deposits with current liabilities to the bank is an additional driver of this cartelization. To the extent that depositors are aware of this rule, they can maximize their effective deposit protection by borrowing from one bank and keeping deposits at another bank. Such rational behavior implies higher liquidity outflows for the lending institutions, which results into stronger interinstitutional dependence due to the consequently higher interbank exposures.

15. However, Cull et al. (2005) question this conclusion by pointing out that risk-adjusted premia might be time-inconsistent, in which case they fail to contain excessive risk-raking. Their study of the large World Bank cross-country deposit guarantee database arrives at the very critical conclusion that deposit guarantee schemes are an obstacle to both financial sector development and financial stability, except in cases of high-quality rule of law institutions and of strong regulation and

supervision. Other theoretical extensions of the original Diamond–Dybvig framework suggest that investor capital makes government deposit insurance redundant and hence removes moral hazard (Dowd 1993), or that an additional capital requirement is necessary and sufficient to restore the first-best allocation of resources when moral hazard is present (Cooper and Ross 2002). With a similar emphasis on the importance of banks' capital, Keeley (1990) hypothesizes that deposit insurance started showing signs of failure when, to offset the negative wealth effects from lower charter values due to increased competition in the context of financial deregulation, banks responded by increasing their risk appetite. Admittedly, the policy implications of this strand of research have been reflected in the higher capital prudential requirements of Basel III.

16. One detailed empirical overview also notes the wide divide between the strong political support for deposit guarantee schemes and the many economic studies that suggest that "the moral-hazard costs of deposit insurance have outweighed its liquidity-risk-reduction benefits" (Calomiris and Jaremski 2019, 711). The authors establish that in the early 20th century in the United States, deposit insurance i) led to lower cash-to-assets and capital-to-assets ratios, ii) increased risk-taking, and iii) created weaker subsidies for risk-taking when it was voluntary. They consider these results as a conservative measure of the current risk-increasing incentives of modern government-guaranteed deposit insurance, which is significantly more pervasive. The authors conclude that "The history of deposit insurance in the United States and internationally has been a process of increasing systemic risk in the name of reducing liquidity risk" (ibid., 751). White (1989) presents the most comprehensive plan, focused on solving the moral hazard problem, for a constructive reform of government deposit guarantee schemes.

17. An impaired assets measure refers to a state-funded investment vehicle (bad bank) that acquires impaired assets from the banks, thereby cleaning their balance sheets. The Irish National Asset Management Agency (NAMA) or the Spanish Sociedad de Gestión de Activos Procedentes de la Reestructuración Bancaria (SAREB) are two paramount examples.

18. For an economic analysis of the causes of the 2009–2010 euro area crisis and a discussion of the associated break-up risks, see Bagus (2010).

19. The balance-of-payments assistance instrument was activated in the case of Hungary (October 2008, EUR 6.5 billion), Latvia (December 2008, EUR 7.5 billion), and Romania (May 2009, EUR 5 billion). Further details on these programs, their timeline, policy content, and the actual amounts disbursed can be found here: https: //ec.europa.eu/info/business-economy-euro/economic-and-fiscal-policy-coordination /financial-assistance-eu_en.

20. In the context of the COVID-19-related pandemic, the euro area ministers approved a Pandemic Crisis Support credit line in May 2020 equivalent to 2% of euro area members' GDP, or about EUR 240 billion for the 19 countries concerned. The credit line is provided upon request by the MS and is conditional only on the requirement to use the funds for healthcare costs related to the pandemic. So far, no MS has requested the activation of its quota in the credit line.

21. So far Greece has repaid around 8% to its total 2012–2015 EFSF support of EUR 141 billion and less than 4% of its total 2015–2018 ESM support of EUR 61.7

billion. Portugal and Spain have repaid, respectively, around 7% and 43% of the received assistance.

22. A financial sector program, like the one in Spain, focuses exclusively on financial sector conditionality and has a shorter duration of 18 months.

23. The Troika refers colloquially to the IMF, the ECB, and the EC in this context. In fact, after the setup of the ESM as an independent institution, a reference to the quartet would have been more adequate.

24. For a very comprehensive presentation of the gist of these programs, with a focus on the financial sector, see European Commission (2017).

25. For a model-based analysis of the bank-sovereign amplification loop that presents the ESM as part of the solution rather than of the problem, see Fontana and Langedijk (2019).

26. Notice also that this triggered another wealth effect, through the revaluation of the securities in investors' portfolios, which is another aspect, often passed unnoticed, of the public bailouts. Even institutional investors in the Greek sovereign debt, for example, other NCBs from the Eurosystem, recorded exceptional profits through this channel.

27. Moreover, the closure of commercial banks triggers three types of problems, associated with the special status of deposits. First, the lost savings create a political problem, as small savers often complain of being expropriated by big capitalists. Second, deposit contraction triggers the economic problem of likely deflation. Third, the need to repay the guaranteed deposits may become challenging for the state budget.

28. The official resolution objectives refer to i) ensuring the continuity of critical functions, such as access to deposits and payments systems, ii) avoiding significant adverse effects to financial stability, iii) protecting public funds, iv) protecting deposits, and v) protecting client funds and client assets. The resolution authority should always seek to minimize the cost of resolution, thus avoiding the destruction of value as much as possible.

29. For the shareholders, who would have lost everything in regular insolvency, the rule holds always. For the creditors to the bank, in particular the holders of bail-inable senior debt, this might not always be the case. Generally, the NCWO rule holds if the problem bank has issued enough subordinate debt, which a regular insolvency would have wiped out anyway, thereby creating a protection cushion for the senior debt.

30. Typically, the good bank assumes all deposits, thereby ensuring their protection, which explains why this approach is often referred to as "purchase and assumption."

31. For complex banking groups, and especially with reference to the bail-in tool, the resolution schemes might be either single point of entry (SPE) or multiple point of entry (MPE). In an SPE scheme, the resolution occurs at the highest level of consolidation of the holding entity. In an MPE scheme, several resolution authorities might intervene at the level of the respective subgroups or subsidiaries. This distinction is relevant for cross-border groups, where national interests might lead domestic authorities to prefer to ring-fence the operation of a local entity, that is, to exclude it from resolution, especially if it is not facing a FOLTF issue on its own. For a political economy discussion of these two approaches, see Goodhart (2014, 99–102).

32. The G-SIBs must meet, as of January 2022, a minimum TLAC requirement amounting to 18% of their RWAs, which should also be at least 6.75% of the Basel III leverage ratio denominator (TLAC leverage ratio exposure minimum). The application date for the G-SIBs headquartered in emerging markets is January 2028. In its midterm implementation review, the FSB (2019) found that the G-SIBs have met or even exceeded their intermediary January 2019 targets (of 16% of RWAs and 6% of the leverage ratio denominator).

33. The formula considers both Pillar 1 and Pillar 2 supervisory requirements (SRB 2021a, 10–11). By analogy to the calculation of the TLAC, a leverage-based MREL complements the risk-based MREL.

34. Total MREL in the BU amounted to 31.07% of RWAs as of mid-2021, which is 5 percentage points above the average requirement. However, due to lack of full compliance by some institutions, the SRB reports also an aggregate shortfall, including the combined buffer amount, of 0.56% of RWAs.

35. As from 2022, a further backstop to the SRF has been introduced. This additional emergency fund, that could be called upon, doubles the actual size of the SRF and is provided through public money initially, to be repaid ex post by all banks in the BU.

36. In particular, the SRF can be used to i) guarantee assets and liabilities, ii) to make loans to the bank under resolution or to purchase assets from it, iii) to make contributions to a bridge institution or to an asset management vehicle, iv) to make a contribution to the bank instead of the write-down or conversion of certain creditors under specific conditions, and v) to compensate shareholders and creditors, if losses exceed those under normal insolvency proceedings.

37. The SRB and the NRAs prepare these plans within the internal resolution teams (IRTs), which operate like the JSTs in the supervisory pillar of the BU.

38. Further details on these cases and on the reasoning followed by the SRB can be found on the dedicated web page: https://www.srb.europa.eu/en/cases.

39. Ultimately, the bail-in, that is, the conversion of debt into equity, to the extent that it is not based on private contracts, is a forced purchase.

40. The repercussion of losses on other banks might be direct, in the case of cross-bank holdings of eligible liabilities, or indirect, through the balance sheet deterioration of other banks' debtors who might hold the eligible liabilities of the bank under resolution.

Conclusion

The economic analysis of banking regulation developed in this book took its inspiration from Walter Bagehot's unsurpassed study of the operation of the banking sector in the 19th century. Beyond its numerous and still topical insights, Bagehot's major legacy was to emphasize the link between the organization of the monetary regime and the operation of the banking system. The principles that govern the production of money have a tremendous influence on banks' balance sheets, with repercussions on the broader economy. Bagehot applied this insight to the monetary system of his time, that is, paper currency issued by a single reserve bank with the promise to convert it into gold upon demand. Having identified the pitfalls and weaknesses of such a monetary system, Bagehot drew some relevant implications on how banks should be regulated to minimize their chronic instability. His book was a call for a regulatory reform of banks, impressively simple by modern standards, on the assumption that the monetary system itself, irrespective of its many imperfections, could not be changed.

Our economic approach to the recent evolution of banking regulation in the EU revives Bagehot's analysis and applies it to the present-day monetary and banking systems. Today, a number of independent central banks produce fiat monies that are not convertible into anything. The principles that rule their production escape any market-driven limitations and follow policy-determined administrative rules. Commercial banks' liquid reserves back only a tiny fraction of their overall liabilities, which depositors use for payments in daily transactions. Hence, these so-called fractional-reserve banks participate, by their very nature, into the production of money in the broader sense. As a result, the business operations of modern banks have implications for the political goals pursued by the public authorities through the conduct of their monetary policies. Under these circumstances, it becomes of paramount importance for governments to ensure that the banking system is organized, and behaves, in a way that it does not contradict their broader policy objectives. In a nutshell, the nature of modern money and the principles of its production imply already that the banking sector must be regulated in a specific way. This is the central insight of this book.

Though consistent with a long-established tradition in the theory of money and banking, this focus on the essence of money as necessary to understand bank regulation happens currently to be somewhat foreign to the economic profession. Indeed, contemporary economists have scarcely approached banking regulation from the angle of its relation to monetary matters. Instead, the question of how best to regulate banks has become a standalone branch of specialized studies in finance and is drawing on findings from many other branches of economics, except monetary theory, for example, the economics of information or of market organization. Our aim here has been to reverse this modern tendency and to put the economic analysis of banking regulation where it belongs, that is, within the theory of money and the study of its broader macroeconomic implications. To that end, the first chapter develops an analytical framework that exhibits the key features of the present-day monetary regime. This lays down the foundations for a very realistic description of what banking regulation actually is, what it can achieve and how it differs from what it would have been in an alternative monetary regime where governments would have no, or a much more limited, role to play.

The proposed alternative economic approach to the study of banking regulation, with strong roots in monetary theory, has several advantages. First, this type of analysis is realistic, and exclusively descriptive and comparative. Thus, it avoids necessarily subjective judgments of value about what the regulatory norms should be. That way, a great deal of subjectivism and arbitrariness has been avoided, given that agreement on such normative questions is rarely achievable as it lacks scientific basis. Second, the economic approach adopted in this book creates a unified intellectual framework that fosters an integrated understanding of the plethora of bank regulatory requirements. Indeed, banking rules have been growing consistently, in both variety and complexity, especially after the Great Financial Crisis of 2007–2008. Too often academics and policy-makers have discussed the various regulatory rules in isolation from each other, only in relation to their respective individual objectives. On the contrary, the unified framework of the economic approach proposed here offers a broader understanding of banking regulation as a whole. That way, the various norms and standards turn out interconnected in two important ways.

First, each specific regulatory requirement appears to address a particular vulnerability that is only a specific aspect of a general, structural weakness of the contemporary banking system. This systemic fragility stems from fiat money itself and banks' fractional reserve, both of which create the illusion that more resources are available in the economy than there are in reality. This systemic discrepancy between perception of scarcity and actual scarcity leads to permanent risk underestimation, concentration of exposures to booming sectors and clustered defaults, all of which pose a major risk to banks' capital. Similarly, the fractional reserve implies, by its very nature, a structural mismatch between assets and liabilities, as well as the likelihood of institutional illiquidity and systemic contagion. From that perspective, the post-GFC evolution of banking regulation, which expanded both in scope and in complexity, resembles a patchwork that plugs individual holes at the surface, but never arrests the ongoing leakage at the root.

Second, this broader economic framework for comprehending banking regulation sheds new light on its efficiency. Authorities have been introducing new requirements or refining the old ones precisely because, relentlessly, the existing rules had failed to deliver the promised result of macro-financial stability. As the analysis presented in this book suggests, this systematic failure is due to the inherent instability embedded in the present-day banking and monetary systems. As long as money and banking are not reformed in their essential and defining features, the successive bank regulatory requirements are bound to disappoint expectations. From that perspective, it could be said that one regulatory rule, through its own failure, leads to the next one. Hence, the growing web of ever more varied and complex regulatory norms is directly imputable to the preset-day organization of the monetary system.

From the outset, the first chapter identifies the liquidity-based regulation of banks' credit expansion by central banks as the very first instance of regulating the banking activity. It concludes that this liquidity-based control turns out, at the end, imperfect and incomplete, or even dysfunctional. Banks can escape central banks' restrictive policies through financial engineering techniques, and notably through the interbank market or the securitization of loans. At the same time, the very existence of a lender of last resort creates a serious moral hazard problem that incentivizes banks to neglect some of the costs of their individual own actions, which leads to risk mispricing. The regular expansionary monetary policies, especially in the present-day context of very low interest rates and massive excess liquidity, further deteriorate the robustness of banks' balance sheets. These adverse effects show that, even from the regulator's own point of view and objectives, the liquidity-based regulation of banks is insufficient. This finding provides an economic rationale for a significantly more invasive institution- and industry-based regulation of the banking sector.

These more invasive requirements, which are tantamount to very specific standards of operation to which no other industry is subject to that extent, constitute the so-called micro- and macro-prudential regulation of banks. The subsequent three chapters review, to some degree of detail and with an open critical mind, the content, justification and consequences, including on the broader economy, of the most relevant of these requirements. Four broad observations are worth the emphasis in this general conclusion.

First, these requirements are formulated based on the related assumptions that economic value is objective and that all future risks are calculable. These two assumptions, which originate in a strictly accounting view of banks' balance sheets, are in stark contrast with the most basic postulates of modern economic science as it has developed since the late nineteenth century. Indeed, modern economic theory evolved out of the understanding that economic value is subjective, that it stems from the acting subjects' choices rather than from the inanimate objects' features, and that the future is uncertain, in the sense that it cannot be known in advance. This means that the main banking requirements, such as the capital adequacy ratios, liquidity ratios, procyclical capital add-ons, and so on, do not pass the test of conformity with the foundations of modern economic science. Why is this important? Economics is, above all, a realistic depiction of real human action as it occurs in our world. Failure to comply with the foundations and conclusions of economics is a sure recipe for repeated errors and disappointments. Thus, as banking regulation is rooted in a questionable understanding of how the world in general and banks in particular operate, it is prone to err and to miss its own objectives. Many of our concrete findings, for instance, the impossibility to determine the optimal level of capital requirements, the self-contradictory nature of pre-determined risk weights or the failure of sophisticated liquidity requirements to prevent illiquidity, illustrate this point.

Second, due to the subsequent tension between the targeted results and the actual outcomes of banking regulation, supervision becomes a necessary complement to regulation and brings intrusiveness in banks' operation to yet another level. The objectification of asset valuation and of risk assessment, in particular, through the now standardized asset quality reviews and stress tests, naturally brings about the need to verify that the banks apply the prescribed norms faithfully and consistently. Supervisors become so much involved in the extensive and continuous monitoring of the various aspects of the banking business that they cannot avoid assuming the ultimate responsibility, both technically and politically, for the financial health and stability of the individual institutions under their surveillance. In turn, this justifies that the public authorities grant the supervisors such extraordinary powers to direct and restructure the banks that make them de facto co-managers of the institutions, despite them having no ownership rights. This outcome is yet another cause of generalized moral hazard, whereby bankers rely on the supervisors for ensuring the soundness of their institutions, up to being ready to "give the keys of the bank" in the event of a crisis.

Third, moral hazard pervades all aspects of banking. The availability of a lender of last resort, the rigidity of regulatory requirements, the daily involvement of supervision, and the myriad of other guarantees and safety nets incentivize banks not to take full account of the costs related to their actions. The resulting socialization of the business-related costs necessarily implies an overexpansion of the banking sector and underprovisioning for risks and potential losses. The latest reforms in the EU, especially as regards the safety nets and the principles of bank restructuring, do not alleviate this fundamental cost socialization. If anything, they bring it to a higher level through the further centralization and mutual redistribution of the costs of bank failures and crises. Hence, to the extent that bank regulation actually promotes moral hazard, it has become one of the drivers of bank crises.

Fourth, the much talked about macro-financial stability, in particular at the system's level, will continue to be the chimera of banking regulation. None of the banking rules address the most fundamental cause of bank instability, that is, the fractional reserve, at its heart. If anything, the growing sophistication and continuous evolution of banking regulation actually contributes to legitimize the current state of play. From that perspective, the failure of regulatory and supervisory requirements to bring about financial stability is, above all, of intellectual origin. The theoreticians of banking regulation spend much time and efforts in building complex mathematical models of alleged market failures and banking sector externalities that would justify broader government interventions at the level of the whole system. Yet they remain utterly unaware of the essentials of monetary theory, which clearly demonstrates the destabilizing effects of fiat money regimes and fractional-reserve banks themselves. Ironically, macro-prudential policy and regulation can then be seen as an antidote to the monetary policy-driven weakening of banks' balance sheets. Given their (common) objective to control credit cyclicality, macro-prudential and monetary policies are akin. We could wonder then whether macro-prudential regulation has not become the (complementary) monetary policy in the new world of excess liquidity and around-zero interest rates. One way or another, as long as economists and financial practitioners search for systemic risk and instability in the market only and never in government monopoly and privileges, financial stability is bound to remain a chimera.

What, then, would be a genuine alternative to the current administrative approach to alleviating financial sector risks? The only viable alternative seems to be a return to market discipline, understood in the widest possible sense. In particular, that would imply a return to a market-based commodity money and a revision of the contractual aspects of the present-day bank deposit contract in line with an unconditional respect for private property. This would rule out fractional-reserve banks, as we know them, and would trigger the abolition of many financial sector institutions and rules, including central banks, that would have become obsolete or unnecessary. In other words, a fully fledged monetary and banking reform rather than an overhaul of banking regulation and supervision would be the right response to the next banking crisis.

Bibliography

Acemoglu, Daron. 2009. "The Crisis of 2008: Lessons for and from Economics." *Critical Review* 21(2–3): 185–94.

Acharya, Viral. 2003. "Is the International Convergence of Capital Adequacy Regulation Desirable?" *Journal of Finance* 58(6): 2745–81.

Acharya, Viral. 2009. "A Theory of Systemic Risk and Design of Prudential Bank Regulation." *Journal of Financial Stability* 5: 224–55.

Acharya, Viral, and Matthew Richardson. 2009. "Causes of the Financial Crisis." *Critical Review* 21(2–3): 195–210.

Acharya, Viral, Katharina Bergant, Matteo Crosignani, Tim Eisert, and Fergal McCann. 2020. "The Anatomy of the Transmission of Macroprudential Policies." *IMF Working Paper* WP/20/58.

Admati, Anat, and Martin Hellwig. 2013. *The Bankers' New Clothes*. Princeton, NJ: Princeton University Press.

Agénor, Pierre-Richard, Leonardo Gambacorta, Enisse Kharroubi, and Luiz A Pereira da Silva. 2018. "The Effects of Prudential Regulation, Financial Development, and Financial Openness on Economic Growth." *BIS Working Papers* No 752.

Aikman, David, Jonathan Bridges, Anil Kashyap, and Caspar Siegert. 2019. "Would Macroprudential Regulation Have Prevented the Last Crisis?" *The Journal of Economic Perspectives* 33(1): 107–30.

Allen, Franklin, and Elena Carletti. 2013. "What Is Systemic Risk?" *Journal of Money, Credit and Banking* 45: 121–27.

Allen, Franklin, Elena Carletti, Itay Goldstein, and Agnese Leonello. 2015. "Moral Hazard and Government Guarantees in the Banking Industry." *Journal of Financial Regulation* 1:30–50.

Allen, Linda, Turan Bali, and Yi Tang. 2012. "Does Systemic Risk in the Financial Sector Predict Future Economic Downturns?" *Review of Financial Studies* 25(10): 3000–3036.

Altavilla, Carlo, Miguel Boucinha, and José-Luis Peydro. 2018. "Monetary Policy and Bank Profitability in a Low Interest Rate Environment." *Economic Policy* October: 531–86.

Arnaboldi, Francesca. 2020. *Risk and Regulation in Euro Area Banks: Completing the Banking Union*. Switzerland: Palgrave Macmillan.

Bagehot, Walter. [1873] 1979. *Lombard Street: A Description of the Money Market.* Westport, CT: Hyperion Press.

Bagus, Philipp. 2003. "Deflation: When Austrians Become Interventionists." *Quarterly Journal of Austrian Economics* 6(4): 19–35.

Bagus, Philipp. 2009. "The Quality of Money." *Quarterly Journal of Austrian Economics* 12(4): 22–45.

Bagus, Philipp. 2010. *The Tragedy of the Euro.* Auburn, AL: von Mises Institute.

Bagus, Philipp. 2012. "Modern Business Cycle Theories in Light of the ABCT." In *Theory of Money and Fiduciary Media: Essays in Celebration of the Centennial,* edited by Guido Hülsmann, pp. 229–46. Auburn, AL: Mises Institute.

Bagus, Philipp. 2015. *In Defense of Deflation.* New York, NY: Springer.

Bank for International Settlements. 2011. "Macroprudential Regulation and Policy." *BIS Papers* No 60.

Bank for International Settlements. 2016. "Macroprudential Policy." *BIS Papers* No 86.

Barth, Andreas, and Isabel Schnabel. 2013. "Why Banks Are Not Too Big to Fail—Evidence from the CDS Market." *Economic Policy* 28(74): 337–60.

Basel Committee for Banking Supervision. 1975. *Report on the Supervision of Banks' Foreign Establishments—Concordat.* https://www.bis.org/publ/bcbs00a.htm

Basel Committee for Banking Supervision. 1983. *Principles for the Supervision of Banks' Foreign Establishments (Concordat)* https://www.bis.org/publ/bcbsc312.htm.

Basel Committee for Banking Supervision. 1988. *International Convergence of Capital Measurement and Capital Standards.* https://www.bis.org/publ/bcbs04a.htm

Basel Committee for Banking Supervision. 1990. *Exchanges of Information between Supervisors of Participants in the Financial Markets.* https://www.bis.org/publ/bcbs07a.htm

Basel Committee for Banking Supervision. 1992. *Minimum Standards for the Supervision of International Banking Groups and Their Cross-border Establishments.* https://www.bis.org/publ/bcbsc314.htm

Basel Committee for Banking Supervision. 2006. *Basel II: International Convergence of Capital Measurement and Capital Standards: A Revised Framework—Consolidated Version.* https://www.bis.org/publ/bcbs128.htm

Basel Committee for Banking Supervision. [1997] 2012. *Core Principles for Effective Banking Supervision.* https://www.bis.org/publ/bcbs230.htm

Basel Committee for Banking Supervision. 2018. *Global Systemically Important Banks: Revised Assessment Methodology and the Higher Loss Absorbency Requirement.* https://www.bis.org/bcbs/publ/d445.pdf.

Basel Committee for Banking Supervision. 2019. "The Costs and Benefits of Bank Capital—A Review of the Literature." *BIS Working Paper* 37. https://www.bis.org/bcbs/publ/wp37.pdf.

Basel Committee for Banking Supervision. 2021. *The Basel Framework.* https://www.bis.org/basel_framework/index.htm

Belkhir, Mohamed, Sami Ben Naceur, Bertrand Candelon, and Jean-Charles Wijnandts. 2020. "Macroprudential Policies, Economic Growth, and Banking Crises." *IMF Working Paper* WP/20/65.

Benes, Jaromir, and Michael Kumhof. 2012. "The Chicago Plan Revisited." *IMF Working Paper* WP/12/202.

Bernanke, Ben, and Cara Lown. 1991. "The Credit Crunch." *Brookings Papers on Economic Activity* 2 (1991): 205–39.

Bernanke, Ben, and Mark Gertler. 1995. "Inside the Back Box: The Credit Channel of Monetary Policy Transmission." *Journal of Economic Perspectives* 9(4): 27–48.

Bhattacharya, Sudipto, and Anjan V. Thakor. 1993. "Contemporary Banking Theory." *Journal of Financial Intermediation* 3: 2–50.

Bhattacharya, Sudipto, Arnoud Boot, and Anjan V. Thakor. 1998. "The Economics of Bank Regulation." *Journal of Money, Credit and Banking* 30(4): 745–70.

Bikker, Jacob, and Tobias Vervliet. 2017. "Bank Profitability and Risk-Taking under Low Interest Rates." *International Journal of Financial Economics* 22:3–18.

Bodenhorn, Howard. 2015. "Double Liability at Early American Banks." *NBER Working Paper* 21494.

Borio, Claudio, Juan Contreras, and Fabrizio Zampolli. 2020. "Assessing the Fiscal Implications of Banking Crises." *BIS Working Papers* 893, https://www.bis.org/publ/work893.pdf.

Brewer, Elijah, and Thomas Mondschean. 1994. "An Empirical Test of the Incentive Effects of Deposit Insurance: The Case of Junk Bonds at Savings and Loan Associations." *Journal of Money, Credit and Banking* 26(1): 146–64.

Bruno, Valentina, and Hyun Song Shin. 2014. "Assessing Macroprudential Policies: Case of South Korea." *The Scandinavian Journal of Economics* 116(1): 128–57.

Busch, Dany, and Guido Ferrarini (edited by). 2020. *European Banking Union.* Oxford: Oxford University Press.

Calomiris, Charles. 1990. "Is Deposit Insurance Necessary? A Historical Perspective." *Journal of Economic History* 50(2): 283–95.

Calomiris, Charles. 2012. "Getting the Right Mix of Capital and Cash Requirements in Prudential Bank Regulation." *Journal of Applied Corporate Finance* 24(1): 33–41.

Calomiris, Charles, and Matthew Jaremski. (2019). "Stealing Deposits: Deposit Insurance, Risk-Taking, and the Removal of Market Discipline in Early 20th-Century Banks." *Journal of Finance* 74(2): 711–54.

Cantillon, Richard. [1734] 2001. *Essay on the Nature of Commerce in General.* New Brunswick, NJ: Transaction Publishers.

Canuto, Otaviano, and Matheus Cavallari. 2013. "Monetary Policy and Macroprudential Regulation: Wither Emerging Markets." *World Bank Policy Research Working Paper* WPS6310.

Cebula, Richard. 1993. "The Impact of Federal Deposit Insurance on Savings and Loan Failures." *Sothern Economic Journal* 59(4): 620–28.

Cecchetti, Stephen, and Kermit Schoenholtz. 2017. "Regulatory Reform: A Scorecard." *CEPR Discussion Paper* 12465. https://cepr.org/active/publications/discussion_papers/dp.php?dpno=12465.

Chiti, Mario, and Vittorio Santoro (edited by). 2019. *The Palgrave Handbook of European Banking Union Law*. Switzerland: Palgrave Macmillan.

Cihak, Martin, and Erlend Nier. 2014. "Resolving Problem Banks: A Review of the Global Evidence." In *Central Banking at a Crossroads: Europe and Beyond*, edited by Goodhart, Charles et al., 109–22. London, UK: Anthem Press.

Claessens, Stijn. 2014. "An Overview of Macroprudential Policy Tools." *IMF Working Paper* WP/14/214.

Claessens, Stijn, Nicholas Coleman, and Michael Donnelly. 2018. "'Low-For-Long' Interest Rates and Banks' Interest Margins and Profitability: Cross-Country Evidence." *Journal of Financial Intermediation* 35:1–16.

Clement, Piet. 2010. "The Term 'Macroprudential': Origins and Evolution." *BIS Quarterly Review* March: 59=67.

Cline, William. 2016. "Benefits and Costs of Higher Capital Requirements for Banks." *Peterson Institute for International Economics Working Paper* WP 16–6. https://www.piie.com/system/files/documents/wp16-6.pdf.

Condillac, Etienne Bonnot de. [1776] 1966. *Le Commerce et le Gouvernement*. In *Mélanges d'Economie Politique*, edited by Eugène Daire and Gustave de Molinari. Osnabrück: Otto Zeller.

Constancio, Vitor (edited by). 2019. "Macroprudential Policy at the ECB: Institutional Framework, Strategy, Analytical Tools and Policies." *ECB Occasional Paper Series* 227. https://www.ecb.europa.eu/pub/pdf/scpops/ecb.op227~971b0a4996.en.pdf.

Cooper, Russell, and Thomas Ross. 2002. "Bank Runs: Deposit Insurance and Capital Requirements." *International Economic Review* 43(1): 55–72.

Crockett, Andrew. 1997. "The Theory and Practice of Financial Stability." *Essays in International Finance* 203. Princeton, NJ: Princeton University Press.

Cull, Robert, Lemma Senbet, and Marco Sorge. 2005. "Deposit Insurance and Financial Development." *Journal of Money, Credit and Banking* 37(1): 43–82.

Danielsson, Jon, Kevin James, Marcela Valenzuela, and Ilknur Zer. 2016. "Can We Prove a Bank Guilty of Creating Systemic Risk? A Minority Report." *Journal of Money, Credit and Banking* 48(4): 795–812.

Das, Sanjiv Ranjan, and Raman Uppal. 2004. "Systemic Risk and International Portfolio Choice." *Journal of Finance* 59(6): 2809–34.

Demirgüç-Kunt, Asli, and Harry Huizinga. 1999. "Determinants of Commercial Bank Interest Margins and Profitability: Some International Evidence." *World Bank Economic Review* 13(2): 379–408.

Demirgüç-Kunt, Asli, and Enrica Detragiache. 2002. "Does Deposit Insurance Increase Banking System Stability? An Empirical Investigation." *Journal of Monetary Economics* 49: 1373–406.

Demirgüc-Kunt, Asli, and Edward Kane. 2002. "Deposit Insurance around the Globe: Where Does It Work?" *Journal of Economic Perspectives* 16(2): 175–95.

De Nicolo, Gianni, Giovanni Favara, and Lev Ratnovski. 2012. "Externalities and Macroprudential Policy." *IMF Staff Discussion Note* SDN/12/05.

Dewatripont, Mathias, and Jean Tirole. 1994. *The Prudential Regulation of Banks*. Cambridge, MA: The MIT Press.

Diamond, Douglas, and Philip Dybvig. 1983. "Bank Runs, Deposit Insurance, and Liquidity." *Journal of Political Economy* 91(3): 401–419.

Dowd, Kevin. 1993. "Re-Examining the Case for Government Deposit Insurance." *Southern Economic Journal* 59(3): 363–70.

Dowd, Kevin. 1997. "The Regulation of Bank Capital Adequacy." In *Advances in Austrian Economics, Volume 4*, edited by Peter Boettke and Steven Horwitz, 95–110. Howard House, UK: Emerald Group Publishing.

Dorobat, Carmen. 2015. *Cantillon Effects in International Trade: The Consequences of Fiat Money for Trade, Finance and the International Distribution of Wealth.* PhD Thesis, University of Angers. https://core.ac.uk/download/pdf/217717782 .pdf.

Eichberger, Jürgen, and Martin Summer. 2005. "Bank Capital, Liquidity, and Systemic Risk." *Journal of the European Economic Association* 3(2): 547–55.

Estrella, Arturo. 2002. "Securitization and the Efficacy of Monetary Policy." *Federal Reserve Bank of New York Economic Policy Review* 8(1): 1–13.

European Banking Authority. 2014. *Guidelines on the Criteria to Determine the Conditions of Application of Article 131(3) of Directive 2013/36/EU (CRD) in Relation to the Assessment of Other Systemically Important Institutions.* https:// www.eba.europa.eu/regulation-and-policy/own-funds/guidelines-on-criteria-to-to -assess-other-systemically-important-institutions-o-siis-.

European Banking Authority. 2019. *2020 EU-Wide Stress Test: Methodological Note.* https://www.eba.europa.eu/sites/default/documents/files/documents/10180 /2841396/ba66328f-476f-4707-9a23-6df5957dc8c1/2020%20EU-wide%20stress %20test%20-%20Draft%20Methodological%20Note.pdf?retry=1.

European Banking Federation. 2019. *EBF Summary of Basel IV in Europe.* https: //www.ebf.eu/wp-content/uploads/2020/10/EBF_033787-EBF-summary-paper-on -Basel-IV-in-Europe.pdf.

European Central Bank. 2015. "The Fiscal Impact of Financial Sector Support during the Crisis." *ECB Economic Bulletin* 6/2015, 74–87. https://www.ecb.europa.eu/pub /pdf/ecbu/eb201605.en.pdf.

European Central Bank. 2018a. *SSM Supervisory Manual.* https://www .bankingsupervision.europa.eu/ecb/pub/pdf/ssm.supervisorymanual201803.en.pdf.

European Central Bank. 2018b. *Asset Quality Review Phase 2 Manual.* https://www .bankingsupervision.europa.eu/ecb/pub/pdf/ssm.assetqualityreviewmanual201806 .en.pdf.

European Central Bank. 2021. *Targeted Review of Internal Models: Project Report.* https://www.bankingsupervision.europa.eu/ecb/pub/pdf/ssm.trim_project_report ~aa49bb624c.en.pdf.

European Central Bank. 2022. *Supervisory Banking Statistics: Second Quarter 2022.* https://www.bankingsupervision.europa.eu/ecb/pub/pdf/ssm .supervisorybankingstatistics_second_quarter_2022_202210~2041cf3796.en.pdf.

European Commission. 2013a. *Banking Communication.* 2013/C 216/01. https:// eur-lex.europa.eu/LexUriServ/LexUriServ.do?uri=OJ:C:2013:216:0001:0015:EN: PDF.

European Commission. 2013b. *EC Press Release on State Aid*. IP/13/1301, https://ec .europa.eu/commission/presscorner/detail/en/IP_13_1301.

European Commission. 2017. "Coping with the International Financial Crisis at the National Level in a European Context: Impact and Financial Sector Policy Responses in 2008–2015." *Commission Staff Working Document*. https://ec.europa .eu/info/sites/default/files/eucountries-responses-to-financial-crisis.pdf.

European Court of Auditors. 2020. *Control of State Aid to Financial Institutions in the EU: In Need of a Fitness Check (Special Report)*. https://www.eca.europa.eu/Lists /ECADocuments/SR20_21/SR_state_aid_EN.pdf.

European Systemic Risk Board. 2018. *The ESRB Handbook on Operationalizing Macroprudential Policy in the Banking Sector*. https://www.esrb.europa.eu/pub/ pdf/other/esrb.handbook_mp180115.en.pdf

European Systemic Risk Board. 2021. *A Review of Macroprudential Policy in the EU in 2020*. https://www.esrb.europa.eu/pub/reports/review_macroprudential_policy/ html/index.en.html.

Financial Stability Board. 2019. *Review of the Technical Implementation of the Total Loss-Absorbing Capacity (TLAC) Standard*. https://www.fsb.org/wp-content /uploads/P020719.pdf.

Financial Stability Board. 2020. *2020 List of Global Systemically Important Banks (G-SIBs)*. https://www.fsb.org/wp-content/uploads/P111120.pdf.

Fontana, Alessandro, and Sven Langedijk. 2019. "The Bank-Sovereign Loop and Financial Stability in the Euro Area." *Joint Research Center Working Papers in Economics and Finance*, 2019/10, https://publications.jrc.ec.europa.eu/repository /handle/JRC115569.

Fontana, Giuseppe. 2002. "The Making of Monetary Policy in Endogenous Money Theory: An Introduction." *Journal of Post Keynesian Economics* 24(4): 503–509.

Freixas, Xavier, Bruno Parigi, and Jean-Charles Rochet. 2000. "Systemic Risk, Interbank Relations, and Liquidity Provision by the Central Bank." *Journal of Money, Credit and Banking* 32(3): 611–38.

Freixas, Xavier, and Jean-Charles Rochet. 2008. *Microeconomics of Banking*. Cambridge, MA: The MIT Press.

Freixas, Xavier, Luc Laeven, and José-Luis Peydro. 2015. *Systemic Risk, Crises and Macroprudential Regulation*. Boston, MA: MIT Press.

Gersbach, Hans, and Jean-Charles Rochet. 2012. "Aggregate Investment Externalities and Macroprudential Regulation." *Journal of Money, Credit and Banking* 44(2): 73–109.

Gertchev, Nikolay. 2009. "Securitization and Fractional Reserve Banking." In *Property, Freedom and Society: Essays in Honour of Hans-Hermann Hoppe*, edited by Guido Hülsmann and Stephan Kinsella, 283–300. Auburn, AL: Mises Institute.

Gertchev, Nikolay. 2012. "The Inter-Bank Market in the Perspective of Fractional Reserve Banking." In *Theory of Money and Fiduciary Media: Essays in Celebration of the Centennial*, edited by Guido Hülsmann, 209–228. Auburn, AL: Mises Institute.

Goodhart, Charles. 2014. "Bank Resolution in Comparative Perspective: What Lessons for Europe?" In *Central Banking at a Crossroads: Europe and Beyond,* edited by Goodhart, Charles et al., 97–108. London, UK: Anthem Press.

Gorton, Gary, and Ellis Tallman. 2016. "Too Big to Fail Before the Fed." *American Economic Review* 106(5): 528–32.

Grigaite, Kristina, Cristina Dias, and Marcel Magnus. 2020a. "Institutional Set-up of Macroprudential Policy in the European Union." *European Parliament Briefing* PE 645.701.https://www.europarl.europa.eu/RegData/etudes/BRIE/2020/645701/ IPOL_BRI(2020)645701_EN.pdf.

Grigaite, Kristina, Cristina Dias, and Marcel Magnus. 2020b. "Macroprudential Policy Toolkit for the Banking Sector." *European Parliament Briefing* PE 645.702. https://www.europarl.europa.eu/RegData/etudes/BRIE/2020/645702/ IPOL_BRI(2020)645702_EN.pdf.

Grossman, Richard. 1992. "Deposit Insurance, Regulation, and Moral Hazard in the Thrift Industry: Evidence from the 1930's." *American Economic Review* 82(4): 800–821.

Grubel, Herbert. 1971. "Risk, Uncertainty and Moral Hazard." *Journal of Risk and Uncertainty* 38(1): 99–106.

Haldane, Andrew. 2014. "Constraining Discretion in Bank Regulation." In *Central Banking at a Crossroads: Europe and Beyond,* edited by Goodhart, Charles et al., 15–32. London, UK: Anthem Press.

Hanson, Samuel, Anil Kashyap, and Jeremy Stein. 2011. "A Macroprudential Approach to Financial Regulation." *Journal of Economic Perspectives* 25(1): 3–28.

Hayek, Friedrich. [1931] 1967. *Prices and Production.* New York, NY: Augustus M. Kelly.

Heimbüchel, Bernd, Ute Heimbüchel, and Urs Lendermann. 2018. *Banking Union Essential Terms: Technical Abbreviations and Glossary.* Brussels, BE: European Parliament. https://www.europarl.europa.eu/RegData/etudes/STUD/2018/619028/ IPOL_STU(2018)619028_EN.pdf.

Hellwig, Martin. 1995. "Systemic Aspects of Risk Management in Banking and Finance." *Swiss Journal of Economics and Statistics* 131(4/2): 723–37.

Hellwig, Martin, and Jürg Blum. 1995. "The Macroeconomic Implications of Capital Adequacy Requirements for Banks." *European Economic Review* 39: 739–49.

Hook, Andrew. 2022. "Examining Modern Money Creation: An Institution-Centered Explanation and Visualization of the 'Credit Theory' of Money and Some Reflexions on Its Significance." *Journal of Economic Education* 53(3): 210–31.

Hoppe, Hans-Hermann. 1994. "How is Fiat Money Possible?—or, the Devolution of Money and Credit." *Review of Austrian Economics* 7(2): 49–74.

Howarth, David, and Joachim Schild (edited by). 2020. *The Difficult Construction of European Banking Union.* London, UK: Routledge.

Huber, Joseph. 2017. *Sovereign Money: Beyond Reserve Banking.* Cham, Switzerland: Springer.

Huerta de Soto, Jésus. 1995. "A Critical Analysis of Central Banks and Fractional-reserve Free Ban king from the Austrian School Perspective." *Review of Austrian Economics* 8(2): 25–38.

Huerta de Soto, Jésus. 2005. *Money, Bank Credit, and Economic Crises*. Auburn, AL: Mises Institute.

Hülsmann, Jörg Guido. 1997. "Political Unification: A Generalized Progression Theorem." *Journal of Libertarian Studies* 13(1): 81–96.

Hülsmann, Jörg Guido. 1998. "Toward a General Theory of Error Cycles." *Quarterly Journal of Austrian Economics* 1(4): 1–23.

Hülsmann, Jörg Guido. 2000. "Banks Cannot Create Money." *The Independent Review* 5(1): 101–110.

Hülsmann, Jörg Guido. 2004. "Legal Tender Laws and Fractional-Reserve Banking." *Journal of Libertarian Studies* 18(3): 33–55.

Hülsmann, Jörg Guido. 2006. "The Political Economy of Moral Hazard." *Politicka Ekonomie* 1: 35–47.

Hülsmann, Jörg Guido. 2008a. *Deflation and Liberty*. Auburn, AL: Mises Institute.

Hülsmann, Jörg Guido. 2008b. *The Ethics of Money Production*. Auburn, AL: Mises Institute.

Hülsmann, Jörg Guido. 2017. "Moral Hazard." In *The SAGE Encyclopedia of Political Behavior*, edited by Fathali M. Moghaddam, 496–97. Thousand Oaks, CA: SAGE Publications.

Hume, David. [1777] 1987. *Essays: Moral, Political, and Literary*. Indianapolis, IN: Liberty Fund.

International Monetary Fund. 2009. *Global Financial Stability Report: Responding to the Financial Crisis and Measuring Systemic Risk*. https://www.imf.org/-/media/Websites/IMF/imported-full-text-pdf/external/pubs/ft/gfsr/2009/01/pdf/_text.ashx.

International Monetary Fund. 2013. "Key Aspects of Macroprudential Policy." *IMF Policy Paper* PP 4803. https://www.imf.org/en/Publications/Policy-Papers/Issues/2016/12/31/Key-Aspects-of-Macroprudential-Policy-PP4803.

Ireland, Peter. 2005. "The Monetary Transmission Mechanism." *Federal Reserve Bank of Boston Working Papers* N°06–1.

Iyer, Rajkamal, Thais Jense, Hiels Johannesen, and Adam Sheridan. 2019. "The Distortive Effects of Too Big to Fail." *Review of Financial Studies* 32(12): 4653–95.

Jablecki, Juliusz, and Mateusz Machaj. 2009. "The Regulated Meltdown of 2008." *Critical Review* 21(2–3): 301–328.

Jeanne, Olivier. 2016. "The Macroprudential Role of International Reserves." *The American Economic Review* 106(5): 570–73.

Jeffs, Jennifer. 2008. "The Politics of Financial Plumbing: Harmonization and Interests in the Construction of the International Payments System." *Review of International Political Economy* 15(2): 259–88.

Kahane, Y. 1977. "Capital Adequacy and the Regulation of Financial Intermediaries." *Journal of Banking and Finance* 1(2): 207–218.

Kara, Gazi, and Mehmet Ozsoy. 2020. "Bank Regulation under Fire Sale Externalities." *Review of Financial Studies* 33: 2554–84.

Kareken, John. 1986. "Federal Bank Regulatory Policy: A Description and Some Observations." *The Journal of Business* 59(1): 3–48.

Kashyap, Anil, Richard Berner, and Charles Goodhart. 2011. "The Macroprudential Toolkit." *IMF Economic Review* 59(2): 145–61.

Keeley, Michael. 1990. "Deposit Insurance, Risk, and Market Power in Banking." *American Economic Review* 80(5): 1183–200.

Keister, Todd. 2016. "Bailouts and Financial Fragility." *Review of Economic Studies* 83: 704–736.

Kuznetsov, Yuri. 2005. "Fiat Money as an Administrative Good." *Review of Austrian Economics* 10(2): 111–14.

Kydland, Finn, and Edward Prescott. 1990. "Business Cycles: Real Facts and a Monetary Myth." *Federal Reserve Bank of Minneapolis Quarterly Review* 14(2): 3–18.

Langfield, Sam, Marco Pagano, Jan Pieter Krahnen, and Wolf Wagner. 2016. "Bank Bias in Europe." *Economic Policy* 31(85):51–106.

Lavoie, Marc. 1984. "The Endogenous Flow of Credit and the Post Keynesian Theory of Money." *Journal of Economic Issues* 18(3): 771–97.

Leonello, Agnese. 2018. "Government Guarantees to Financial Institutions: Banks' Incentives and Fiscal Sustainability." In *Achieving Financial Stability: Challenges to Prudential Regulation*, edited by Evanoff, Douglas et al., 305–316. Singapore: World Scientific.

Levine, Ross. 1997. "Financial Development and Economic Growth: Views and Agenda." *Journal of Economic Literature* 35(2): 688–726.

Liang, Nellie. 2013. "Systemic Risk Monitoring and Financial Stability." *Journal of Money, Credit and Banking* 45(1): 129–35.

Löffler, Gunter, and Peter Raupach. 2018. "Pitfalls in the Use of Systemic Risk Measures." *Journal of Financial and Quantitative Analysis* 53(1): 269–98.

Macey, Jonathan, and Geoffrey Miller. 1992. "Double Liability of Bank Shareholders: History and Implications." *Wake Forest Law Review* 27: 31–62.

Macovei, Mihai. 2016. "The Austrian Business Cycle Theory: A Defense of Its General Validity." *Quarterly Journal of Austrian Economics* 18(4): 409–435.

McLeay, Michael, Amar Radia, and Ryland Thomas. 2014. "Money Creation in the Modern Economy." *Bank of England Quarterly Bulletin* 2014(Q1): 14–27.

Meltzer, Allan H. 1967. "Major Issues in the Regulation of Financial Institutions." *Journal of Political Economy* 75(4): 482–501.

Menger, Carl. [1871] 1994. *Principles of Economics*. Grove City, PA: Libertarian Press.

Menger, Carl. 1892. "On the Origins of Money." *Economic Journal* 2: 239–255.

Mishkin, Frederic. 1995. "Symposium on the Monetary Transmission Mechanism." *Journal of Economic Perspectives* 9(4): 3–10.

Mishkin, Frederic. 2006. "How Big a Problem Is Too Big to Fail? A Review of Gary Stern and Ron Feldman's 'Too Big to Fail: The Hazards of Bank Bailouts.'" *Journal of Economic Literature* 44(4): 988–1004.

Mishra, Rabi. 2019. *Systemic Risk and Macroprudential Regulations*. New Delhi, India: SAGE Publications.

Mises, Ludwig von. [1912] 1980. *The Theory of Money and Credit*. Indianapolis, IN: Liberty Classics.

Mises, Ludwig von. [1920] 1990. *Economic Calculation in the Socialist Commonwealth.* Auburn, AL: Mises Institute.

Mises, Ludwig von. [1944] 1996. *Bureaucracy.* Grove City, PA: Libertarian Press.

Mises, Ludwig von. [1940] 1998a. *Interventionism: An Economic Analysis.* Irvington-on-Hudson, NY: The Foundation for Economic Education.

Mises, Ludwig von. [1949] 1998b. *Human Action: A Treatise on Economics.* Auburn, AL: Mises Institute.

Mises, Ludwig von. [1933] 2003. *Epistemological Problems of Economics.* Auburn, AL: Mises Institute.

Mizen, Paul, Margarita Rubio and Philip Turner. 2020. *Macroprudential Policy and Practice.* Cambridge, UK: Cambridge University Press.

Moore, Basil. 1988. "The Endogenous Money Supply." *Journal of Post Keynesian Economics* 10(3): 372–85.

Nier, Erlend, and Ursel Baumann. 2006. "Market Discipline, Disclosure and Moral Hazard in Banking." *Journal of Financial Intermediation* 15: 332–61.

O'Hara, Maureen, and Wayne Shaw. 1990. "Deposit Insurance and Wealth Effects: The Value of Being 'Too Big to Fail.'" *Journal of Finance* 45(5): 1587–600.

Palley, Thomas. 1991. "The Endogenous Money Supply: Consensus and Disagreement." *Journal of Post Keynesian Economics* 13(3): 397–403.

Pecchenino, Rowena. 1992. "Risk-based Deposit Insurance: An Incentive Compatible Plan." *Journal of Money, Credit and Banking* 24(4): 499–510.

Posner, Eric, and E. Glen Weyl. 2013. "Benefit-Cost Analysis for Financial Regulation." *American Economic Review: Paper and Proceedings 2013*, 103(3): 393–97.

Reinhart, Carmen, and Kenneth Rogoff. 2009. *This Time is Different: Eight Centuries of Financial Folly.* Princeton, NJ: Princeton University Press.

Rochet, Jean-Charles, and Jean Tirole. 1996. "Interbank Lending and Systemic Risk." *Journal of Money, Credit and Banking* 28(4): 733–62.

Rosengren, Eric. 2011. "Defining Financial Stability and Some Policy Implications of Applying the Definition." *Keynote Remarks at the Stanford Finance Forum.* Boston, MA: Boston Fed. https://www.bostonfed.org/-/media/Documents/Speeches/PDF/060311.pdf.

Rothbard, Murray. 1956. "Toward a Reconstruction of Utility and Welfare Economics." In *On Freedom and Free Enterprise: The Economics of Free Enterprise*, edited by Mary Sennholz, 224–62. Princeton, N.J: D. Van Nostrand).

Rothbard, Murray. [1962] 1991. *The Case for a 100 Percent Gold Dollar.* Auburn, AL: Mises Institute.

Rothbard, Murray 1994. *The Case Against the Fed.* Auburn, AL: Mises Institute.

Rothbard, Murray. [1974] 2000. *Egalitarianism As a Revolt Against Nature.* Auburn, AL: von Mises Institute.

Rothbard, Murray. [1983] 2008. *The Mystery of Banking.* Auburn, AL: Mises Institute.

Rothbard, Murray. [1962] 2009. *Man, Economy, and State with Power and Market: The Scholar's Edition.* Auburn, AL: Mises Institute.

Salerno, Joseph. 1991. "Two Traditions in Monetary Theory." *Journal des Economistes et des Etudes Humaines* 2(2): 337==79.

Salerno, Joseph. 2010. *Money, Sound and Unsound*. Auburn, AL: Mises Institute.

Santos, Joao. 2000. "Bank Capital Regulation in Contemporary Banking Theory: A Review of the Literature." *BIS Working Papers* No 90.

Say, Jean-Baptiste. 1841. *Traité d'Economie Politique*. Paris, France: Guillaumin.

Schenk, Catherine. 2014. "Summer in the City: Banking Failures of 1974 and the Development of International Banking Supervision." *The English Historical Review* 129(540): 1129–56.

Shleifer, Andrei, and Robert Vishny. 2010. "Unstable Banking." *Journal of Financial Economics* 97: 306–318.

Single Resolution Board. 2016a. *MREL: Approach Taken in 2016 and Next Steps*. https://www.srb.europa.eu/system/files/media/document/srb_mrel_approach_2016_post_final.pdf.

Single Resolution Board. 2016b. *The Single Resolution Mechanism: Introduction to Resolution Planning*. https://www.srb.europa.eu/system/files/media/document/intro_resplanning.pdf.pdf.

Single Resolution Board. 2021a. *Minimum Requirement for Own Funds and Eligible Liabilities (MREL): SRB Policy under the Banking Package*. https://www.srb.europa.eu/system/files/media/document/mrel_policy_may_2021_final_web.pdf.

Single Resolution Board. 2021b. *SRB MREL Dashboard—Q2.2021*. https://www.srb.europa.eu/system/files/media/document/2021-12-02_SRB-MREL-Dashboard-Q2.pdf.

Sinn, Hans-Werner. 2020. *The Economics of Target Balances: From Lehman to Corona*. Cham, Switzerland: Palgrave Macmillan.

Sinn, Hans-Werner, and Timo Wollmershäuser. 2012. "Target Loans, Current Account Balances and Capital Flows: The ECB's Rescue Facility." *International Tax Public Finance* 19: 468–508.

Sironi, Andrea. 2018. "The Evolution of Banking Regulation Since the Financial Crisis: A Critical Assessment." *Baffi Carefin Center Working Paper* 103. https://repec.unibocconi.it/baffic/baf/papers/cbafwp18103.pdf.

Smith, Adam. [1776] 1994. *The Wealth of Nations*. New York, NY: The Modern Library.

Strahan, P. 2013. "Too Big to Fail: Causes, Consequences, and Policy Responses." *Annual Review of Financial Economics* 5: 43–61.

Strigl, Richard von. [1934] 2000. *Capital and Production*. Auburn, AL: Mises Institute.

Teixeira, Pedro Gustavo. 2020. *The Legal History of the European Banking Union*. New York, NY: Hart Publishing.

Thornton, Mark. 2003. "Apoplithorismophobia." *Quarterly Journal of Austrian Economics* 6(4): 5–18.

Thornton, Mark. 2012. "Cantillon on the Cause of the Business Cycle." *Quarterly Journal of Austrian Economics* 9(3): 45–60.

Turgot, Anne Robert Jacques. [1766] 1997. *Formation et Distribution des Richesses*. Paris, France: Flammarion.

Turner, Philip. 2018. "The Macroeconomics of Macroprudential Policies." In *Macroprudential Policy and Practice*, edited by Paul Mizen, Margarita Rubio and Philip Turner, 19–45. Cambridge, UK: Cambridge University Press.

Ulate, Mauricio. 2021. "Going Negative at the Zero Lower Bound: The Effects of Negative Nominal Interest Rates." *American Economic Review* 111(1): 1–40.

Wagster, John. 1996. "Impact of the 1988 Basle Accord on International Banks." *The Journal of Finance* 51(4): 1321–46.

Wallison, Peter. 2009. "Cause and Effect: Government Policies and the Financial Crisis." *Critical Review* 21(2–3): 365–76.

Wheelock, David, and Paul Wilson. 1995. "Explaining Bank Failures: Deposit Insurance, Regulation, and Efficiency." *Review of Economics and Statistics* 77(4): 689–700.

White, Lawrence. 1989. "The Reform of Federal Deposit Insurance." *Journal of Economic Perspectives* 3(4): 11–29.

White, Lawrence. 2009. "The Credit-Rating Agencies and the Subprime Debacle." *Critical Review* 21(2–3): 389–99.

Zukauskas, Vytautas. 2021. "Measuring the Quality of Money." *Quarterly Journal of Austrian Economics* 24(1): 110–46.

Zukauskas, Vytautas, and Jörg Guido Hülsmann. 2019. "Financial Asset Valuations: The Total Demand Approach." *Quarterly Review of Economics and Finance* 72: 123–31.

Index

asset quality review (AQR), 7, 59, 86–88, 96n37, 154
asset-backed securities (ABSs), 39–40

backstops, 126, 132–37
Bagehot, Walter, 3–4, 6, 10nn5–6, 13, 48n19, 151
bail-in principle, 137, 139
bailouts, 8, 124–5, 129–32, 137
bank credit, 24–26;
    contraction, 30, 101, 106;
    expansion, 27, 30, 37, 40–41, 72–73, 105–6, 108–9
banking crises, 76–78, 102, 97n41, 123–25, 129, 145
banking union (BU), 2, 56, 61, 84, 96n20, 98n50, 129, 137, 140
banks-sovereign loop, 2, 124, 135, 145
Basel framework, 2, 56–60, 75, 96n36
boom-bust cycle, 27–28, 41, 43, 49n25, 74, 101, 105, 109
burden-sharing, 130–31.
    See also bail-in principle

Cantillon effects, 17, 24, 28, 73
capital, 27, 43, 56, 61, 68.
    See also own funds
capital buffers, 59, 68, 89, 114–16

capital requirements, 62–63, 93n9, 96n38, 97n43, 154;
    definition of, 68–70;
    impact on monetary transmission, 73;
    influence on bank credit, 70–73;
    issues with, 75–76;
    optimality of, 76–79;
    part of the SREP decision, 84
central bank, 3–4, 7, 25–26, 28–31, 35–39, 42, 55, 108–9, 151–55
commodity money, 17–18, 23, 25, 49n24, 155
competent authority (CA), 62, 84, 88–89
comprehensive review (CR), 86–88
contagion, 4, 20, 37, 46, 56–57, 100, 102–4, 113, 119n7, 119n11, 123, 137, 139, 144, 153
coverage ratio, 98n53, 98n54;
    See also provisions
credit crunch, 104–8
credit institution, 61
credit procyclicality, 101, 104–5, 108–9, 115

De Larosière report, 100–101
deflation, 5, 11, 33, 100, 105, 123, 149n27
deposit guarantee. *See* deposit insurance

169

Index

About the Author

Nikolay Gertchev holds a PhD in monetary economics from the University of Paris II Panthéon-Assas. His scholarly contributions have appeared in the *Quarterly Journal of Austrian Economics*, *Journal of Libertarian Studies*, and *Libertarian Papers*. Recently he has lectured on international economics at the ICHEC Management School in Brussels, Belgium, and on financial regulation in the EU at the University of Angers, France. Since 2007, he has been working for the European Commission, notably on the design and follow-up of the banking sector reforms in Ireland, Cyprus, and Greece in the aftermath of the Global Financial Crisis.

He lives in Brussels with his wife and two children.

Milton Keynes UK
Ingram Content Group UK Ltd.
UKHW011315240424
441691UK00006B/62

9 781666 937190